The Politics of Education in Developing Countries

The Politics of Education in Developing Countries

From Schooling to Learning

Edited by
Sam Hickey and Naomi Hossain

OXFORD
UNIVERSITY PRESS

OXFORD
UNIVERSITY PRESS

Great Clarendon Street, Oxford, OX2 6DP,
United Kingdom

Oxford University Press is a department of the University of Oxford.
It furthers the University's objective of excellence in research, scholarship,
and education by publishing worldwide. Oxford is a registered trade mark of
Oxford University Press in the UK and in certain other countries

First Edition published in 2019

Impression: 1

Published in the United States of America by Oxford University Press
198 Madison Avenue, New York, NY 10016, United States of America

British Library Cataloguing in Publication Data
Data available

Library of Congress Control Number: 2018961975

ISBN 978–0–19–883568–4

Printed and bound in Great Britain by
Clays Ltd, Elcograf S.p.A.

To my parents, Maureen and Brian Hickey, for helping to make the value of learning clear to me, and to so many others.

To Samer and Sophia, for all they have taught me about schooling and learning.

Preface and Acknowledgements

This manuscript brings together the findings and analysis from a project entitled 'The Politics of Social Provisioning' that was undertaken within the Effective States and Inclusive Development Research Centre (ESID) between 2011 and 2016. ESID is based at the Global Development Institute, The University of Manchester, and consists of researchers located across the global North and South. Since 2011, its aim has been to identify the political conditions under which elites become committed to, and states become capable of, delivering inclusive development. ESID has examined the politics of development across several different policy domains, including growth, natural resource governance, social protection, gender equity, urban governance and health, as well as the topic of education that we focus on here (www.effective-states.org).

Undertaking comparative research and publishing the results in an edited collection relies heavily on a great deal of teamwork and goodwill, and we have been fortunate to find these qualities in abundance amongst the colleagues we have worked with on this study. As editors, our first and foremost round of thanks goes to the stellar cast of researchers and authors who contributed such fascinating country case studies to the collection. From the initial meetings in Buxton and Manchester, where the ideas were set in place, through the research design workshop in Nairobi and sharing of initial drafts in Cape Town, the research team has been a pleasure to work with.

In addition to the chapters produced by the ESID-education research team, we are delighted to include chapters from two leading authorities in the field, namely Merilee Grindle and Lant Pritchett, both of Harvard University. Our decision to engage with the 'learning crisis' as a critical problem facing countries in the global South owed much to Lant's ground-breaking work on this topic, whilst our decision to do so from a political perspective that focused on the critical role of coalitions owed a great deal to Merilee's landmark (2004) text on the politics of educational reform in Latin America. We were grateful and honoured when both agreed to contribute critical commentaries to help close the book by identifying what the collection contributes, what it misses and where work on the politics of the learning crisis should move to next. Our thanks to them both for taking on this challenge and delivering in such style.

We have accumulated many other debts along the way, and are particularly grateful to the ESID research associates who have provided outstanding support at different stages of the project. Early on, Sophie King produced an excellent literature review on the politics of education that saved us priceless time and identified the gaps in the field to take aim at. Towards the end, David Jackman helped us to convert the last of the extensive working papers into much shorter and sharper book chapters, ensuring integration between the chapters, liaising with the publishers, and the many other time-consuming tasks required to bring a book project through to completion. So swift and incisive was his grasp of our material that he joined us as co-author for the closing chapter, much improving the product in the process.

The ideas within this book have been sharpened by many fruitful intellectual exchanges along the way, at seminars, conferences, and workshops. These include seminars at the School of Advanced International Studies at Johns Hopkins University and the World Bank in Washington DC, at the German Development Institute in Bonn, and at academic conferences in Bath, Oxford, San Diego, and Barcelona, all of which encouraged us to take this work forward and think harder about how to frame the findings. Our thanks go to the many anonymous reviewers who gave their time to offer peer review comments on our early working papers, and in particular to Professor Leon Tikly of Bristol University who offered insightful comments on early versions of all of the country papers. Samer Al-Samarrai provided valuable insights into the policy debates about the learning crisis, and on indicators and data sources.

The ESID network has provided many opportunities for this work to be pored over, critiqued and sharpened, and we thank our colleagues for their critical comments and encouragement, including Kunal Sen, David Hulme, Pablo Yanguas, Sohela Nazneen, Abdul-Gafaru Abdulai, Badru Bukenya, and Fred Golooba-Mutebi. The initial framing of the project flowed directly from the (2013) ESID Working Paper on 'Researching the Politics of Social Provisioning' produced by Brian Levy and Mike Walton, to whom we owe a significant intellectual debt. We have also benefitted from the guidance of the Centre's Advisory Group, including David Booth, Barbara Harriss-White, Duncan Green, Margaret Kakande and Peter Evans (at Brown University) as well as Peter Evans (at the Research Department in DFID). Our thanks to these esteemed colleagues and to those who also acted as critical discussants and participants at our various workshops, including Nic van de Walle, Heather Marquette, Anu Joshi, and Merilee Grindle. An initial discussion with Steve Kosack at Harvard in 2011, just before his own excellent book on the politics of education was published, helped to orientate the project in the very early stages.

At Manchester many people have assisted with the management of this project. They have facilitated our meetings, organized workshops, handled budgets, and done all the other administrative work without which research—especially international collaborative and comparative research—would not be possible. In particular, we are grateful to Kat Bethell, Julia Brunt, Clare Degenhardt, Julie Rafferty, and Anna Webster. Finally, our thanks to Adam Swallow at OUP for supporting the project from the outset and to his colleague Katie Bishop for guiding it through contracting and production.

Sam Hickey, *Manchester* Naomi Hossain, *Washington, DC*

This document is an output from a project funded by UK Aid from the UK Government for the benefit of developing countries. However, the views expressed and information contained in it are not necessarily those of, or endorsed by, the UK Government, which can accept no responsibility for such views or information, or for any reliance placed on them.

Contents

List of Figures

List of Tables

List of Abbreviations

ANC	African National Congress (South Africa)
ASEAN	Association of South East Asian Nations
BBS	Bangladesh Bureau of Statistics
BECE	Basic Education Certificate Examination
CAMPE	Campaign for Popular Education
CAO	Chief Administrative Officer
CDD-Ghana	The Ghana Centre for Democratic Development
CDRI	Cambodia Development Research Institute
CFS	Child Friendly School
COSATU	Congress of South African Trade Unions
CPP	Cambodian People's Party
CSO	Civil Society Organization
DA	District Assembly (Ghana)
DA	Democratic Alliance (South Africa)
DCE	District Chief Executive
DED	District Education Directorate
DEO	District Education Officer
DEOC	District Education Oversight Committee
DET	Department of Education and Training (South Africa)
DFID	Department for International Development
DHS	Demographic and Health Survey
DPE	Directorate of Primary Education (Bangladesh)
DRC	Democratic Republic of Congo
EA	Expatriate Advisor
ECDoE	Eastern Cape Department of Education
ELRC	Education Labour Relations Council (South Africa)
ERC	Education Research Council (Cambodia)
ESID	Effective States and Inclusive Development Research Centre

FBO	Faith-based Organization
FG	Focus Group
FGD	Focus Group Discussion
FMRP	Financial Management Reform Programme
FUNCINPEC	*Front Uni National pour un Cambodge Independent Neutre Pacifique et Cooperatif* (Cambodia)
GDP	Gross Domestic Product
GDPPC	Gross Domestic Product Per Capita
GED	General Economics Division
GES	Ghana Education Service
GoB	Government of Bangladesh
GPS	Government Primary School
HoR	House of Representatives
IRI	International Republican Institute
IS	International Scholar
JICA	Japan International Cooperation Agency
KG	Kindergarten
KPRP	Kampuchean People's Revolutionary Party
LC	Local Council
MDGs	Millennium Development Goals
MINALOC	Ministry of Local Government (Rwanda)
MINECOFIN	Ministry of Finance and Economic Planning (Rwanda)
MINEDUC	Ministry of Education (Rwanda)
MMDA	Metropolitan Municipal and District Assembly
MoE	Ministry of Education
MoEYS	Ministry of Education, Youth and Sport (Cambodia)
MOPME	Ministry of Primary and Mass Education (Bangladesh)
MP	Member of Parliament
MPAT	Management Performance Assessment Tool
NDC	National Democratic Congress (Ghana)
NE	National Expert
NER	Net Enrolment Ratio
NGO	Non-governmental Organization
NISR	National Institute of Statistics Rwanda
NM	National Ministry of Education Youth and Sport official (Cambodia)
NPP	New Patriotic Party (Ghana)
NRM	National Resistance Movement (Uganda)

OECD	Organisation for Economic Co-operation and Development
PEDP3	Third Primary Education Development Programme
PIRLS	Progress on International Literacy Study
PMO	Prime Minister's Office
PTA	Parent–Teacher Association
PTC	Parent–Teacher Committee
PTI	Primary Training Institute
RDC	Resident District Commissioner
REB	Rwandan Education Board
RMG	Readymade Garment
RNGPS	Registered Non-Government Primary School
RPF	Rwandan Patriotic Front
RSA	Republic of South Africa
RWF	Rwandan Franc
SACMEQ	South African Consortium on Monitoring Education Quality
SADTU	South African Democratic Teachers Union
SASA	South African School Act
SBM	School-based mentorship
SDGs	Sustainable Development Goals
SEO	Sector Education Officer
SGB	School Governing Body
SIP	School Improvement Plan
SMC	School Management Committee
SSA	Sub-Saharan Africa
TDMS	Teacher Development and Management System
TIMSS	Trends in International Mathematics and Science Study
TPAP	Teacher Policy Action Plan
TTC	Teacher Training College
TTCA	Teacher Training College Province A
TVET	Technical and Vocational Education and Training
UNATU	Uganda National Teachers' Union
UNESCO	United Nations Educational, Scientific and Cultural Organization
UNICEF	United Nations Children's Fund
UPE	Universal Primary Education
USAID	United States Agency for International Development
WCED	Western Cape Education Department
WDR	World Development Report

List of Contributors

Khondoker Shakhawat Ali is a sociologist, researcher and part-time faculty member at ASA University Bangladesh. At present he is the Chief Executive of Knowledge Alliance and Executive Editor of Protichinta—a quarterly on society, economy and state. Presently, he is also working at the Bangladesh Institute of Development Studies (BIDS) on Mobile Financial Service Impact Study (2017–2018) as a Senior Sociologist. His published books are: *Mobile Financial Services in Bangladesh: Success, Prospect and Challenges* and *'Antonio Gramsci: Life Struggle and Theory'* (Editor); *Fotoya: 1991–1995* (Co-editor). He studied sociology at Chittagong University, Bangladesh and development studies from the University of Wales, Swansea, UK.

Edward Ampratwum is a PhD Candidate at the Rory and Elizabeth Brooks Doctoral college at the Global Development Institute (GDI), The University of Manchester, UK. He is currently researching the politics of social protection implementation in Ghana, with a focus on power and political dynamics at the sub-national level in Ghana. His research interests include politics of social service delivery, decentralization, governmental transparency and social accountability, and democratic governance.

Mohammed Awal is Research and Program Officer at the Ghana Center for Democratic Development (CDD-Ghana), a research and policy think tank based in Accra, Ghana. His research and policy interests focus on democratic politics, social accountability, decentralization, and the politics of public service delivery. He is a member of the CDD-Ghana ESID Research Team.

Robert Cameron is Professor of Public Administration in the Department of Political Studies, University of Cape Town. He has published multiple books, journal articles and book chapters on local government, public administration and public service reform. He is a Senior Fellow at the Global Cities Institute, University of Toronto. He was a member of the South African Municipal Demarcation Board (1999–2004) which demarcated non-racial local government boundaries for the democratic South Africa.

Chuong Chantha is a government officer working for the Ministry of Education, Youth and Sport, Cambodia. He is mainly responsible for data processes, analysis, and report writing. He participated in the Lead analyst programme at the OECD for PISA-D data analysis and report writing in France. His latest report is *Results of Grade 8 Student Achievement from the National Assessment in 2017*. His responsibilities and interests are on large-scale student learning assessments in Cambodia. He holds a Master's degree in Science education from Hiroshima University, Japan.

Merilee S. Grindle is Edward S. Mason Professor of International Development, Emerita at the Harvard Kennedy School at Harvard University. She is a specialist on the comparative analysis of policymaking, implementation, and public management in developing countries, with particular reference to Latin America. Her most recent book is *Jobs for the Boys: Patronage and the State in Comparative Perspective.* She is also the author of: *Going Local: Decentralization, Democratization, and the Promise of Good Governance; Despite the Odds: The Contentious Politics of Education Reform; Audacious Reforms; Challenging the State; State and Countryside; Searching for Rural Development;* and *Bureaucrats, Politicians, and Peasants in Mexico,* as well as numerous articles on governance and the policy process.

Mirza M. Hassan is a political economist currently based at the BRAC Institute of Governance and Development (BIGD), BRAC University, Bangladesh. His research focuses on political settlements, private sector development, state–business relations, national and local governance, and human rights. He has worked as a consultant for various international agencies—UNDP, the Asia Foundation, the World Bank, DFID, CARE, in Bangladesh and in countries in North Africa and the Asia Pacific. His three most recent publications are on the political economy of tax reform in Bangladesh in the *Journal of Development Studies,* political settlement and democratic transition in Bangladesh in the *Conflict, Security and Development* and the political economy of state–business relations in Bangladesh (book chapter in 'Deals and Development'). He is currently leading action research on social accountability in the public procurement process for BIGD, which received an international award from the World Bank.

Sam Hickey is Professor of Politics and Development in the Global Development Institute, The University of Manchester, and Research Director of the DFID-UK-funded Effective States and Inclusive Development Research Centre (ESID). His recent work on the politics of development has been published in *African Affairs, Journal of Development Studies,* and *World Development.* He has edited or co-edited six collections, the most recent being *The Politics of Inclusive Development: Interrogating the Evidence,* with Kunal Sen and Badru Bukenya.

Ursula Hoadley is Associate Professor in the School of Education at the University of Cape Town. Her extensive published research explores the relation between education and social stratification and differential social and academic outcomes, with a focus on pedagogy, curriculum, and school organization at the primary level. Ursula participates in multiple professional education associations, fora, and boards, including South Africa's Ministerial Review Committee of 2009 which led to the revision of the outcomes-based national curriculum. She is currently working on a book 'Pedagogy in poverty: 20 years of curriculum reform in South Africa'.

Naomi Hossain is a political sociologist and a Research Fellow at the Institute of Development Studies at the University of Sussex. Her research focuses on the social and political impacts of the global food crisis, and on the political economy of human development, including education, in Bangladesh. She has researched elite perceptions of poverty, accountability for public services, women's empowerment, and food riots and food rights struggles. Recent books include *The Aid Lab: Understanding Bangladesh's Unexpected Success* and *Food Riots, Food Rights and the Politics of Provisions,* co-edited with Patta Scott-Villiers.

Md. Sajidul Islam is an educationist, researcher and full-time employee with UNICEF Bangladesh. He started his professional career in the education sector with UNICEF in early 1996, and currently works for the organization in Cox's Bazar managing the

Rohingya children's education programme. He has also worked for the World Bank and Asian Development Bank. He holds a Master's in Chemistry from Chittagong University and is a Master of Education from the Institute of Education and Research at Dhaka University.

David Jackman is an ESRC Postdoctoral Research Fellow at the School of Oriental and African Studies (SOAS). His research examines the political economy of violence in South Asia, with a focus on brokerage, party politics, and crime in Bangladesh. His work has been published in the journals Development and Change, Environment and Urbanization, and European Journal of Development Research. He holds a PhD in International Development from the University of Bath and was Research Associate for ESID between 2017–2018.

Tim Kelsall is a Research Fellow at the Overseas Development Institute in London, who specializes in political economy analysis and political anthropology. He has published extensively on issues of politics and development in Africa and Asia, is an alumnus of the East-West Center in Hawai'i, and an Honorary Research Fellow of the School of Environment, Education and Development at The University of Manchester. His latest book is *Business, Politics, and the State in Africa: Rethinking the Orthodoxies on Growth and Transformation*.

Sothy Khieng is a Research Fellow and head of the Education Unit at the Cambodia Development Resource Institute (CDRI). His major publications include the co-edited volume on Cambodia *Education 2015: Employment and Empowerment*. He was a Visiting Scholar at the Melbourne Centre for Study of Higher Education and at Griffith University. His current research projects and interests are on teaching and learning and diversity of higher education institutions in Cambodia. He has a PhD in Organization Sciences from Vrije Universiteit Amsterdam and an MA in International Development Studies from Ohio University.

Anne Mette Kjær is an Associate Professor in the Department of Political Science, at Aarhus University. She is Principal Investigator on the DANIDA-funded research programme of Political Settlements and Revenue Bargaining. She has published in journals such as *Development Policy Review, World Development, Public Administration, and Democratization*. She has recently co-authored *The Politics of African Industrial Policy* and co-edited *Perspectives on Politics, Production, and Public Administration in Africa*.

Brian Levy is Professor of the Practice of International Development, School of Advanced International Studies, Johns Hopkins University in Washington, DC and Academic Director, Graduate School of Development Policy and Practice, University of Cape Town. He worked at the World Bank from 1989 to 2012. His books include *Working with the Grain: Integrating Governance and Growth in Development Strategies* (co-edited with Sahr Kpundeh) and *Building State Capacity in Africa*. He completed his BA (Hons) at the University of Cape Town in 1976, and PhD in economics at Harvard University in 1983.

Nansozi K. Muwanga is a Senior Lecturer and former Head of Department, Department of Political Science and Public Administration, Makerere University. A Fulbright New Century Scholar, she holds a PhD in Political Science from the University of Toronto and a Master's degree in Area Studies, from London University. Nansozi has extensive multi-disciplinary research interests and consultancy experience in the areas of governance and education policy reform. Her most recent publications include an article in *The African Journal of Public Administration*, and 'The Metropolitanization, Decentralization and Local Democracy in Uganda', co-authored with Christopher Gore in the *Journal of Urban Development*.

Tieng Tek Muy is a Research Assistant within the Education Unit at the Cambodian Development Resource Institute (CDRI). Her latest article is 'How do Cambodian Academic Leaders Define and Perceive Higher Education Internationalisation'. Her research interests revolve around educational policies, international education, students' mobility, and educational leadership. Currently she is a graduate student at the Beijing Normal University, China, and her Master's thesis is investigating international students' experience in post-secondary studies in China. She majored in Teaching English as a Foreign Language in her bachelor programme at the Royal University of Phnom Penh, Cambodia.

Vinothan Naidoo is Senior Lecturer in the Department of Political Studies, University of Cape Town. His research explores South Africa's challenges of institutional transformation and public sector reform, policy coordination and implementation, political–administrative relations, and inter-governmental relations. He completed a PhD in Public Administration at the University of Cape Town.

Franklin Oduro is Deputy Executive Director and Director of Programs at the Ghana Center for Democratic Development (CDD-Ghana), a research and policy think tank based in Accra, Ghana. His research interests include democratic governance, public policy and public affairs management, and comparative national systems and development politics. Dr Oduro is the coordinator for all ESID research at CDD-Ghana.

Lant Pritchett is Professor of the Practice of Economic Development at the Harvard Kennedy School at Harvard University and is a Senior Fellow of the Center for Global Development. He has authored (either alone or with one of his fifty co-authors) over a hundred articles, with over 35,000 citations on development-related topics ranging from economic growth to education, population, social capital, health, migration, and state capability. His most recent books are *Building State Capability: Evidence, Analysis, Action* (with Matt Andrews and Michael Woolcock) and *The Rebirth of Education: Schooling Ain't Learning*.

Muhammad Ashikur Rahman is a PhD student at the University of Leicester, UK. His research focuses on the labour internationalism and its implication in the local context particularly in the Ready-made Garment (RMG) sector of Bangladesh. His recent publication includes a book chapter titled *'Framing "food riots": subsistence protests in international and national media, 2007–2012'* (co-authored with Hossain et al.), in *Food Riots, Food Rights and the Politics of Provisions*, edited by Naomi Hossain and Patta Scott-Villiers.

Timothy P. Williams is an Honorary Research Fellow in the School of Environment, Education and Development at The University of Manchester, and Adjunct Professor in global practice at Boston College School of Social Work. His recent work on the politics of education and development has been published in *Journal of Development Studies*, *World Development*, *Journal of East African Studies*, and *International Journal of Educational Development*. He has served as a consultant for the Center for Universal Education at the Brookings Institution and for the World Bank's 2018 World Development Report.

1

The Problem of Education Quality in Developing Countries

Naomi Hossain and Sam Hickey

Introduction

Universal basic education was set to be one of the great development successes of the twentieth century, as countries all around the world enthusiastically expanded provision, enrolling ever more of their young in primary and secondary schools. Yet by the early 2000s, it was already evident that not only were millions still out of school, but that a majority dropped out early, attended sporadically, or learned little while there (UNESCO 2014). As one observer summarized it, 'schooling ain't learning' (Pritchett 2013): there is more to learning than placing children in schools. The 'learning crisis' is acknowledged in the Sustainable Development Goal 4 to 'ensure inclusive and quality education for all and promote lifelong learning',[1] an emphasis on quality and equality in contrast to the focus on access in Millennium Development Goal 2. This learning crisis is widely yet unevenly spread, varying between countries, classes, genders, and social groups (World Bank 2017). But whereas expanding primary schooling was a comparatively popular and measurably successful policy goal, addressing poor quality teaching and low levels of learning has so far proven less so (Bruns and Schneider 2016). A few countries have managed to expand their education systems while enhancing learning. But it is easier to build schools, abolish fees, recruit more teachers, and instruct parents to send their children, than it is to ensure that schools, teachers, and students are equipped and motivated for teaching and learning once there.

[1] http://un.org/sustainabledevelopment/education/ (accessed 12 June 2017).

This book contributes to making sense of this global learning crisis, by exploring the conditions under which reforms likely to shift education provisioning onto a higher-quality pathway are undertaken and enacted. It takes as its starting point the view that politics is likely to matter in explaining why this is the case. As a recent review put it, education reform is:

> a highly charged and politicized process; what gets implemented—and its impact—depends as much or more on the politics of the reform process as the technical design of the reform. (Bruns and Schneider 2016, 5)

There are good reasons to believe that variations in how countries adopt and implement reforms necessary to promote learning relate to differences in their political economies. These differences may play out in the design of reforms that are attempted and adopted, and in what gets implemented—including that it is more politically popular and less taxing of often weak state capacities to expand school provision than to improve learning outcomes. Yet, barring some notable exceptions (e.g. Grindle 2004), there has been little political analysis of education in general (Busemeyer and Trampusch 2011; Gift and Wibbels 2014), and still less on the political economy of education quality in developing countries—a gap that has been noted and bemoaned in several recent reviews (Kingdon et al. 2014; Nicolai et al. 2014; Wales, Magee, and Nicolai 2016; Bruns and Schneider 2016). As a contribution to filling this critical gap, this book sets out and tests hypotheses about how different types of political context interact with the education policy domain in ways that shape the uptake and implementation of reforms designed to improve learning outcomes.

The book features comparative analysis of the politics of education quality reforms across six low- to middle-income countries—Bangladesh, Cambodia, Ghana, Rwanda, South Africa, and Uganda—all of which were relatively successful at rapidly expanding access to primary schooling, but which have all found it much harder to improve learning outcomes, in part (we suggest) because of the variable levels of political commitment that exist in each context for reforms aimed at improving the quality of education. In this volume, we understand political commitment to reflect the incentives and ideas that predominate amongst political elites, and which are shaped by the underlying character of politics and power in specific contexts. The concept we use to describe 'the balance or distribution of power between contending social groups and social classes, on which any state is based' (di John and Putzel 2009, 4) is a 'political settlement', and we have chosen our cases to represent different types of these settlements.

The comparison explores how different distributions of power shaped incentives and ideas around education quality reforms and the institutions and processes of implementation, tracing the politics of reform from the political centre down through different levels of governance to the school, taking into account the impact of the external environment (for example, aid) and the policy legacies and challenges in each context. What we want to examine here is less the broad question of 'how politics shapes educational outcomes' per se, than the ways in which politics shapes the commitment and capacity of elites and governments in developing countries to promote reforms that are aimed at improving learning outcomes. In particular, and following several systematic reviews of what works to improve learning outcomes in developing countries (e.g. Glewwe et al. 2011; Tikly and Barrett 2013), we focus on efforts to improve the level and management of resourcing accorded to schools, and the quality and presence of teachers through training, incentives, and oversight mechanisms.

What we know about quality reforms is that they are inherently more difficult to design and to 'sell' to the public: there is less certainty about 'what works' and results are harder to measure (Nelson 2007). It is easier to design and implement top-down command-and-control responses to build more schools and recruit more teachers and children than to devise workable solutions to the 'craft' challenge of the interpersonal, transactional nature of effective teaching and learning (Pritchett 2013). Strengthening local accountability is difficult. Teachers, the group whose interests are most likely to suffer from reforms to enhance their performance accountability, tend to be well-organized, influential, and equipped to resist them (Corrales 1999, 2006; Moe and Wiborg 2017; Kingdon et al. 2014; Béteille, Kingdon, and Muzammil 2016). Parents and communities, particularly in developing countries, are often less well-equipped and informed to articulate demand for quality improvements from their political leaders or frontline providers (Dunne et al. 2007; Mani and Mukand 2007). This means that for parents and communities, both the 'long route' (via the process of political representation) and the 'short route' (via relationships with frontline providers, teachers, and schools) to accountability for the delivery of high quality education, may be obstructed or subverted (World Bank 2003). A recent review concluded that three features of the politics of education are particularly relevant in analysing the prospects for reform: (i) the strength of teacher unions compared with other education stakeholders or labour unions; (ii) the 'opacity of the classroom'—the need for reforms to shape teacher behaviour in the classroom, over which direct control is impossible; and (iii) the slow or lagged nature of the results of quality reforms (compared, for example, with the abolition of fees, learning reforms will yield no instant or obvious political return) (Bruns and Schneider 2016).

The World Bank identifies children's unreadiness to learn, along with teacher and school management skills, and inadequate school inputs, as the proximate determinants of the learning crisis (World Bank 2017). It argues that the intractability of education quality reforms is not inherently a matter of inadequate resources, although many failing systems are also under-resourced (UNESCO 2014; World Bank 2017). Instead, it is a problem of 'mis-alignment' between learning goals, policies, and practices, in which the dominant role of teacher unions and other forms of 'unhealthy politics' plays an important and persistent role (World Bank 2017). It concludes that 'healthier' forms of politics—in particular the use of information to increase 'the political incentives for learning' and broad-based pro-reform coalitions—are critical to align goals, policies, and practices around improved learning. While highlighting the significance of the politics of teacher and school management on the frontline of the learning crisis, the emphasis on 'alignment' sidelines the significance of contention in education reform, and fails to address the questions to which it gives rise: under what conditions do broad-based, pro-reform coalitions come about? In which political contexts does information about education performance become embedded in functioning mechanisms of accountability? Why do some states visibly devote more capacity to learning and more political resources to quality reforms than others?

This book seeks to pick up the analysis at the point where the World Development Report (WDR) 2018 leaves off, pursuing a political explanation of the misalignments and contentions that shape the uptake of learning reforms. The analysis seeks to test assumptions that political settlements where elites have shorter time-horizons (competitive and clientelistic settlements, such as those in Ghana and Bangladesh) are less likely to take up the politically intractable task of redistributing power in the education system than those (the dominant settlements of Cambodia and Rwanda) where elites are better insulated, can adopt longer-term horizons and might be more likely to take up developmentally important projects. It also seeks to explore how different political settlements interact with systems of governance within the domain of education, ranged from traditional hierarchically organized bureaucracies to multi-stakeholder models, to create a range of different outcomes in 'the many layers within a specific sector in between the top levels of policymaking and the service provision frontline' (Levy and Walton 2013, 4).

Following this introductory chapter, Chapter 2 sets out the intellectual rationale for a political settlement-based approach to the analysis of education quality reforms, and establishes the theoretical framework and methodological approach used to research the politics in the cases presented here. Chapters 3 through 8 comprise the set of six country cases, each of which gives an account of the quality of basic education and its development in that country; of the political settlement and its influences on education policy and the reform agenda; and of the implementation of policies aimed at improving learning from the national level downwards through sub-national levels of governance and, in most cases, through to schools themselves. Chapter 9 draws together the theoretical, methodological, and empirical findings from the comparative analysis, and points towards areas for further conceptual development and empirical research. The book concludes with two commentaries from leading authorities in the field on the arguments and cases presented in the book.

The Global Learning Crisis

From an access point of view, progress towards universal primary education in low-income countries accelerated markedly in the past two decades (see Figure 1.1). Globally, 93 per cent of children now attend primary school at the appropriate age, up from 84 per cent in 1999. By 2015, 20 million more developing country children had completed primary school than would have done so had the rate of school expansion before 2000 continued. In seventeen countries, age-correct enrolment rates increased by more than 20 per cent between 1999 and 2012, implying a remarkably rapid expansion. And gains were concentrated in the poorest world regions of Sub-Saharan Africa (where the net enrolment ratio [NER] rose from 59 per cent in 1999 to 79 per cent in 2012) and South and West Asia (where it went from 78 to 94 per cent over the same period). Between 2000 and 2010, NER increased from 27 to almost 64 per cent in Niger, from 42 to 76 per cent in Guinea, and in Burundi, from less than 41 to 94 per cent in 2010. The proportion of children who had never attended

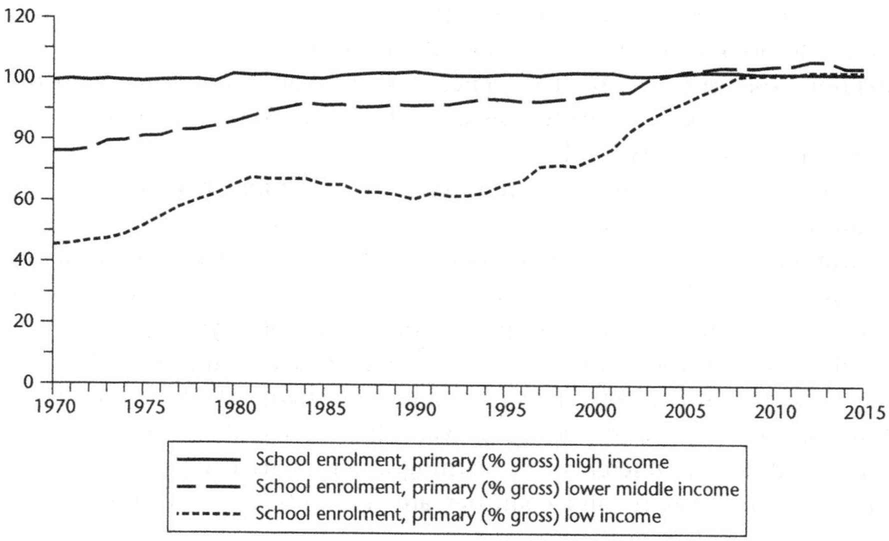

Figure 1.1 Primary enrolment rates worldwide, 1970–2015
Source: World Development Indicators (accessed 12 July 2017).

school dropped in Ethiopia from 67 per cent in 2000 to 28 per cent in 2011, and in Tanzania from 47 per cent in 1999 to 12 per cent in 2010. Globally, gender parity in enrolment was achieved at primary level and almost achieved at secondary level over the period, in part due to the push on girls' education from MDG3 on gender equality; of countries with data, 69 per cent were set to achieve gender parity at primary level, but only less than half at secondary level by 2015.[2]

However, the idea that mass education was 'one of the successes of the MDGs' has been tempered by 'more sobering trends' (Unterhalter 2014, 181). Large numbers of children remain excluded from school, with 58 million children aged six to eleven unenrolled in 2012, many in conflict-affected regions. At least one-fifth of all children were likely to drop out before completing primary in 32 countries, most of them in Sub-Saharan Africa (UNESCO 2015). And rural–urban location, socio-economic class, and marginalization and social exclusion continued to determine which children enrolled and stayed on in school. Despite gains in gender parity on literacy in many places, progress towards adult literacy has been slow; in fact, almost all gains have been due to the transition of schooled youth into adulthood, rather than programmes of learning for adults. About half a billion women still lacked basic literacy in 2015 (UNESCO 2015). And while most children in most countries can now attend school, in a great many, a minority learn as much as their governments expect them to. By their own standards, a large number of developing country school systems are failing to endow their students with even minimum competencies of reading, writing, and arithmetic. Globally, some 125 million children do not attain functional literacy or numeracy even after four years of school, while the majority—in some cases the vast majority—of primary school students in many education systems do not attain even the basic competencies in reading or arithmetic needed to continue their learning (World Bank 2017).

The poor quality of the education received by the majority in developing countries is of particular concern because of the potential role of good quality education in reversing—or reinforcing—economic and related inequalities. The quality of education is increasingly understood to be a more powerful driver of economic growth than the size of an education system, and higher-quality basic education is associated with more inclusive and equitable forms of growth (Hanushek 2009; Hanushek and Woessmann 2007). However, the learning crisis aggravates, and is aggravated by, social and economic inequalities of all kinds. Differences in learning attainments between lower- and higher-income regions and countries are substantial, as a comparison of

[2] All figures here are from UNESCO's 2015 *Global Monitoring Report*, which took stock of all progress towards the EFA goals over the period (UNESCO 2015).

PISA (Programme for International Student Assessment) test scores shows: the average student in a low-income country performs worse than 95 per cent of students in OECD countries—that is, would require remedial lessons in any developed country school system. Differences within a region can also be significant: Colombian students attain basic literacy six years earlier than their Bolivian counterparts, while only 19 per cent of young Nigerian primary school completers can read, compared with 80 per cent in Tanzania (World Bank 2017). Girls, rural students, and children from minority or other socially marginalized groups generally learn less, compared with boys, city children, and other advantaged groups (World Bank 2017). This reflects how gender and class disadvantage, remote geography, and membership of marginalized social groups amplify unequal learning outcomes; these then accumulate as children transition through the education system and on into the labour market (UNESCO 2012, 2014). Nonetheless, some countries outperform others on learning indicators: Vietnam, for instance, performs much better than predicted by its per capita income; students in Latvia and Albania similarly learn more than expected from their other social and economic indicators (World Bank 2017). This again reinforces the sense that the drivers of educational quality are not simply related to economic or cultural factors, and that political factors are likely to play a significant role here.

Roots of the Learning Crisis: Lessons from Efforts at Reform

Why is the learning crisis so pervasive and apparently stubborn, when policies of educational expansion were so rapidly and enthusiastically adopted across the developing world? Improving quality is recognized to be more expensive and more difficult than increasing school places, and there is a perceived trade-off between keeping unit costs low and maximizing learning achievement (Nicolai et al. 2014, 2). Enabling high quality learning is particularly challenging amongst low-income populations because of: institutional or personal biases against children from poor or marginalized groups (UNESCO 2010); challenges in the home environment (Smith and Barrett 2011); the adverse cognitive effects of early and chronic malnourishment (Crookston et al. 2010, 2013; World Bank 2017); and dropout, poor attendance, child labour, and other characteristic features of childhoods lived in extreme poverty (Rose and Dyer 2008). School meals tend to raise participation and attendance rates, for instance, but evidence that school meals improve learning outcomes is more mixed (Adelman, Gilligan, and Lehrer 2008; Snilstveit et al. 2015). Poverty and inequality may be the biggest obstacles to education quality (Tikly and Barrett 2013), but while good quality education may be the surest pathway out of poverty and towards more equitable societies, there are few simple solutions to raising education standards in such settings. There is, in any case, limited consensus about what works to improve learning, as a recent 'review of reviews' found (Evans and Popova 2016).

Under-resourced and poorly managed systems lead to persistently poor quality basic education, but more finance is not necessarily the answer. Low- and middle-income countries typically spend too little on education: only 41 of 150 countries for which data is available spend the recommended 6 per cent of Gross Domestic Product (GDP) on education, and 25 countries spend less than half that. Globally, the average proportion of public spending on education was only 15 per cent (against a recommended 20 per cent), a proportion that has barely changed since 1999; in some low- and middle-income countries, the share of education in public spending dropped below 5 per cent of GDP during the MDG period (UNESCO 2014). Under-resourcing does not explain all of the problems of education quality, but it helps to explain why fewer than 5 per cent of Tanzanian students have their own reading textbook, why 130 Malawian students cram into the average first-year classroom, and why only one in four Chad schools has a toilet (UNESCO 2014).

Yet the extent to which resources shape education quality is known to be highly variable, depending on how they are governed and managed at the different levels of education systems. The resources that do reach schools are often poorly deployed, usually because of over-centralized control, so that the meagre resources are inefficiently and ineffectively used, and the evidence on how more resources contribute to better learning via lower pupil–teacher ratios and more qualified teachers is mixed and context-specific (Glewwe et al. 2011). In their review of seventy-nine studies in developing countries, Glewwe et al. (2011, 41) concluded that a reasonably functional physical classroom tended to matter, but so did teachers with more subject knowledge, longer school days, and the provision of tuition; by contrast, teacher absence had a 'clear negative effect'. Many teachers freelance as private tutors or find other ways to supplement their income (Bray 2006). Leakage is common, particularly through loss of public sector employee time (Chaudhury et al. 2004).

Where teachers do show up, they are often themselves too poorly educated to impart high quality learning: most new teachers in The Gambia, Botswana, Lesotho, Chad, Togo, Guinea-Bissau, and Cameroon did not even meet secondary school minimum qualifications for teachers in the 1990s (UNESCO 2004). And, despite massive investments in teacher training in the 2000s, in one-third of countries less than 75 per cent of teachers are trained even up to (often quite low) national standards (UNESCO 2014). Tikly and Barrett (2013, 4) found that while low reading and mathematics attainments were closely linked to poverty and inequality, 'schools can make a difference', even more so in lower-income countries than in richer countries, particularly through effective school leadership and teacher management. As the World Bank (2017) summarized it, the four determinants of the learning crisis are: (i) children do not arrive ready to learn; (ii) teachers often lack the needed skills and motivation; (iii) school management skills are low; and (iv) school inputs have failed to keep pace with expansion. A critical lesson is that learning crises are systemic, not merely errors at the margin: entire education systems generally fail to deliver adequate levels of learning. This reflects the 'misalignment' of the goals and practices of the education system with the learning outcomes it needs to generate, notably on matters such as setting learning objectives and responsibilities, monitoring learning, financing, and the motivations and incentives of key actors within the system (World Bank 2017).

What causes these misalignments? The World Development Report 2004, *Making Services Work for Poor People*, undertook a political analysis of service delivery failures, linking them to weak or dysfunctional relationships of accountability between citizens and service-users (with respect to education, parents, and students) and service providers (teachers, officials, politicians) (World Bank 2003). Four dimensions of accountability most needed strengthening in relation to education performance: (i) voice, or how well citizens could hold the state—politicians and policymakers—accountable for performance in discharging its responsibility for education; (ii) compacts, or how well and how clearly the responsibilities and objectives of public engagement were communicated to the public, and to private organizations that provide services (Ministries of Education, school districts); (iii) management, or the actions that created effective frontline providers (teachers, administrators) within organizations; and (iv) client power, or how well citizen-clients could increase the accountability of schools and school systems (World Bank 2003, 113). Central insights included that accountability for public service provision could be exercised via the 'long route to accountability', whereby citizens and civil society mandate political actors to provide education services, politicians then direct state actors to design such services, and the central state then tasks local governments and frontline service to deliver the services (and they are potentially punished electorally for failures at education service delivery); or via the 'short route', through which service-users hold frontline providers directly to account, through the use of their powers as consumers or rights-bearing citizens to demand services and sanction failures (World Bank 2003).

Recognizing the central importance of accountability, efforts to strengthen the 'short route' to accountable education provision took the form of interventions and experiments to promote community participation in school-based management; induce community monitoring of school quality indicators, such as enrolment, attendance, and performance; introduce vouchers and other 'school choice' initiatives; and efforts to monitor teacher performance, amongst others. It seems clear that teachers perform best when motivated and monitored to do so (Bruns, Filmer, and Patrinos 2011; Bruns and Luque 2014), yet efforts to enhance learning by strengthening 'client power' have yielded mixed results (Bruns et al. 2011; Carr-Hill et al. 2015; Snilstveit et al. 2015; World Bank 2017). Carr-Hill et al. (2015) found that community participation in school management yielded positive and large effects in middle-income countries, but smaller and more uneven results in poorer countries, where, amongst other things, community members lacked the capacities or incentives to engage with school performance (see also Dunne et al. 2007).

Some of these interventions, particularly the quasi-experimental efforts at information and monitoring, were introduced with limited reference to the political contexts within which they needed to operate, something which recent reviews of social accountability have found to be critical (Devarajan, Khemani, and Walton 2011; Hickey and King 2016). These 'widgets'—pared-down tools for project intervention that failed to engage with the deeper and wider politics of school provision—had little prospect of strengthening accountability for public service delivery (Joshi and Houtzager 2012). Citizen power involves a transformation of political relationships, not merely the 'teeth' or consumer power to make choices at the frontline, but the 'voice' to mandate public action, and to demand accountability (Fox 2015). In the terms of the WDR 2004, the short route to accountability needs the 'voice' of political claims- and policymaking for it to be effective, while at the local level, education service delivery only has 'teeth'—the ability to punish failures—when citizens and service-users have the capacities to demand, and receive, improved performance on the frontline (see also Westhorp et al. 2014).

These bottom-up pressures also need to be backed up by top-down pressure from within the political and bureaucratic system (Booth 2012), often through combined forms of diagonal accountability that join up oversight mechanisms in pursuit of more responsive and effective performance (Goetz and Jenkins 2005; Joshi and Houtzager 2012). The nature of the 'craft' in the interpersonal activity of teaching and learning means that effective school systems need to be organized like starfish—independently functional and responsive to differences in environment, yet connected to the whole—rather than, as most are, like spiders, directly controlled from the centre (Pritchett 2013). Yet central control remains an important political objective in many school systems, whether under democratic or authoritarian rule, and whether state capacity can be judged strong or weak.

These lessons have renewed attention to the politics of the 'long route' to accountability in education provision. In the first World Development Report on education (World Bank 2017) the roots of the learning crisis are framed as both technical and political. In one important example, national learning assessments are seen as vital to create 'measures *for* learning [to] guide action' as well as 'measures *of* learning [to] spur action', by increasing public participation and awareness of school performance; providing parents with evidence needed to make better choices; and raising voice via 'the long route of accountability, where learning metrics may help citizens use the political process to hold politicians accountable for learning' (World Bank 2017, 94). Yet, while 'political impetus' has been critical to the adoption and implementation of learning reforms, powerful political incentives, including 'unhealthy' relationships between teacher unions and political and bureaucratic interests, can also ensure the goals and practices of the system remain misaligned with those of children's learning (World Bank 2017).

Understanding the Political Economy of Education Quality Reforms

It may be true that 'education systems are what they are, and indeed, the schools are what they are—everywhere in the world, regardless of the nation—because politics makes them that way' (Moe and Wiborg 2017). Yet political science has paid little attention to education, for reasons that include lack of data and the specific disciplinary challenge (for political science) of accessing household dynamics and decision-making processes at multiple levels (Gift and Wibbels 2014; Busemeyer and Trampusch 2011; Ansell 2010). There has been some interest in the comparative politics of education, including in developing countries (for instance, Baum and Lake 2003; Brown and Hunter 2004), but it remains a new thematic area for the discipline, and one in which theorizing is in its infancy. The next section briefly discusses existing political science theories of education provision in light of the distinct challenges and concerns of developing countries, before moving on to the literature on the politics of education quality in developing country settings. This includes a discussion of the need to maintain a distinction between the politics of education in advanced, industrialized societies with long-established systems of mass education, and the politics of education in societies whose population includes many first-generation learners, where mass education is still a novelty and where transnational influences may be stronger.

Gift and Wibbels (2014) argue that the basis for a political science theory of education is as a function of the interaction between demand and supply: how much education a society receives is a function of: (a) the demand for skills emanating from the labour market and the economy; and (b) how, and the extent to which, those skills are supplied through the education system. Parents are assumed to 'naturally prefer' schools that are good for their children, and, to a greater or lesser extent, to mandate politicians to deliver them. How successfully they organize to assert their demands will determine what states provide. Ansell (2010) similarly notes that a political theory of education must rest on insights (a) that education is essentially redistributive and, depending on how resources are spent, can be progressive or otherwise; and (b) that 'public education policy is heavily affected by the nature of the global market for educated labor' (Ansell 2010, 3).

Not all the assumptions made by Gift and Wibbels (2014) hold in contexts where mass formal schooling is still new. Gift and Wibbels view the outcome as a matter of magnitude, with the dependent variable being public spending on education. But if the heart of the problem is that schools and teachers are unaccountable to the parents and pupils they are supposed to serve, this implies a change in the relative political power of these groups, and not—or not only—more resources. In fact, more resources may exacerbate the problem, entrenching public sector interests in the existing system, making teacher unions stronger, expanding poorly managed services to an even wider population. Parents may know neither what to expect nor what to demand (for instance, Martínez 2012; Dunne et al. 2007; Mani and Mukand 2007). The capacity of citizens to demand and achieve improved levels of service provision is in general closely shaped by issues of poverty, exclusion, and inequality (Hickey and King 2016).

In developing countries with limited state capacity, the strongest demand for an educated population may come from the state itself. Many developing countries lack the human resources to staff the state; as we have already seen, many low-income countries cannot recruit enough educated teachers. Education provision may thus be insulated against state weaknesses and/or the problems of personalized as opposed to programmatic policy regimes, but with limited implications for quality: 'in an environment of weak state capacity, democracy may prompt governments to increase education access, but not education inputs' (Harding and Stasavage 2014, 230). The likely absence of programmatic education agendas in developing countries may also be related to the general absence of programmatic class-based parties; the political history of education in developed countries indicates that parties and coalitions on the left and centre are more likely to promote wider access to education, and are associated with higher public spending on education (Busemeyer 2014).

Demand for educated labour from employers may be weak in low-income developing countries with large 'reserve army' populations, or because low-capital enterprises generally need little skilled labour. It seems clear that the 'Varieties of Capitalism' approach to understanding differences in education policy on the basis of 'a functional complementarity between skill formation and welfare state policies' (Busemeyer 2014, 35) offers limited insights into situations where the relationship between labour, capital, and the state is informal, paternalistic, and unorganized. Corrales argues that it is possible that 'more exposure to capitalism prompts governments and constituents to protect education expenditures', but that how domestic politics interacts with opportunities and constraints in the global economy shapes the politics of investment in education (Corrales 2006, 240). Doner and Schneider (2016, 635) note that informality, inequality, and a reliance on foreign direct investment can fragment business and labour, and 'undercut the potential demand for upgrading institutions'.

Of the available scholarship that does focus on the political economy of education in developing countries,[3] it is possible to differentiate between those studies which focus on how national-level politics shapes educational policies in broad terms (e.g. Stasavage 2005; Kosack 2009; Kosack 2012) and those that look more specifically at how politics (e.g. Grindle 2004) and governance arrangements (Pritchett 2013) play out within education systems. Within each of these literatures, there is a further distinction between a focus on formal institutional arrangements (e.g. Ansell 2008 and Stasavage 2005 on democracy; Pritchett 2013 on education sector governance; World Bank 2003 on formal accountability structures) and those that focus on informal power and politics (e.g. Kosack 2012 on political coalitions; Grindle 2004 on policy coalitions; also, Wales et al. 2016).

Analysis of the relationship between democracy and education tends to find that democracy exerts a positive influence on governments' financial commitments to education (Stasavage 2005; Ansell 2008). But this may not advance understanding of reforms aimed at learning, as opposed to access. Nelson (2007) argues that competitive elections may create pressures to increase but not to improve or reallocate provision, because the political incentives to do so are so weak and non-urgent. Kosack (2012) also goes beyond regime-type explanations in search of a less formal and institutional analysis, arguing that none of the three most common political–economic explanations (relating to regime type, education cultures, and governmental commitment to economic performance) predict the realities of education policies. In his analysis of Taiwan, Ghana, and Brazil, Kosack concludes that answers to two questions can explain patterns of education investment: whose support does a government need to stay in power? What sort of education do those citizens want? Kosack identifies situations in which political entrepreneurs help disorganized groups to organize around common interests on education, as through the formation of coalitions between populist leaders and rural constituencies (Kosack 2012; also Corrales 1999). By

[3] We are grateful to Sophie King for producing an excellent annotated bibliography on the politics of education in developing countries, on which this section is based.

extension of the same logic regarding the role of coalitions in shaping policy preferences, it may well be that developing countries lack the kinds of organized groups that might constitute a coalition in favour of a better trained citizenry and labour force (e.g. middle-class parents, organized capitalists).

This focus on informal forms of politics seems to characterize the most insightful comparative work to date on education politics. Merilee Grindle's (2004) seminal work on education sector reform in Latin America notes that whereas access reforms were '"easy" from a political economy perspective' (Grindle 2004, 6), reforms aimed at improving quality in the 1990s:

> involved the potential for lost jobs, and lost control over budgets, people, and decisions. They exposed students, teachers, and supervisors to new pressures and expectations. Teachers' unions charged that they destroyed long existing rights and career tracks. (Grindle 2004, 6)

The wider literature supports the presumption that teachers are typically the best organized and most vocal group empowered to influence education policy and reforms, and that influence is not always benign (Moe and Wiborg 2017; Bruns and Schneider 2016; Kingdon et al. 2014; Rosser and Fahmi 2018; Béteille et al. 2016). Nevertheless, Grindle's cases of education quality reforms in Latin America show that reforms could succeed, depending on how they were introduced, designed, approved, and implemented. Reform-oriented coalitions within the education sector were particularly important in her cases. Corrales (1999) similarly suggests that policy entrepreneurs tend to emerge in response to high-level government commitment to reforms. But a recent review of the politics of education quality in developing countries found that the visibility and 'political returns' of educational investments, information asymmetries, particularly around performance assessment, and patterns of demand and accountability, including capacities for collective action, tended to limit commitment to quality reforms (Nicolai et al. 2014, 5).

In terms of studies on the significance of formal governance arrangements within the education sector, there has been a focus on both the national- and local-level systems, and within each of these on the appropriate balance between top-down and bottom-up forms of accountability mechanisms. Pritchett (2013) argues that school systems are often highly centralized, which can work well to deliver expanded provision quickly, but which may exclude local parents and teachers from influence, and so deliver schooling without learning. A similar point is made by Tikly and Barrett (2013, 20), who conclude that 'weighting accountability towards top-down control...can constrain the space for teacher autonomy, reducing responsive inclusion and curricula relevance at the classroom level'.

However, formal governance arrangements rarely play out according to design in developing countries (Andrews 2013). Kingdon et al. (2014, 2) note that the supposed benefits of decentralization 'do not accrue in practice because in poor rural areas the local elite closes up the spaces for wider community representation and participation in school affairs'. They suggest the effects of decentralization are 'especially problematic when accountability systems are weak, and there is little parental information or awareness of how to hold schools responsible' (Kingdon et al. 2014, 28). A good deal of work has been undertaken at the level of schools themselves, particularly in terms of the type of oversight and accountability measures associated with improved levels of performance. Westhorp et al.'s (2014) systematic review of the circumstances under which decentralization, school-based management, accountability initiatives, and community schools influence education outcomes, particularly for the poor, found that a wide range of approaches had achieved some degree of success. These include the introduction of rewards in conjunction with sanctions; performance monitoring by the community members, including traditional authorities and politicians; and the introduction of direct accountability relationships, including the power to hire and fire between school management committees and staff. However, school-level interventions are rarely enough on their own: to work, they depend on a supportive political context, an adequately-resourced education sector with a strong national system for assessment, and high-capacity local actors, including school management committees, head teachers, and local community actors.

Some research into the politics of education in developing countries has focused more on the ideas (rather than only the incentives) that shape elite behaviour. A good deal of work on elite perceptions and commitment has identified education as being an area that attracts a high level of consensus from ruling elites, as compared with other aspects of social policy (e.g. Hossain 2005; Hossain and Moore 2002). Contemporary developing countries are part of a world system in which mass education is, or is becoming, the norm, so that integration into that world system depends on the provision of mass education, and provision of mass education legitimates state authority (Boli, Ramirez, and Meyer 1985; Meyer, Ramirez, and Soysal 1992; see also Corrales 2006; Tikly 2001). Policy and political elites may 'demand' education as part of a developmentalist agenda of nation building or economic development, or as an instrument for achieving other social policy goals (e.g. fertility control: Colclough 2012; Ansell 2010).

Finally, international actors have played a significant role in driving up the levels of investment in education in developing countries, and in ensuring that a significant effort is made to target this provision at poorer groups. This is in part through the transnational advocacy coalition that comprised the Global Campaign for Education (Gaventa and Mayo 2009), as well as the strong pressures that international aid agencies have often exerted over education policy within countries that rely on overseas development finance. The Millennium Development Goals helped to provide further impetus here. However, the influence of aid agencies within the global South is declining, and there is little evidence to date that donors or international agencies have succeeded in promoting reforms targeted at improving the quality of education, despite efforts in this direction (Wales et al. 2016), including through the Sustainable Development Goals.

Overall, then, there have been some important studies of the politics of educational quality in developing countries, even if these are few in nature. Of these, the ones that most closely address our concern with the politics of promoting difficult reforms aimed at tackling the learning crisis have tended to emphasize the role of informal as well as formal institutional processes, ideas as well as incentives, and actors operating at multiple scales, from the global through to the local, and often in the form of coalitions. Given that none have presented a conceptual framework that can help capture these multiple factors, we try to address this failing in the next chapter, where we set out an approach that helped guide the studies reported on here and which we hope can be of some use in guiding further work in the field.

Conclusion: Understanding Education Quality Reform Demands a Political Approach

The global learning crisis manifests itself in low learning attainments in each of the six countries studied here. Their experiences are reflected across the struggles faced by low- and middle-income countries to grow their education systems in an increasingly competitive global economy dependent on skills. This book helps to make sense of the global learning crisis by exploring the proposition that politics matters, centrally, in explaining why some countries are doing better at raising the quality of education than others. But how might politics matter? Political analysis of education is limited, both empirically and theoretically, and both in developed and in developing countries. While there are good reasons to believe that the difference in the uptake of quality reforms and their implementation relates to differences of a political nature, there is little conceptual work with which to build a theoretical framework for analysing how that works, or evidence to test it. This book contributes both evidence of how politics influences reforms in developing countries, and to the construction of theory about how this comes about. It does this by setting out and testing hypotheses about how the political settlement and its relationship to the domain of education have shaped the uptake, success, or failure of recent efforts to bring about education quality reform.

Education quality reforms tend to be less politically tractable than programmes of expansion. The nature and distribution of power over the vital resource involved in education quality—teaching—are necessarily at the centre of this analysis. Quality reforms are difficult to design and difficult to deliver: less is known about 'what works' and achievement is hard to measure. Weak state capacity has not prevented children from attending school, but it is very likely to shape what happens once they get there. Yet strong state capacity in relation to education may not necessarily or only mean centralized power; effective education systems must be responsive and adaptive to local needs, granting enough autonomy for schools to be accountable to the local communities they seek to educate. The governance and institutional reforms needed to build effective schools are intensely political and involve struggles over power, whether in terms of the authority to define the content and direction of nation building, the power to deploy the vast national teaching force, or the resources to spend on school buildings and teachers' pay.

The following chapters look at how politics is shaping the level of capacity and commitment of elites to improving the quality of public education and its governance in developing countries. These chapters explore variations in the extent to which countries have adopted and implemented reforms aimed at improving learning outcomes, and in how those reforms have played out in terms of improved learning. Next, Chapter 2 develops a theoretical framework for understanding the politics of education in developing countries within which such analysis can be conducted.

References

Adelman, S., D. Gilligan, and K. Lehrer. 2008. *How Effective Are Food for Education Programs? A Critical Assessment of the Evidence from Developing Countries*. Washington, DC: International Food Policy Research Institute.

Andrews, M. 2013. *The Limits of Institutional Reform in Development: Changing Rules for Realistic Solutions*. Cambridge: Cambridge University Press.

Ansell, B. W. 2008. 'Traders, Teachers, and Tyrants: Democracy, Globalization, and Public Investment in Education'. *International Organization*, 62(2): 289–322.

Ansell, B. W. 2010. *From the Ballot to the Blackboard: The Redistributive Political Economy of Education*. Cambridge: Cambridge University Press.

Baum, M. A., and D. A. Lake. 2003. 'The Political Economy of Growth: Democracy and Human Capital'. *American Journal of Political Science*, 47(2): 333–47.

Béteille, T., G. G. Kingdon, and M. Muzammil. 2016. 'Teacher Unions in India: Diverse and Powerful'. In *The Comparative Politics of Education*. Edited by T. Moe and S. Wiborg, 239–68. Cambridge: Cambridge University Press.

Boli, J., F. O. Ramirez, and J. W. Meyer. 1985. 'Explaining the Origins and Expansion of Mass Education'. *Comparative Education Review*, 29(2): 145–70.

Booth, D. 2012. 'Development as Collective Action Problem. Addressing the Real Challenges of African Governance'. *Synthesis Report for the Africa Power and Politics Programme*. London: Overseas Development Institute.

Bray, M. 2006. 'Private Supplementary Tutoring: Comparative Perspectives on Patterns and Implications'. *Compare: A Journal of Comparative and International Education*, 36(4): 515–30.

Brown, D. S., and W. Hunter. 2004. 'Democracy and Human Capital Formation Education Spending in Latin America, 1980 to 1997'. *Comparative Political Studies*, 37(7): 842–64.

Bruns, B., and J. Luque. 2014. *Great Teachers: How to Raise Student Learning in Latin America and the Caribbean*. Washington, DC: World Bank.

Bruns, B., and B. R. Schneider. 2016. 'Managing the Politics of Quality Reforms in Education Policy: Lessons from Global Experience'. *The Learning Generation Background Paper*. New York: The Education Commission.

Bruns, B., D. Filmer, and H. A. Patrinos. 2011. *Making Schools Work: New Evidence on Accountability Reforms*. Washington, DC: World Bank.

Busemeyer, M. R. 2014. *Skills and Inequality: Partisan Politics and the Political Economy of Education Reforms in Western Welfare States*. Cambridge: Cambridge University Press.

Busemeyer, M. R., and C. Trampusch. 2011. 'Review Article: Comparative Political Science and the Study of Education'. *British Journal of Political Science*, 41(2): 413–43.

Carr-Hill, R., C. Rolleston, T. Pherali, and R. Schendel. 2015. 'The Effects of School-based Decision Making on Educational Outcomes in Low and Middle Income Contexts: A Systematic Review'. *3ie Grantee Final Review*. London: International Initiative for Impact Evaluation.

Chaudhury, N., J. Hammer, M. Kremer, K. Muralidharan, and F. Rogers. 2004. 'Teacher and Health Care Provider Absence: A Multi-Country Study'. Washington, DC: World Bank DEC.

Colclough, C. 2012. 'Education, Poverty and Development—Mapping their Interconnections'. *Comparative Education*, 48(2): 135–48.

Corrales, J. 1999. *The Politics of Education Reform: Bolstering the Supply and Demand; Overcoming Institutional Blocks*. Washington, DC: World Bank.

Corrales, J. 2006. 'Political Obstacles to Expanding and Improving Schooling in Developing Countries'. In *Educating All Children: A Global Agenda*. Edited by Cohen, J. E., D. E. Bloom, and M. B. Malin, 231–99. Cambridge, MA: MIT Press.

Crookston, B. T., K. A. Dearden, S. C. Alder, C. A. Porucznik, J. B. Stanford, R. M. Merrill, T. T. Dickerson, and M. E. Penny. 2010. 'Impact of Early and Concurrent Stunting on Cognition'. *Journal of Maternal and Child Nutrition*, 7(4): 397–409.

Crookston, B. T., W. Schott, S. Cueto, K. A. Dearden, P. Engle, A. Georgiadis, E. A. Lundeen, M. E. Penny, A. D. Stein, and J. R. Behrman. 2013. 'Postinfancy Growth, Schooling, and Cognitive Achievement: Young Lives'. *The American Journal of Clinical Nutrition*, 98(6): 1555–63.

Devarajan, S., S. Khemani, and M. Walton. 2011. *Civil Society, Public Action and Accountability in Africa*. Washington, DC: World Bank.

Di John, J., and J. Putzel. 2009. 'Political Settlements: Issues Paper'. Birmingham: Governance and Social Development Resource Centre (GSDRC), University of Birmingham.

Doner, R. F., and B. Ross Schneider. 2016. 'The Middle-Income Trap: More Politics than Economics'. *World Politics*, 68(4): 608–44.

Dunne, M., K. Akyeampong, S. Humphreys, and Transitions and Equity Consortium for Research on Educational Access. 2007. *School Processes, Local Governance and Community Participation: Understanding Access*. Brighton: Consortium for Research on Educational Access, Transitions and Equity.

Evans, D. K., and A. Popova. 2016. 'What Really Works to Improve Learning in Developing Countries? An Analysis of Divergent Findings in Systematic Reviews'. *The World Bank Research Observer*, 31(2): 242–70.

Fox, J. A. 2015. 'Social Accountability: What Does the Evidence Really Say?' *World Development*, 72(C): 346–61.

Gaventa, J., and M. Mayo. 2009. 'Spanning Citizenship Spaces through Transnational Coalitions: The Case of the Global Campaign for Education'. IDS Working Paper 327. Brighton: Institute of Development Studies, University of Sussex.

Gift, T., and E. Wibbels. 2014. 'Reading, Writing, and the Regrettable Status of Education Research in Comparative Politics'. *Annual Review of Political Science*, 17(1): 291–312.

Glewwe, P. W., E. A. Hanushek, S. D. Humpage, and R. Ravina. 2011. 'School Resources and Educational Outcomes in Developing Countries: A Review of the Literature from 1990 to 2010'. NBER Working Paper 17554. Cambridge, MA: National Bureau of Economic Research.

Goetz, A., and R. Jenkins. 2005. *Reinventing Accountability: Making Democracy Work for Human Development*. London: Palgrave Macmillan.

Grindle, M. S. 2004. *Despite the Odds: The Contentious Politics of Education Reform*. Princeton, NJ: Princeton University Press.

Hanushek, E. A. 2009. 'School Policy: Implications of Recent Research for Human Capital Investments in South Asia and Other Developing Countries'. *Education Economics*, 17(3): 291–313.

Hanushek, E. A., and L. Woessmann. 2007. 'The Role of Education Quality for Economic Growth'. Policy Research Working Paper 4122. Washington, DC: World Bank.

Harding, R., and D. Stasavage. 2014. 'What Democracy Does (and Doesn't Do) for Basic Services: School Fees, School Inputs, and African Elections'. *The Journal of Politics*, 76(01): 229–45.

Hickey, S., and S. King. 2016. 'Understanding Social Accountability: Politics, Power and Building New Social Contracts'. *The Journal of Development Studies*, 52(8): 1225–40.

Hossain, N. 2005. 'Productivity and Virtue: Elite Categories of the Poor in Bangladesh'. *World Development*, 33(6): 965–77.

Hossain, N., and M. Moore. 2002. 'Arguing for the Poor: Elites and Poverty in Developing Countries'. IDS Working Paper 148. Brighton: Institute of Development Studies, University of Sussex.

Joshi, A., and P. P. Houtzager. 2012. 'Widgets or Watchdogs? Conceptual Explorations in Social Accountability'. *Public Management Review*, 14(2): 145–62.

Kingdon, G. G., A. Little, M. Aslam, S. Rawal, T. Moe, H. Patrinos, T. Béteille, R. Banerji, B. Parton, and S. K. Sharma. 2014. 'A Rigorous Review of the Political Economy of Education Systems in Developing Countries. Final Report'. *Education Rigorous Literature Review*. London: Department for International Development.

Kosack, S. 2009. 'Realising Education for All: Defining and Using the Political Will to Invest in Primary Education'. *Comparative Education*, 45(4): 495–523.

Kosack, S. 2012. *The Education of Nations: How the Political Organization of the Poor, Not Democracy, Led Governments to Invest in Mass Education*. Oxford: Oxford University Press.

Levy, B., and M. Walton. 2013. 'Institutions, Incentives and Service Provision: Bringing Politics Back In'. ESID Working Paper 18. Manchester: Effective States and Inclusive Development Research Centre, The University of Manchester.

Mani, A., and S. Mukand. 2007. 'Democracy, Visibility and Public Good Provision'. *Journal of Development Economics, Special Issue: Papers from a Symposium: The Social Dimensions of Microeconomic Behaviour in Low-Income Communities*, 8(2): 506–29.

Martínez, M. A. F. 2012. 'From the Streets to the Classrooms: The Politics of Education Spending in Mexico'. PhD thesis. Durham, NC: Duke University.

Meyer, J. W., F. O. Ramirez, and Y. N. Soysal. 1992. 'World Expansion of Mass Education, 1870–1980'. *Sociology of Education*, 65(2): 128–49.

Moe, T. M., and S. Wiborg. 2017. 'Introduction'. In *The Comparative Politics of Education*. Edited by T. M. Moe, and S. Wiborg, 1–23. Cambridge: Cambridge University Press.

Nelson, J. M. 2007. 'Elections, Democracy, and Social Services'. *Studies in Comparative International Development*, 41(4): 79–97.

Nicolai, S., L. Wild, J. Wales, S. Hine, and J. Engel. 2014. 'Unbalanced Progress'. ODI Development Progress Working Paper 5. London: Overseas Development Institute.

Pritchett, L. 2013. *The Rebirth of Education: Schooling Ain't Learning*. Washington, DC: Center for Global Development Books.

Rose, P. M., and C. Dyer. 2008. 'Chronic Poverty and Education: A Review of Literature'. CPRC Working Paper 131. Manchester: Chronic Poverty Research Centre, University of Manchester.

Rosser, A., and M. Fahmi. 2018. 'The Political Economy of Teacher Management Reform in Indonesia'. *International Journal of Educational Development*, 61(July): 72–81.

Smith, M., and A. M. Barrett. 2011. 'Capabilities for Learning to Read: An Investigation of Social and Economic Effects for Grade 6 Learners in Southern and East Africa'. *International Journal of Educational Development*, 31(1): 23–36.

Snilstveit, B., J. Stevenson, D. Phillips, M. Vojtkova, E. Gallagher, T. Schmidt, H. Jobse, M. Geelen, M. G. Pastorello, and J. Eyers. 2015. 'Interventions for Improving Learning Outcomes and Access to Education in Low-and Middle-Income Countries: A Systematic Review'. *3ie Final Grantee Final Review*. London: International Initiative for Impact Evaluation.

Stasavage, D. 2005. 'Democracy and Education Spending in Africa'. *American Journal of Political Science*, 49(2): 343–58.

Tikly, L. 2001. 'Globalisation and Education in the Postcolonial World: Towards a Conceptual Framework'. *Comparative Education*, 37(2): 151–71.

Tikly, L., and A. M. Barrett. 2013. 'Education Quality and Social Justice in the Global South: Towards a Conceptual Framework'. In *Education Quality and Social Justice in the Global South: Challenges for Policy, Practice and Research*. Edited by L. Tikly, and A.M. Barrett, 11–25. London: Routledge.

UNESCO (United Nations Educational, Scientific and Cultural Organisation). 2004. *The Quality Imperative: Education for All 2005 Global Monitoring Report.* Paris: UNESCO.

UNESCO. 2010. *Reaching the Marginalised: Education for All 2010 Global Monitoring Report.* Paris: UNESCO, and Oxford: Oxford University Press.

UNESCO. 2012. *Youth and Skills: Putting Education to Work: Education for All 2012 Global Monitoring Report.* Paris: UNESCO.

UNESCO. 2014. *Teaching and Learning: Achieving Quality for All. Education for All 2013/14 Global Monitoring Report.* Paris: UNESCO.

UNESCO. 2015. *Education for All 2000–2015: Achievements and Challenges. Education for All 2015 Global Monitoring Report.* Paris: UNESCO.

Unterhalter, E. 2014. 'Measuring Education for the Millennium Development Goals: Reflections on Targets, Indicators, and a Post-2015 Framework'. *Journal of Human Development and Capabilities*, 15(2–3): 176–87.

Wales, J., A. Magee, and S. Nicolai. 2016. 'How Does Political Context Shape Education Reforms and Their Success?' ODI Dimension Paper 6. London: Overseas Development Institute.

Westhorp, G., B. Walker, P. Rogers, N. Overbeeke, D. Ball, and G. Brice. 2014. *Enhancing Community Accountability, Empowerment and Education Outcomes in Low and Middle-Income Countries: A Realist Review.* London: Department for International Development.

World Bank. 2003. 'Making Services Work for Poor People: World Development Report 2004'. Washington, DC: World Bank.

World Bank. 2017. 'World Development Report 2018: Learning to Realize Education's Promise'. Washington, DC: World Bank.

2

Researching the Politics of Education Quality in Developing Countries

Towards a New Conceptual and Methodological Approach

Sam Hickey and Naomi Hossain

Introduction

> The literature on the political economy of education is underdeveloped in geographical scope, robustness of methods utilised and theoretical richness . . . large parts of the world, especially most countries of Africa and South-east Asia, remain virtually untouched by research on the ways in which political economy forces affect their education sector decisions, processes and outcomes.
>
> (Kingdon et al. 2014, 46)

That politics plays a major role in shaping educational outcomes in the global South is increasingly recognized within academic and policy communities alike. However, there is little agreement on which forms of politics really matter, how to conceptualize these factors, and how to actually investigate them in practice. The quote above, drawn from the most systematic survey of existing scholarly work on the politics of education in developing countries, emphasizes how far we still need to go to arrive at a more rigorous and complete sense of this important field. The analysis of the learning crisis in developing countries suffers not only from large empirical gaps, but also from the lack of theoretical frameworks specifically oriented towards understanding the politics of educational quality (Wales, Magee, and Nicolai 2016) and from systematic and comparative analysis of how these relationships unfold in practice (Kingdon et al. 2014).

In Chapter 1, we reviewed the small body of work that does exist in this area, and drew out the main dimensions and factors to which it draws attention. This chapter sets out a new framework for analysing the political economy of education in developing countries that foregrounds these factors, and which can help guide comparative work on the politics of educational reform in developing countries. We also describe the methodological approach that was deployed to undertake the research presented in this volume. It is important at this stage to re-emphasize what this volume is trying to explain, namely the political factors that shape the extent to which elite actors become committed to adopting and implementing educational reforms aimed at improving learning outcomes. This means we are not addressing the question of how political factors help shape the nature and extent of the learning crisis per se, or of educational outcomes (which would need a very different methodological approach), but rather the political conditions under which elites decide to tackle this crisis and how politics shapes the nature and success of this response. To close the gap between this question and actual learning outcomes, we focus on those reforms that recent reviews suggest have a strong chance of tackling the sources of the learning crisis, particularly those aimed at tackling deficits in teacher training, problems of teacher absenteeism, and issues of oversight and performance management.

Rethinking the Politics of Education: A 'Domains of Power' Approach

> Studies (on the political economy of education) have tended to employ a very general understanding of 'political economy'... future work needs to develop more conceptual clarity and more nuanced political theories about change and particularly about how alternative structural, historical and institutional conditions determine varied possibilities and constraints within which actors in different polities have to work thereby generating differing developmental paths.
>
> (Kingdon et al. 2014, 46–7)

The task of formulating a conceptual framework that can capture the ways in which politics shape processes of educational reform in developing countries is, then, a considerable one. Here we set out one possible response to the challenge set out by Kingdon et al. (2014), by trying to capture the most salient political factors that seem to shape educational reform and outcomes in developing countries within a coherent conceptual framework. To recap the findings of the literature reviewed in Chapter 1, these factors include the ways in which material aspects of a country's political economy shape the capacity of different groups to make demands; the powerful role played by informal as well as formal institutions in developing countries; the particular forms of political agency (e.g. leadership, coalitions) required to navigate these structural conditions at multiple levels; the role of governance arrangements and relationships within the state, as well as between the state and citizens; and the role played by ideas as well as the incentives in shaping elite behaviour. A framework for understanding the politics of education in developing countries would also need to avoid the methodological nationalism that pervades much political analysis, and incorporate a sense of how transnational factors also shape domestic policy processes.

Our conceptual effort to capture these features, which draws on recent theoretical advances aimed at understanding the politics of development, is termed the 'domains of power' framework. This seeks to capture the interaction between the *political settlement*, which refers to the broad configuration of power within society, and the *policy domain*, in this case the domain of education (see Figure 2.1). This focus on domains of power represents an effort to go beyond a focus on how formal institutional arrangements shape development processes and outcomes (e.g. World Bank 2003), and an effort to bring together the approaches used within the most insightful and (importantly) comparative work on the political economy of education discussed in Chapter 1 (Grindle 2004; Kosack 2012).

Political Settlements

Going beyond the mantra that 'institutions matter', development theory has increasingly recognized the central role that politics plays in shaping uneven

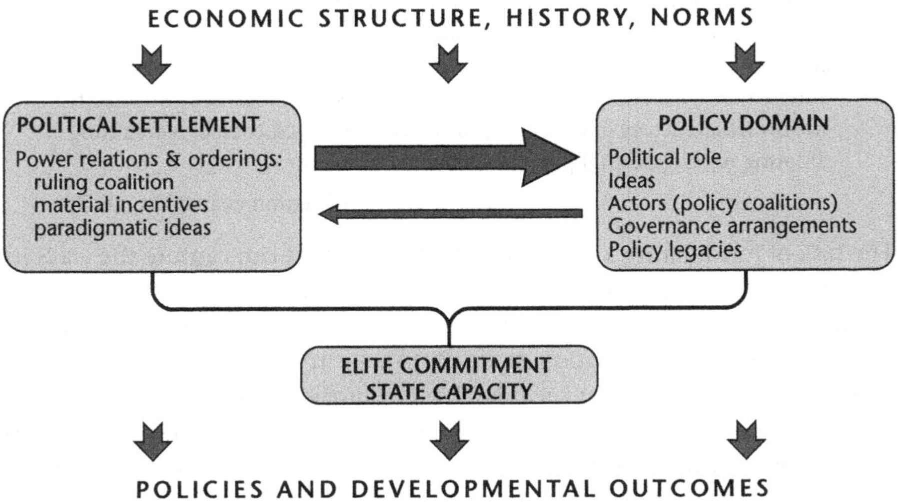

Figure 2.1 Domains of power

patterns of development between different countries and the economic and social progress that countries are able to make. Major contributions have centred on the forms of politics and power relations that shape which kinds of institutions emerge and how they actually function in practice (Acemoglu and Robinson 2012; North, Wallis, and Weingast 2009; Khan 2010). A shared focus within this body of work is on the significance of inter-elite bargaining, whereby powerful groups within society struggle with each other for influence over the rules of the game that distribute resources and status. The nature of these struggles and their outcomes is critical to understanding why similar forms of institutions, including rules regarding the exchange of political power and the distribution of resources, function in very different ways in different contexts. Within this increasingly influential body of literature,[1] the conceptual approach that has been subject to the greatest level of theory-testing (Whitfield et al. 2015), and which goes furthest in terms of incorporating a strong political economy perspective (Gray 2016), is the political settlements approach advanced by Mushtaq Khan (2000, 2010, 2017).

Political settlements analysis focuses on how the balance of power between social groups tends to ensure that institutions function primarily to distribute goods and status to powerful groups, in order to maintain their agreement with the basic rules of the game.[2] Political settlements are shaped by 'the relative holding power of different groups and organizations contesting the distribution of resources', with holding power 'partly based on income and wealth but also on historically rooted capacities of different groups to organize' (Khan 2010, 1). A political settlement, in terms of political order and relative stability, emerges when enough elites are sufficiently satisfied that status and resources are being distributed in line with the prevailing balance of power in society. The historical moments at which such settlements become established, or experience some kind of rupture, have been identified as creating the conditions for significant shifts in policy approach, including within the domain of education. For example,

> In their comparative study of African countries, Evans et al. (1995) underline the role of political imperatives and contexts in 'triggering' reviews of education policy between the 1970s and early 1990s. National reviews of education arose in Benin, Mali and Uganda after a new, often revolutionary and/or newly elected democratic government came to power (Benin, Mali, Uganda). They also arose at the end of a period of conflict or war (Mozambique, Uganda), when public

[1] For example, this new turn to politics within mainstream development theory has had a direct influence on successive flagship publications from the World Bank, most notably the 2017 World Development Report on 'Governance, Law and Development' (also World Bank 2011).

[2] For a political settlements analysis of education in Ghana, see Abdulai and Hickey (2016), from which the following paragraph is substantially derived.

dissatisfaction with the condition of education could no longer be ignored (Benin, Ghana, Guinea). (From Kingdon et al. 2014, 35)

To this, we can add the case of South Africa, whereby prior to the reforms that accompanied the move towards a multi-racial democracy in 1994 (see Chapter 6), the threats to the apartheid era political settlement generated by the 1976 Soweto uprising, school boycotts, industrial unrest, and skilled labour shortages triggered wholesale reforms of the education and training system (Chisholm 1983).

The personalized processes of bargaining between powerful actors leads to 'deals' rather than 'rules', in the first instance, and helps explain why formal institutions, such as multi-party elections and rational bureaucratic processes for allocating budgetary resources, may not easily displace the 'informal' logics of the personalized and clientelist rule that preceded them (Khan 2010; North et al. 2009). This makes it difficult for institutions to operate on an 'impersonal' basis, and likely that they will instead take on highly personalized modes of functioning (Levy 2014).

Going further, Khan (2010, 2017) argues that the predominance of informal institutions in developing countries is underpinned by the nature of their political economy, whereby relatively small formal sectors are outweighed by the much larger informal economy. This has two types of effect on the realm of politics and governance.

First, the limited size and scope of the formal productive economy means that governments lack the tax base required to allocate resources to powerful groups, other than through informal, off-budgetary processes. This helps ensure that processes of rent-seeking and the clientelist distribution of public resources and positions are systemic features of such political economies, in ways that directly undermine the quality of the public bureaucracy and of service provision in domains such as education.

Second, the limited scope of the formal sector reflects the limited level of capitalist development that characterizes most developing countries, most of which lack a domestic capitalist class of any significant size or influence. This means that most developing countries lack organized social groups with the capacity to accumulate wealth other than through their relationship with political elites, on whom they rely for various rent-seeking opportunities (involving subsidies, contracts, procurement opportunities, and so on).

Again, the nature of the political economy helps ensure that the politics of patronage and rent-seeking are structural (rather than cultural) features of governance in most developing countries. Importantly for our focus on education, this means that not only are public institutions frequently turned to purposes other than distributing resources in line with a broad public interest, but also that developing countries lack a critical mass of capitalists with sufficient 'holding power' to pressure governments into producing more highly skilled workers through educational 'upgrading' (Doner and Schneider 2016; Kosack 2012).

These two features—the configuration of power and the nature of institutions, and how they interact—constitute the central features of a political settlement. We briefly discuss each here, before setting out how they can be used to construct a typology of political settlements whereby different countries can be understood as representatives of heuristic types, each of which establishes different conditions for achieving development.

The configuration of power amongst different social groups in society plays a significant role in shaping the capacity and commitment of those in control of political power, a group that Khan refers to as the 'ruling coalition'. If the ruling coalition considers itself vulnerable to threats from excluded factions with significant holding power, it is more likely to be driven by short-term calculations than to undertake institutional reforms and distribute resources with a longer-term vision of the national interest in mind (Khan 2010; also Kelsall 2012). Khan argues that the highest levels of state capacity for development are likely to occur where the vulnerability of ruling elites is low, due to the absence of powerful excluded factions and also strong lower-level factions which may be able to block reforms. This level of regime security can encourage these 'dominant coalitions' to adopt a longer-term time horizon, and reduces the transaction costs involved in implementing policies. Conversely, where there is a credible threat to the ruling coalition from powerful excluded groups, who may be able to wrest power away from them (e.g. through elections), and where lower-level factions are strong enough to make multiple demands on the centre, then the prospects for developmental governance are diminished. Within this 'competitive clientelist' type of political settlement, elite incentives are loaded towards the use of public institutions for securing short-term political gains (Khan 2010; also Levy 2014).[3] In terms of education, this may involve strong incentives to invest more in the quantity and visibility of provision (e.g. school buildings), rather than the quality of provision, which may involve challenging the interests of groups with significant holding power (e.g. teachers' unions).

Through their interaction with the configuration of power in society, institutions are mutually constitutive of political settlements. The nature of institutions can be arranged along a continuum that runs from being 'personalized' to 'impersonal' (Levy 2014). Institutions here refer to the 'rules of the game' that help govern and shape the behaviour of actors in

[3] The triggers of educational reform have been associated with many factors that would be captured within the political settlements analysis proposed here, including threats to political stability, changes between ruling coalitions, and the ideological preferences of leaders.

economic, political, and social spheres (North 1990), including firms, political parties, bureaucratic organizations, and civic associations. Where institutions are highly personalized, such organizational forms largely exist as the vehicles of particular interests, rather than on the basis of a wider and programmatic platform, as is generally the case with political parties in many developing countries.

The interaction between these two dimensions of any given political settlement is critical. On the one hand, the configuration of power can shape the extent to which institutions function in more or less personalized ways. Where the ruling coalition is relatively dominant, it may be willing to undertake investments in building bureaucratic capability and enable institutions to function in ways that are largely impersonal and can constrain the behaviour of elites as well as ordinary citizens (e.g. through ensuring that the rule of law applies to all). Conversely, where levels of elite cohesion are low and exacerbated by high levels of inter-elite competition for power, the incentives for rulers to use institutions to distribute public goods and positions to maintain political survival are much higher.

The influence can also run in the opposite direction, with the nature of institutions also helping to shape the strategies of rule deployed by elites, as numerous studies of political development have shown. For example, competitive politics can further embed the politics of patronage if it emerges before significant levels of state capacity (in terms of strong and impersonal bureaucratic organizations in particular) have been built, as this presents strong incentives to capture public organizations as a means of ensuring political survival. Conversely, where institutional capacity has been developed, competitive politics can help underpin moves towards meritocratic forms of civil service system (Fukuyama 2016; Grindle 2012).

The interplay between the configuration of power and institutions produces four main types of political settlement that prevail in the majority of developing countries (Figure 2.2). These are countries that have achieved a degree of political order and relative stability that is reflected in some sort of political settlement, but which have not moved towards what North et al. (2009) refer to as 'open access orders', characterized by economic and political institutions that are largely rule-based, impersonal, and open to all. Each of these four types offers different incentives, opportunities, and constraints in terms of governance and development (Levy 2014). Note that political settlements are always in flux, with countries characterized by the same broad type potentially moving in different directions along one or more dimensions; there is no expectation that countries will move forward in a particular direction, with reversals and sideways movements always possible, depending on how the interaction of power relations and institutions plays out.

Type 2: dominant-personalized settlements include countries that have the potential to make rapid developmental advances because elite cohesion

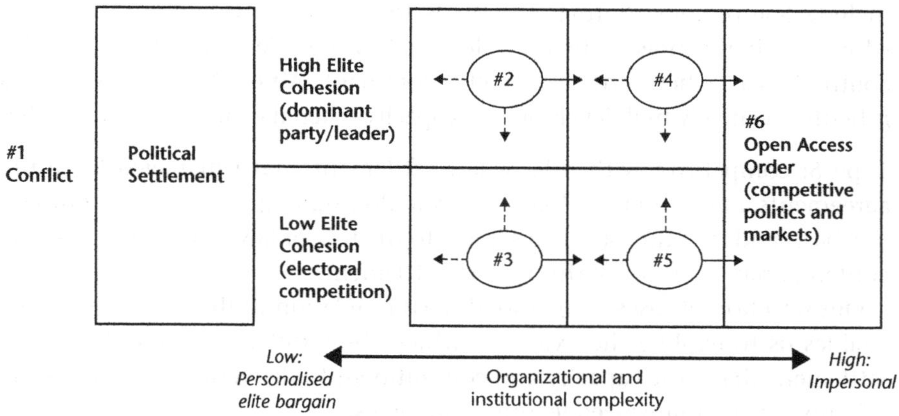

Figure 2.2 A typology of political settlements
Source: Adapted from Levy (2014).

enables rulers to enact and implement reforms in line with a long time-horizon and state-building project, with relatively little opposition (e.g. South Korea in the 1960s). Contemporary examples may include Ethiopia and Rwanda. It is worth noting here that many of the 'score outperformers' on charts of educational attainment (such as South Korea, Vietnam, Japan, Singapore, and several ex-Soviet states) were, for an extended period, under dominant rule systems (see Chapter 10). However, the reliance on particular leaders renders such settlements prone to personalized forms of capture and potential backsliding into instability and conflict (e.g. Democratic Republic of Congo). Unless public organizations are robust, competitive pressures are likelier to incentivize rulers to double-down on the personalized use of institutions to secure political survival (e.g. Uganda), rather than make longer-term investments in building impersonal institutions.

Type 3: competitive clientelist settlements characterize much of the developing world, and illustrate the difficulties of forming credible institutions under the pressures of inter-elite competition for power and resources, with strong incentives for ruling elites to distribute public resources and positions to secure political loyalty. Examples include Bangladesh (before 2009), Malawi, Kenya, and Zambia. However, the iterative process of political power changing hands between elite factions may strengthen political institutions over time (e.g. Ghana).

Type 4: dominant with rule-by-law settlements are generally those dominant-personal settlements that have managed to institutionalize 'rules' around the exchange of political power and distribution of resources. This allows for a degree of accountability while maintaining political continuity. Examples include South Korea during the 1980s to 1990s, Singapore, and arguably China (with the now erstwhile rules limiting presidential terms), and also South Africa, where the electorally dominant Africa National Congress inherited relatively high levels of state capacity when it came to power in 1994.

Type 5: competitive with rule of law settlements have managed to secure agreements amongst elites that power should exchange hands on a competitive basis and that they are also subject to the rule of law. India would be one contemporary example of this type of settlement.

Our selection of cases, which we discuss in relation to this typology below, enables us to explore the extent to which these different types of political settlement shape the capacity and commitment to delivering on educational reforms aimed at improved learning outcomes.

Political settlements analysis thus operates at the broad level of how political power is organized within societies, and how this shapes the functioning of institutions. We have suggested that the ways in which political settlements are formed and shift over time, how the balance of power between different groups is configured within them, and the extent to which institutions operate along personal or impersonal lines, are all likely to play significant roles in shaping the capacity and commitment of elites to different aspects of development, including education. However, the specific ways in which this plays out are likely to differ within different types of policy areas or sectors; for example, the challenge of promoting economic growth, and the vested interests involved in lobbying for different approaches, differs from concerns with social provisioning. As such, and in line with calls for this macro level of analysis to be joined up more effectively with more proximate frames of analysis that are better attuned to capturing the politics of reform at lower levels (Grindle 2017), our conceptual framework includes a second domain of power, namely the 'policy domain'. This will enable us to explore how political drivers interact with the specific character of education as a policy domain. Here we set out some of the general features of a policy domain, before identifying the most salient of these for our focus on education.

Policy Domains

A 'policy domain' can be defined as a meso-level social field of power relations within which actors promote competing agendas.[4] Different types of policy domain will play different roles in terms of maintaining the political

[4] For other efforts to conceptualize how political settlements and policy domains interact, see Bebbington et al. (2018) on natural resources, Hickey and Lavers (2016) on social protection, Nazneen, Hickey, and Sifaki (forthcoming) on women's empowerment, and Pritchett, Sen, and Werker (2013).

settlement, particularly through the provision of the rents and/or popular legitimacy required to keep political elites in power. The nature of this political role is likely to shape the degree of political interference and the relative autonomy that domain-specific actors have to act within their domain. Given that education can deliver both popular legitimacy, particularly in terms of offering access to previously excluded rural voters, and a great many divisible goods that can be distributed directly to favoured regions and groups (e.g. jobs, schools), this suggests that it is a type of policy domain that will be prone to being highly politicized. This leaves open the question of whether this politicization has more or less developmental consequences: for example, too little politicization can lead a policy domain to becoming marginalized when it comes to budgetary allocations and prioritization regarding implementation, whereas too much can generate problems such as political interference and elite capture.

Specific policy domains are further defined by their governance arrangements, the range of actors and ideas (or 'policy frames') involved, and the legacies of past policies. Governance arrangements include the processes through which policies are formulated and implemented, and the mechanisms in place to ensure accountability. These processes, which may be more or less centralized or decentralized, and involve top-down, diagonal, and bottom-up accountability mechanisms, have been identified as central to how different aspects of education reforms are enacted and implemented (World Bank 2003). However, while these formal arrangements provide the institutional architecture within which different types of actors manoeuvre and seek to exert their influence within the domain, in clientelistic political settlements they may only function as intended insofar as they are aligned with the interests of powerful actors (Levy and Walton 2013). Within the domain of education, this often involves a large range of players, including politicians and bureaucrats at multiple levels, teachers' unions and associations, aid agencies, traditional leaders, community-based organizations, and school-level players such as management committees, headteachers, and parent–teacher associations. The incentives of these actors to behave in particular ways will do much to shape the possibilities for different types of reforms to emerge and gain priority. However, the ideological projects of different actors may also matter here, as we go on to discuss in more detail next. Finally, policy legacies can also play an important role in shaping what is politically and technically feasible with regards to contemporary reforms. This may occur through processes of 'policy feedback' (Pierson 1993), whereby first-generation reforms empower particular actors or modes of practice that may then act as obstacles to future generations of reform. For example, a recurring theme across the cases we present here concerns the impact that access-based reforms, such as universal primary education, have had on efforts to promote improved learning outcomes.

The Cross-cutting Role of Ideas

Ideas matter to the politics of development, both in general and with reference to specific policy domains in developing countries. This is particularly true in the case of education. Going beyond a purely materialist and rational-actor sense of what drives political elites and projects, ideas are conceptualized here as integral dimensions of both domains of power within our framework, namely the political settlement and the policy domain. At the level of the political settlement, certain ideas are required to bind elites together, securing their commitment to upholding a certain set of institutions (Blyth 2002), while also being deployed more instrumentally by elites to help secure loyalty amongst followers. Ideas around education have played an important role in both of these regards. For example, nationalist elites, who themselves benefited from a modern education, have often conceived of education as being central to their wider ideological projects of nation building and commitment to development (Hossain 2005), and a commitment to education often cuts across party loyalties. Ruling elites have also often used promises of educational expansion to secure popularity at opportune moments of the electoral cycle, as indicated by the correlation between elections and expenditure in this sector (Stasavage 2005), and as a means of forming ruling coalitions across otherwise disparate social groups (Kosack 2012). Ideas are not simply the preserve of elites, of course, and the strong emphasis that elites often place on education is partially in recognition of the emphasis that many parents place on the value of education for their children.

More specific forms of ideas also matter within the educational policy domain, from campaigns for improved access, through to the proposition of specific solutions to the problem of quality (e.g. around teacher-training and specific accountability mechanisms). There is an important transnational dimension to the flow of ideas around education and education reform, with several international agencies, such as UNESCO and the World Bank, seeking to shape the content and direction of reforms within developing countries through a variety of means. For example, ideas about the value of universal primary education circulated in the international community and influenced national political and bureaucratic elites through aid programming and global conferences (e.g. the 1990 Jomtien Conference on Education for All).

One way to conceptualize the role of ideas within and across these two domains of power is to draw on the field of 'discursive institutionalism' (Schmidt 2008, 2010). Discursive institutionalists conceive of ideas at three main levels:

- *paradigmatic ideas* that offer 'a relatively coherent set of assumptions about the functioning of economic, social and political institutions' (Béland 2005, 8),

- *problem definitions* that frame particular social issues as problems that need to be resolved, and
- *policy ideas* that provide potential solutions to the problems deemed worthy of addressing.

Paradigmatic ideas can be seen as operating primarily at the level of the political settlement, while problem definitions and policy ideas are promoted and struggled over primarily at the level of the policy domain (see Figure 2.1). As discussed in the case study chapters, powerful ideas around education, the social role it plays, and the way the delivery of education should be governed, all play important roles in shaping the extent to which higher-quality learning has been prioritized and achieved in developing countries.

Researching the Politics of Education

Our contention here is that the interaction between particular types of political settlement and the domain of education in a given context will do a good deal to determine the extent to which new reforms, including those aimed at promoting higher-quality learning, gain political priority in terms of both adoption and implementation. In broad terms, this is what we set out in Figure 2.1. However, to explore these interactions in more depth requires a further move towards operationalizing this framework. Here we draw on ground-breaking work by Levy and Walton (2013), which shows how different types of political settlement interact with, and help shape performance within, sectors like education that are involved in social provisioning (Figure 2.3). Throughout the different levels of the framework, from national through sectoral and sub-national levels of governance to the frontline of service delivery, there is a strong focus on the de facto as well as the de jure processes at work here, responding to the sense that powerful actors can often override formal rules in clientelistic political settlements. Their framework also focuses on how ideas and discourse as well as material incentives shape political and policy-related behaviour. This would include, for example, the informal strategies of reform entrepreneurs and coalitions (Corrales 1999; Grindle 2004) as well as formal accountability mechanisms (World Bank 2003). This seeks to overcome the problem of emphasizing formal relationships between formally constituted sets of actors (citizens, bureaucrats, politicians), given that multiple studies of the politics of service delivery (and of politics in developing countries in general) have found that a wider range of players matters and that informal forms of politics, process, and relationships are highly significant. A political settlements perspective explicitly draws attention to these informal as well as formal institutions, and seeks

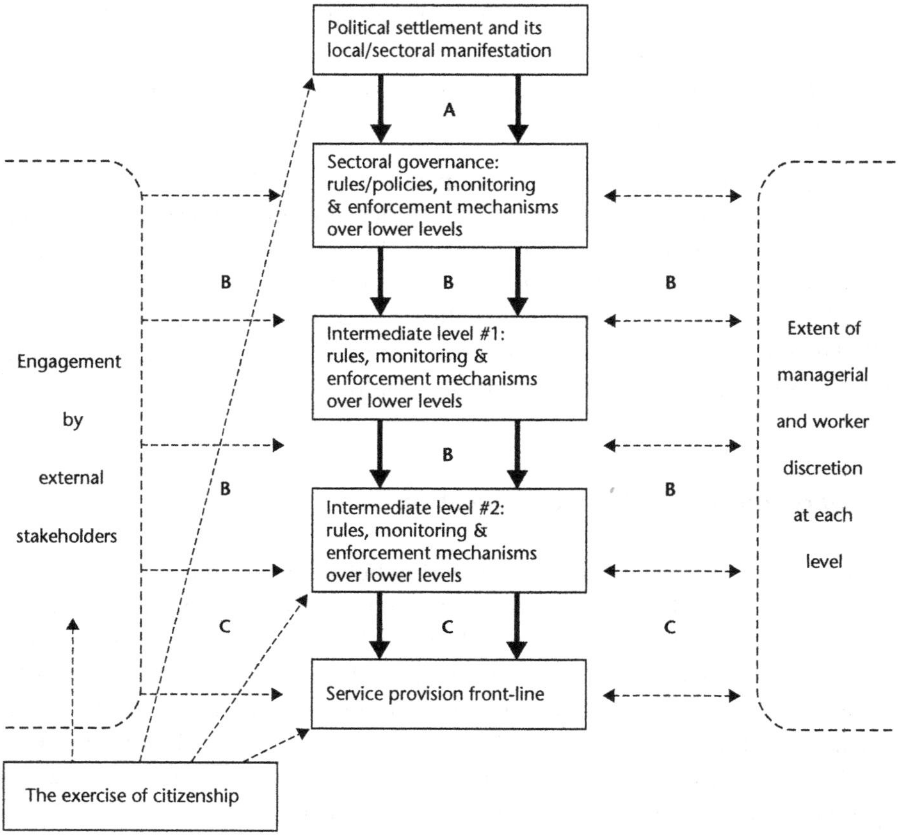

Figure 2.3 A framework for researching the politics of social provisioning
Source: Levy and Walton (2013).

to show that the ways in which they actually function are shaped by underlying sets of power relations. Levy and Walton's effort to operationalize a political settlements approach in the domain of service provision directly encourages a focus on 'the many layers within a specific sector in between the top levels of policymaking and the service provision front line' (Levy and Walton 2013, 4); an important proposition here is that these 'in-between spaces' are major domains of political, stakeholder, and organizational behaviour. This helps identify the 'politically salient stakeholders' that are critical to shaping the success or failure of reforms at localized levels of governance, which our case study analysis shows stretches to traditional actors and local-level coalitions, rather than only to citizens and service providers. This in turn helps to overcome the tendency within political settlements analysis to focus on the role of elite actors at the national level.

Process Tracing and Comparative Case Study Analysis

This conceptual framework is best suited to being deployed and tested within the kinds of small- and medium-n comparative research efforts that have so far been largely absent within research into the politics of education, and of development more generally. This type of approach can help move beyond both the generalities of large-n dataset analysis and the highly context-specific findings from single-shot case studies. The use of a theory-driven typology to select cases can enable theory-testing and also offer more policy-relevant findings that can 'fit' with particular types of context (George and Bennett 2004), as opposed to identifying either one-size-fits-all solutions or exaggerating the unique character of every case.

The comparative research project that we report on here was undertaken in six countries that represent three of the four different types of political settlement identified by Levy (see Figure 2.2).

- Type 2: Rwanda, Uganda, Cambodia: personalized elite bargains and limited institutional complexity, with dominant party/leader. However, each country reflects different levels of dominance and commitment to building impersonal institutions.
  - Rwanda: highly dominant, higher commitment to impersonality
  - Cambodia: dominant, limited commitment to impersonality
  - Uganda: weakly dominant, highly personalized
- Type 3: Bangladesh, Ghana: personalized elite bargains and limited institutional complexity within competitive clientelism.
- Type 4: South Africa: more impersonalized elite bargains and greater institutional complexity within a relatively dominant setting. However, the ruling African National Congress (ANC) coalition in South Africa is itself made up of several factions, which renders it as a 'negotiated' form of dominance; the country is also characterized by significant sub-national variation, whereby some provinces reflect different types of sub-national political settlements, due to differing levels of political competition and institutional legacies. This sub-national variation is exploited through a comparative study of the Western and Eastern Cape Provinces in Chapter 6.

The aim was to help enable the identification not only of different rates and levels of progress made *between* different types of political settlement, but also to test whether similar types of political settlement that were experiencing different dynamics led countries to go down similar pathways or trajectories of policy reform. These cases also reflect a diversity of geographical, historical, and cultural contexts, which should further help to test the extent to which a political settlements framework can explain similarities across these differences. It is important to stress here that we did not choose these cases because they represent particular forms or levels of the learning crisis, and nor do we set out to offer an explanation for actual learning outcomes within these countries or the variance between them. This would have required a different research design and the selection of a much wider set of country cases, and it is not clear that the available data on outcomes would have allowed for this in the types of countries engaged with here. Instead, we wanted to examine the conditions under which elites and governments become more or less committed to, and capable of addressing, the learning crisis, and how politics shapes this process. This choice of our research focus is further validated by the fact that while there is some consensus on what kinds of reform are likely to have positive impacts on learning outcomes (such as reforms aimed at teacher-training and accountability mechanisms designed to enhance performance), we know far less about whether elites are likely to commit to deliver on these reforms, or what it takes to enact them effectively. In focusing on how committed and capable elites and states are to deliver reforms aimed at improving educational quality, we are able to gain traction on an important route through which learning outcomes can improve in developing countries.

To test whether the nature of a political settlement has an influence on elite commitment and state capacity to improve learning outcomes, as we have hypothesized above, we therefore needed to choose countries that reflect different types of political settlement. Here we briefly identify some of the key ways in which these cases, while also being different in other significant respects, represent these types of political settlement.[5] The categorization of cases into different types of political settlements is not a precise science; the configurations of power that define political settlements are dynamic, rather than static—particularly concerning the shifting relations of power between social groups and how this interacts with institutions—and therefore subject to change over time.[6] Here we have allocated countries to types based on our reading of the configuration of power in these countries during the main historical period under discussion. In terms of our contextual analysis, our time period covers the post-colonial period as a whole, in order to set the political significance of the educational policy domain within a political

[5] The nature of the educational policy domains in each country is discussed in more depth in the case study countries.

[6] Since we completed the research for this project, the ANC-led ruling coalition in South Africa has become increasingly vulnerable to threats by excluded factions, while the Awami League in Bangladesh has undertaken several measures designed to crush the opposition and secure dominance for itself. Recent elections in Uganda (2016) deepened the sense that its settlement is both increasingly competitive *and* that presidential dominance remains a key feature of the landscape. Elections in Cambodia in 2018 look set to erode the dominance of the ruling party there.

settlements perspective. Within our primary research, we examine the same time period within each country, namely the 20-year period from the mid-1990s until around the early 2010s. This timeframe is important, as it extends over the period in which the international policy agenda on education has shifted from one focused on access, to one that is increasingly concerned with issues of quality (see the shift from the Millennium Development Goals (MDGs) to Sustainable Development Goals (SDGs) on education in this regard, also World Development Report 2018 (World Bank 2017)). Looking across the same timeframe in each country also helps to control for the important role that international actors and ideas have played in shaping policy reforms.

In two of our dominant cases, *Rwanda* and *South Africa*, the respective ruling coalitions have both been in power since 1994, during which time they have largely been able to determine their own priorities, with relatively little organized or substantial opposition from rival elite factions. This dominance has been helped in both cases by the manner in which each ruling coalition took power, which in both cases involved major upheavals to the existing order, and came amidst promises to bring a post-ethnic political order in Rwanda and multi-racial democracy in South Africa. Both countries exhibit strong tendencies towards centralized and top-down modes of governance, even if certain functions have been devolved to local levels. Election results help illustrate the dominance of each ruling party, although the ruling party's regular achievement of over 90 per cent of the vote in Rwanda contrasts with the far more tempered results that flow from South Africa's institutionalized system of multi-party competition—within which the ANC's share of the vote has been declining—and longer-standing modern state bureaucracy (Hirsch and Levy 2018). It is this degree of institutionalization that leads us to characterize South Africa as a 'Type 4' political settlement, where dominance interacts with 'rule-by-law'.

Cambodia and *Uganda* represent similar trajectories, in that periods of civil conflict in both cases were ended when an organized political force gained supremacy, took political power, and sought to impose their dominance on the polity. One of these forces, the National Resistance Movement (NRM) in Uganda has, since the mid-1990s, placed a strong emphasis on increasing access to education—an emphasis that seems to flow from a mixture of genuine ideological commitment to development and a populist appeal to the rural masses on which the NRM relies. However, the last decade or so has seen this political dominance come under increasing threat in both countries as a result of elite defections from each ruling coalition; the development of stronger organizational capacities amongst rival factions; and growing popular pressures from below, including social constituencies brought into the ruling coalition through the promise of free education. Interestingly, whereas heightened levels of competition have tended to generate more personalized forms of governance in Uganda, similar pressures appear to be encouraging a more programmatic and technocratic approach in Cambodia, including in the arena of social service delivery. A graphic illustration of this, as reported in our respective case study countries, is that whereas the threat of increased electoral competition led the President in Cambodia to appoint a technocrat to the position of Education Minister (see Chapter 7), the same pressures in Uganda led the President to appoint his wife to this role, despite her having no prior competence in the domain (see Chapter 8).

Since the early 1990s, both *Bangladesh* and *Ghana* have been largely characterized by political settlements with high degrees of competition over political power between rival factions, each of which is more or less as capable as the other of gaining power. In both settings, formal institutions (constitutional arrangements, multi-party electoral systems) have become closely entwined with, and have arguably deepened, clientelist tendencies, in line with the suggestion that there are strong incentives within competitive clientelist settings for institutions to become highly politicized (Khan 2010; Levy 2014). The result has often been a high level of dysfunctionality within each country's public bureaucracy, as jobs and other resources are exchanged for political loyalty, leading to large gaps between stated policy commitments and actual implementation and outcomes. In the last few years, the ruling party in Bangladesh has sought to assert its dominance over government and other institutions, and appears to have significantly reduced the level of competition for political power, while also increasing the levels of factionalism within the ruling coalition. In Ghana, meanwhile, the fact that there have been three peaceful turnovers of power since 1992, the most recent in 2016, suggests that certain political (if not bureaucratic) institutions may be becoming more impersonalized and rules-based.

In line with Figure 2.3, in-depth qualitative research was undertaken at each level of interaction between the political settlement and educational policy domain, flowing downwards through sector-level politics and governance arrangements to frontline performance in schools. The methods used were primarily key informant interviews with all significant actors, along with focus group discussions and documentary analysis. An important first step involved each team producing detailed mappings of the political settlement and the education domain, in order to assess the relative power of the key actors, incentives, and ideas involved in shaping both policy formulation and policy implementation in education. These mapping exercises were very helpful in identifying leads to pursue with regards to the types of reform undertaken and actors to interview, while also generating substantive findings on the politics of the domain. For example, the mapping revealed a gap between those actors involved in policy adoption and those involved in implementation, which helped to explain at least part of the shortfall between the policy objectives on paper and what was implemented in practice.

To give a concrete focus to the work, and to enable us to process-trace reforms across multiple levels of the education system, each team chose one or more of the key policy reforms identified in the recent literature as being central to efforts to improve quality. In particular, we focused on efforts to improve the quality and level of resources and resource management within schools, and efforts to improve the quality and presence of teachers through training, incentives, and oversight mechanisms (Glewwe et al. 2011; Tikly and Barrett 2013). We did not take such reforms as proxies for achieving improved learning outcomes, but rather sought to identify whether elites are committed to adopting and implementing reforms that are directly targeted at improved learning outcomes.

Matching this menu with actual reforms that had been undertaken within each country led us to focus in particular on investments in human resources (e.g. teacher training) and the kinds of accountability and incentive mechanisms (including transparency and information-based initiatives) employed to monitor and improve performance at local government and school levels.[7] The focus was sharpened further at the frontline, with each team identifying two different socio-economic contexts (one relatively wealthy, one relatively deprived) and then choosing a high- and low-performing school in each of these contexts for further investigation, in order to try and identify the specific effects of politics and governance vis-à-vis other factors (e.g. the class status of pupils and parents). Differing levels of performance were identified via a range of sources, particularly school tests. This level of research enabled us to examine interactions between local levels of governance and the school, including the role of traditional authorities, and also the immediate governance arrangements of the school itself (e.g. senior management committees, parent and teacher associations, unions). A particular focus here fell on efforts to combat leakage of funds, school-based management reforms that give local stakeholders greater control over how schools are run, and teacher incentive reforms, such as different kinds of employment contract arrangements, rewards for attendance, and performance-related pay. The multi-levelled, process-tracing approach adopted here has, we would argue, helped generate useful and original insights into the multiple ways in which political and political economy factors shapes the progress of educational quality reforms.

This approach responds to the challenge set out by Kingdon et al. (2014), by undertaking theoretically driven, comparative, and methodologically robust research on the question of the political economy of education quality

[7] Other reforms include the development of national assessment systems, methodology-based reforms, and early years education.

reforms. The central focus is on how, and the extent to which, the nature of the political settlement helps explain why generating high levels of commitment and capacity to improve basic education quality has been so challenging for developing countries. Given that poor quality provision seems to be fairly typical across low-income countries, the focus is less on the causes of this generalized problem, than on understanding how the political settlement influences whether and how the problem of quality becomes politically salient and to what extent it is effectively addressed; in other words, what shapes capacity and commitment to addressing the learning challenge in developing countries?

By theorizing this problem in terms of the interaction between key 'domains of power', we seek to draw attention to the key forms of politics that shape capacity and commitment to delivering higher-quality learning in developing countries. This includes a focus on informal as well as formal institutions, and on the incentives, ideas, and influence of actors and coalitions at multiple levels of both the political settlement and policy domain. This approach allows us to build on, but also move beyond, the existing literature, much of which has tended to focus on quantitative expansion either of enrolment or numbers (e.g. Ansell 2008; Kosack 2012), or on the influence of organized interests (Moe and Wiborg 2017) and formal accountability mechanisms (World Bank 2003) in the education sector. We hope that by focusing on the political drivers that shape reforms, and by going beyond unions to investigate the roles of bureaucrats and policymakers, we can provide an approach that is policy relevant, while also providing theoretical and empirical clarity to an under-explored area. Nonetheless, we would also acknowledge that the approach could be developed further. For example, and like much political analysis, our approach does not reach down to the most local domains of power that shape educational performance, namely the household and familial dynamics that are crucial to the functioning of education systems (Gift and Wibbels 2014). Further research in this area may therefore consider adding further, more localized domains of power to the framework mapped out here.

Conclusion

The existing literature on the political economy of education remains underdeveloped in all aspects: theoretical, methodological, and empirical. However, the growing range of studies of education in developing countries that have placed politics at the centre of their analysis has started to indicate which forms of politics are likely to matter most. These include the ways in which material aspects of a country's political economy shape not only the capacity of different groups to make demands, but also the nature of its institutions; the powerful role played by informal as well as formal institutions in developing countries; the particular forms of political agency (e.g. leadership, coalitions) required to navigate these structural conditions; the role of governance arrangements and relationships within the state, as well as between the state and citizens; and the role played by ideas as well as the incentives in shaping elite behaviour. This chapter has taken these insights and placed them alongside recent theoretical advances around the politics of development to propose a conceptual framework that can usefully guide work in this area, one which focuses on the interaction between 'domains of power' at national and policy levels. It has also suggested that, particularly at this stage of theorizing the politics of education in developing countries, comparative case study research that uses a typological approach is particularly well suited to testing out and refining certain propositions, and to generating policy implications that are of relevance to different types of political context. In line with the challenge set by Kingdon et al. (2014), the deployment of a 'political settlements' typology seeks to capture how different types of 'structural, historical, and institutional conditions' prevail within different polities. The remainder of this collection deploys this approach to set out new evidence and analysis on the politics of addressing the learning crisis in developing countries, before inviting leading commentators to discuss how far we have helped push forward this important field of enquiry and action, and where attention could usefully turn next.

References

Abdulai, A.-G., and S. Hickey. 2016. 'The Politics of Development under Competitive Clientelism: Insights from Ghana's Education Sector'. *African Affairs*, 115(458): 44–72.

Acemoglu, D., and J. A. Robinson. 2012. *Why Nations Fail: The Origins of Power, Prosperity and Poverty*. London: Profile Books.

Ansell, B. W. 2008. 'Traders, Teachers, and Tyrants: Democracy, Globalization, and Public Investment in Education'. *International Organization*, 62(2): 289–322.

Bebbington, A., A-G. Abdulai, D. H. Bebbington, M. Hinfelaar, and C. Sanborn. 2018. Governing Extractive Industries: Politics, Histories, Ideas. Oxford: Oxford University Press.

Béland, D. 2005. 'Ideas and Social Policy: An Institutionalist Perspective'. *Social Policy and Administration*, 39(1): 1–18.

Blyth, M. 2002. *Great Transformations: Economic Ideas and Institutional Change in the Twentieth Century*. Cambridge: Cambridge University Press.

Chisholm, L. 1983. 'Redefining Skills: Black Education in South Africa in the 1980s'. *Comparative Education*, 19(3): 357–71.

Corrales, J. 1999. *The Politics of Education Reform: Bolstering the Supply and Demand; Overcoming Institutional Blocks*. Washington, DC: World Bank.

Doner, R. F., and B. Ross Schneider. 2016. 'The Middle-Income Trap: More Politics than Economics'. *World Politics*, 68(4): 608–44.

Evans, D. R., R. Sack, and C. P. Shaw. 1995. *Formulating Education Policy: Lessons and Experiences from Sub-Saharan Africa*. Paris: Association for the Development of African Education (DAE) and UNESCO.

Fukuyama, F. 2016. *The Origins of Political Order*. London: Profile Books.

George, A., and A. Bennett. 2004. *Case Studies and Theory Development in the Social Sciences*. Cambridge, MA: MIT Press.

Gift, T., and E. Wibbels. 2014. 'Reading, Writing, and the Regrettable Status of Education Research in Comparative Politics'. *Annual Review of Political Science*, 17(1): 291–312.

Glewwe, P. W., E. A. Hanushek, S. D. Humpage, and R. Ravina. 2011. 'School Resources and Educational Outcomes in Developing Countries: A Review of the Literature from 1990 to 2010'. NBER Working Paper 17554. Cambridge, MA: National Bureau of Economic Research.

Gray, H. 2016. 'Access Orders and the "New" New Institutional Economics of Development'. *Development and Change*, 47(1): 51–75.

Grindle, M. S. 2004. *Despite the Odds: The Contentious Politics of Education Reform*. Princeton, NJ: Princeton University Press.

Grindle, M. S. 2012. *Jobs for the Boys: Patronage and the Politics of Public Sector Reform*. Cambridge, MA: Harvard University Press.

Grindle, M. S. 2017. 'Good Governance, RIP: A Critique and an Alternative'. *Governance: An International Journal of Policy, Administration and Institutions*, 30(1): 17–22.

Hickey, S., and T. Lavers. 2016. 'Conceptualising the Politics of Social Protection Expansion in Low Income Countries: The Intersection of Transnational Ideas and Domestic Politics'. *International Journal of Social Welfare*, 25(4): 388–98.

Hirsch, A. and B. Levy. 2018. 'Elaborate Scaffolding, Weak Foundations: Business–Government Relations and Economic Reform in Democratic South Africa'. ESID Working Paper No. 105. Manchester: University of Manchester.

Hossain, N. 2005. 'Productivity and Virtue: Elite Categories of the Poor in Bangladesh'. *World Development*, 33(6): 965–77.

Kelsall, T. 2012. 'Neo-patrimonialism, Rent-seeking and Development: Going with the Grain?' *New Political Economy*, 17(5): 677–82.

Khan, M. 2000. 'Rent-seeking as a Process'. In *Rents, Rent-seeking and Economic Development*. Edited by Khan, M., and K. S. Jomo, 70–144. Cambridge: Cambridge University Press.

Khan, M. 2010. 'Political Settlements and the Governance of Growth-enhancing Institutions'. Monograph. London: SOAS.

Khan, M. 2017. 'Introduction: Political Settlements and the Analysis of Institutions'. *African Affairs*. Virtual Issue. 1–20.

Kingdon, G. G., A. Little, M. Aslam, S. Rawal, T. Moe, H. Patrinos, T. Beteille, R. Banerji, B. Parton, and S. K. Sharma. 2014. 'A Rigorous Review of the Political Economy of Education Systems in Developing Countries. Final Report'. *Education Rigorous Literature Review*. London: Department for International Development.

Kosack, S. 2012. *The Education of Nations: How the Political Organization of the Poor, Not Democracy, Led Governments to Invest in Mass Education*. Oxford: Oxford University Press.

Levy, B. 2014. *Working with the Grain: Integrating Governance and Growth in Development Strategies*. Oxford: Oxford University Press.

Levy, B., and M. Walton. 2013. 'Institutions, Incentives and Service Provision: Bringing Politics Back In'. ESID Working Paper 18. Manchester: Effective States and Inclusive Development Research Centre, The University of Manchester.

Moe, T. M., and S. Wiborg. 2017. 'Introduction'. In *The Comparative Politics of Education*. Edited by T.M Moe, and S. Wiborg, 1–23. Cambridge: Cambridge University Press.

Nazneen, S., S. Hickey, and E. Sifaki (Eds.). 2019. *Negotiating Gender Equity in the Global South: The Politics of Domestic Violence Policy*. London: Routledge.

North, D. C. 1990. *Institutions, Institutional Change and Economic Performance*. Cambridge: Cambridge University Press.

North, D. C., J. J. Wallis, and B. R. Weingast. 2009. *Violence and Social Orders: A Conceptual Framework for Interpreting Recorded Human History*. Cambridge: Cambridge University Press.

Pierson, P. 1993. 'When Effect Becomes Cause: Policy Feedback and Political Change'. *World Politics*, 45(4): 595–628.

Pritchett, L., K. Sen, and E. Werker (Eds.). 2018. *Deals and Development: The Political Dynamics of Growth Episodes*. Oxford: Oxford University Press.

Schmidt, V. A. 2008. 'Discursive Institutionalism: The Explanatory Power of Ideas and Discourse'. *Annual Review of Political Science*, 11(1): 303–26.

Schmidt, V. A. 2010. 'Taking Ideas and Discourse Seriously: Explaining Change through Discursive Institutionalism as the Fourth "New Institutionalism"'. *European Political Science Review*, 2(1): 1–25.

Stasavage, D. 2005. 'Democracy and Education Spending in Africa'. *American Journal of Political Science*, 49(2): 343–58.

Tikly, L., and A. M. Barrett. 2013. 'Education Quality and Social Justice in the Global South: Towards a Conceptual Framework'. In *Education Quality and Social Justice in the Global South: Challenges for Policy, Practice and Research*. Edited by Tikly, L., and A. M. Barrett, 11–25. London: Routledge.

Wales, J., A. Magee, and S. Nicolai. 2016. 'How Does Political Context Shape Education Reforms and Their Success?' ODI Dimension Paper 6. London: Overseas Development Institute.

Whitfield, L., O. Therkildsen, L. Buur, and A. Mette Kjaer. 2015. *The Politics of African Industrial Policy: A Comparative Perspective*. Cambridge: Cambridge University Press.

World Bank. 2003. 'Making Services Work for Poor People: World Development Report 2004'. Washington, DC: World Bank.

World Bank. 2011. 'Conflict, Security and Development: World Development Report 2011'. Washington, DC: World Bank.

World Bank. 2017. *World Development Report 2018: Learning to Realize Education's Promise*. Washington, DC: World Bank, http://worldbank.org/en/publication/wdr2018, accessed 3 Oct. 2018.

3

Decentralization and Teacher Accountability

The Political Settlement and Sub-national Governance in Ghana's Education Sector

Edward Ampratwum, Mohammed Awal, and Franklin Oduro

Introduction

The question of how politics shapes social services provisioning in Sub-Saharan Africa (SSA) has centred on the extent to which democratization, or at least the consistent holding of elections over time, will lead to higher levels of expenditure on goods and services that benefit non-elite groups (Carbone 2012; Stasavage 2005). Although this is an interesting and worthwhile question, it may obscure the main characteristics of both politics and education, and thus prevent a clear understanding of the links between the two. In terms of politics, this approach tends to ignore the extent to which 'democratization' remains a highly contested process, which has yet to displace other often 'informal' political processes and relationships (Oduro, Awal, and Ashon 2014; Whitfield et al. 2015) that exert more powerful influences over processes of resource allocation and service delivery (Abdulai and Hickey 2016). In terms of education, the approach tends to focus mainly on the provision of access (visible infrastructure and enrolment), rather than on the quality of education that is being delivered (Darvas and Balwanz 2014; Lenhardt, and Rocha Menocal, with Engel 2015).

Ghana is a particularly interesting setting in which to explore the debates around democratization, politics, and education provisioning. Though the country has performed relatively well in terms of increasing access to education (albeit at a slower rate than some other poorer, less democratic countries), it has achieved less in terms of securing outcomes, and there is evidence of a learning crisis. A recent study found that 75 per cent of those leaving school after five to six years could not read, and the youth literacy gap between rich and poor is 50 per cent (Rose 2014). High levels of teacher absenteeism have been identified as one of the key inefficiencies in the education sector, accounting for poor education outcomes (World Bank 2010). Rates of absenteeism amongst teachers for reasons other than sickness increased from 4 per cent in 1988, to 13 per cent in 2003 (World Bank 2004, 2010), and 27 per cent in 2008 (CDD 2008). All of this presents a puzzle, not only because democratic and (lower) middle-income Ghana could be expected to perform better, but also because Ghana has undertaken some key reforms for raising learning outcomes, most notably the decentralization of power and resources within the education sector (Pritchett 2013). This suggests that the problem of educational outcomes in Ghana cannot be understood through a focus on formal political institutions associated with democracy and decentralization per se, but, more importantly, through focusing on kinds of political relationships or relational forms of politics that exist between political elites and poor groups in society (Kosack 2009).

This chapter seeks to unravel this puzzle, following the power domains approach outlined in Chapter 2. This builds on Levy and Walton (2013), who make the case for exploring the political drivers of educational quality through a multi-levelled approach that starts with the nature of the 'political settlement' at the national level and then works through multiple levels of governance arrangements at the sub-national level, right down to the front-line schools. This chapter will therefore examine the local political drivers of quality educational performance through a political settlements lens. From this perspective, the education sector in Ghana needs to be understood not simply in a technical sense, but as a domain of resource allocation that can play a political as well as a developmental function with regards to maintaining the legitimacy and longevity of the ruling coalition.

Taking up the issue of teacher absenteeism, this chapter argues that implementation of education quality reforms is significantly shaped by district-level dynamics in Ghana's political settlement. In particular, the level of inter- and intra-party competition influences the ability for 'developmental coalitions' to emerge at district level, and for the incentives and interests of politicians, bureaucrats, and school-level state and non-state actors to be aligned around collectively addressing the challenge of teacher absenteeism.

The chapter draws on qualitative research conducted between 2012 and 2015, using in-depth case studies of two pairs of schools in two different districts within the Central region of Ghana. The methods used included documentary analysis, school surveys, and thirty-six key informant interviews with stakeholders at national, regional, district, and school levels.[1] Informants

[1] The key informants included former and acting directors of Ghana Education Service, former minister of education, Ministry of Education chief directors, chairman of Education Reform Review

were purposively selected on the basis of a mapping exercise, which identified key actors in the education system at different hierarchical levels. Four focus group discussions, two in each district, with forty key stakeholders[2] at the community and district levels, were also undertaken as part of the field research. The choice of schools and districts is discussed in more detail later in this chapter.

The Political Settlement and the Education Sector in Ghana

The political settlement in Ghana has been defined as 'competitive clientelist' (Oduro et al. 2014), combining elements of multi-party political competition with clientelistic practices.[3] Elections in Ghana have developed into a highly competitive political game since 1992, in which two parties, the National Democratic Congress (NDC) and the New Patriotic Party (NPP), have consistently challenged each other in closely fought national elections. The highly competitive nature of the country's electoral process and the constitutionally imposed four-year-term limits have combined to generate strong pressures for governing parties and elites to answer to the short-term socio-economic needs of voters and their supporters, and the needs of their own short-term political survival. This political context strongly incentivizes ruling elites to adopt a politicized approach to public policy formulation and implementation, resulting in the public bureaucracy becoming increasingly personalized and informal in character.

The fact that the public bureaucracy is personalized rather than programmatic in character, has particular implications for the education sector in Ghana, which has historically been seen by its ruling elites as critical to legitimizing their status and staying in power (Antwi 1992; Casely-Hayford 2000). The political significance of education has seen it become a critical arena within which elite incentives and ideas are played out. Education sector reforms in Ghana over the past three decades have, on paper at least, focused on the twin imperatives of improving both the quality and quantity of education. For example, the Free, Compulsory, Universal Basic Education programme, introduced in 1993 under the NDC regime focused

Committee, civil society actors, district chief executives, district directors of education, circuit supervisors, executives of teacher unions, members of the DEOCs, assembly members, etc.

[2] The FGD participants were representatives of parent teacher associations, school management committees, community-based organizations, faith-based organizations, selected parents, and traditional authorities.

[3] For detailed discussions of Ghana's political settlement and its implications for development, see Mohan and Asante (2015); Oduro et al. (2014); Whitfield (2011); and Whitfield et al. (2015).

on increasing enrolment and expanding physical infrastructure, to the detriment of teacher education and pedagogical resources (Inkoom 2012; Tagoe 2011). Similarly, the NPP government, shortly after gaining political power in 2001, ordered a review of the 'goals and philosophy' of Ghana's education system. This review eventually led to the launch in 2007 of the National Education Reform Programme (Darvas and Balwanz 2014). These reforms reaffirmed the government's responsibility for the implementation of the Free, Compulsory, Universal Basic Education programme, setting out a framework for decentralization, in addition to several initiatives aimed at improving the quality of education (Darvas and Balwanz 2014).

With the electoral pendulum swinging back to NDC regime in 2009, further reforms in the education sector were introduced. Although these reforms were broadly in line with the reforms highlighted in the Education Act of 2008 (Act 778), promulgated and passed into law under the previous NPP regime as part of the National Education Reform Programme, there was a stronger focus on enhancing education delivery and outcomes through the deepening of decentralized structures (Little 2010). Outside the decentralization reforms, which were largely sustained, the NDC regime in 2009 subsequently reversed the NPP's policy of extending secondary education from three to four years. This singular move, in addition to a few other politically engineered initiatives, reinforced the sense that the frequency of reforms within the education sector in Ghana tends to increase under the conditions of intense electoral competition, at the expense of both coherence and technocratic control.

Indeed, many key decisions affecting education continue to be made outside of the Ministry of Education (Darvas and Balwanz 2014). This situation is driven by the increasing politicization of education, as well as bureaucrats' fear of victimization by political actors within the sector (Booth et al. 2005; Casely-Hayford et al. 2007). Politicians and political actors, informed by party manifestos, ultimately drive policy formulation processes in the education sector in Ghana (Casely-Hayford 2011). While a focus on quality has been apparent in the discourse of political and policy stakeholders, this appears to have been outweighed by the political imperatives of providing more tangible goods via the access and quantity agenda. Similarly, ensuring that critical constituencies such as the teaching force and district-level bureaucracies are appeased is essential, with a strong union focused on teacher salaries and welfare issues, and not (unlike the professional teacher associations) on teacher performance (Casely-Hayford 2011; Prempeh 2011). Consequently, the balance of power between the different actors active in the education sector, and their specific interests, helps to explain how reforms actually play out in practice, including why some gain priority over others.

Mapping Key Actors within Decentralized Education Governance in Ghana

Recent efforts to decentralize power and responsibilities within Ghana's education sector need to be understood within the wider context of decentralization that was launched in 1988, and further extended following the return to democracy under the Fourth Republic in 1993. Under this programme, the country has developed a three-tier structure of sub-national governments at the regional, district, and sub-district levels. Institutionally and functionally, the decentralization framework structured local governance around the metropolitan, municipal, and district assemblies (MMDAs, here referred to as district assemblies [DAs]).

The DAs are the highest political authorities entrusted with the political, administrative, and legislative powers to initiate, facilitate, and execute development activities in their respective districts. Reforms aimed at decentralizing line management functions to the District Education Directorates (DEDs) and at devolving decision-making and financing authority to the DAs were first put in place by the Ghana Education Service Act of 1995 (Act 506). Following this, the Education Act of 2008 (Act 778) deepened the decentralization of education service delivery, by creating new mechanisms and structures to empower regional- and district-level stakeholders to play active roles in the management of education service delivery. The Education Act of 2008 (Act 778) provided Ghana with a four-tier structure for the decentralized governance of the education sector, running from regions, through districts to circuits, and then schools (see Figure 3.1).

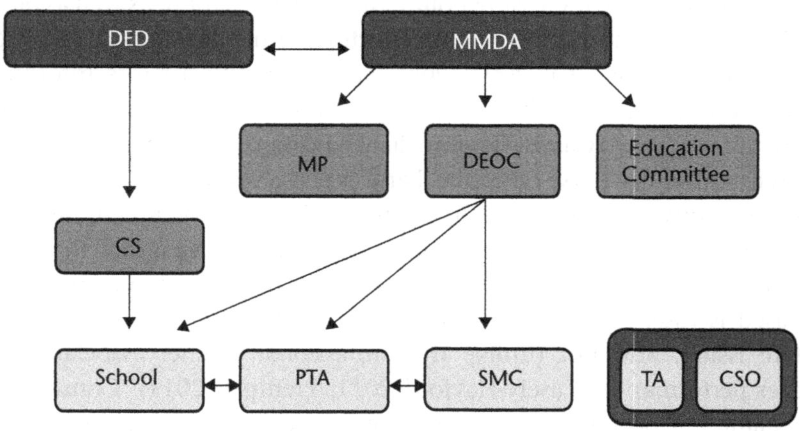

Figure 3.1 Structure of education policy implementation at the district level, Ghana
Source: Authors' construction.

The DAs have broad responsibility for development outcomes, including ensuring education is available and responsive to local needs, across basic, secondary, and functional literacy levels. The DAs are headed by centrally appointed metropolitan, municipal, and district chief executives (here referred to as district chief executives [DCEs]), who are political and development agents of the ruling political party. DCEs are expected to represent the interests of the ruling party and government at the district level. The DAs are made up of elected and appointed members of the various localities under the DAs. The ruling party and government appoint 30 per cent of DA members and these are largely party activists and loyalists. It is also worth noting that although two-thirds of the membership of the DAs are elected on a non-partisan platform, there is anecdotal evidence of the alignment of these assembly members to the two main political parties at the central level of government, the NDC and NPP. Hence, centre–local relations are critical to understanding decentralization and implementation of decentralized reforms in Ghana (Crook 2017).

The decentralization of education sector governance in Ghana has centred on efforts to ensure higher levels of authority for local political actors over more centralized and technical actors, and on empowering non-state actors to be involved in governing the sector. Democratic oversight is organized through the district education oversight committee (DEOC), which is chaired by the central government-appointed DCE, who is also the political head of the District Assembly. Other members of the DEOC include the district director of education, chairperson of the education committee at the DA and representatives from parent–teacher associations (PTAs), school management committees (SMCs), the Private Schools Association, teacher unions, traditional authorities, and faith-based organizations (FBOs). Although the Education Act of 2008 (Act 778) called for the creation of DEOCs and empowered them to directly participate in the management of teachers and the provision of support, in practice they have weak incentives and authority to drive up performance over the long term, and are therefore largely an advisory body. For instance, where the DEOC takes decisions on education at the district level, which may not be in accord with national policy, the committee has no real power to enforce its decisions on education at the district level, leading sometimes to conflict and contestations with the DEDs and implementation challenges at the school level.

Members of parliament (MPs) also mediate between the central and local levels. MPs are ex-officio members of the DA and operate outside the formal structures of the DEOC. MPs are elected on the competitive electoral platforms of political parties and hence are subject to inter- and intra-party pressures, in terms of their decisions, initiatives, and ideas to improve teacher accountability and education performance at the district and community levels. MPs have often undertaken programmes to improve education performance at the local level in partnership with the DEDs and DAs, especially when they represent the ruling party at the central level of government. Where the MPs represent the opposition party, they often directly implement policies without recourse to the DAs, and to some extent the DEDs, which sometimes leads to conflicts and a focus on 'visible' goods to the detriment of quality reforms.

The Ghana Education Service (GES), the technical arm of the Ministry of Education, implements education policy at the district level through the DED in accordance with the GES Act of 1995 (Act 506) (Mankoe 2006; Baffour-awuah 2011). A centrally appointed district director, who is accountable to the central appointing authority at the GES, heads the DED. Relative to other actors at the district level, the DEDs have high powers and strong incentives to influence district education policy- and decision-making. However, the DEDs have no influence in changing national policies affecting education delivery in Ghana. The DED mainly works around existing policies and adapts these policies to suit the needs of their districts. The DED represents a de-concentrated rather than devolved form of governance.

Circuit supervisors operate as the interface between the DED and school authorities, responsible for particular zones within each district[4] and for inspecting school facilities, providing assistance and support to teachers and headteachers, and using the outcomes of training programmes and the centrally produced headteacher appraisal guides to assess performance (Baffour-awuah 2011). Headteachers of both primary and junior high schools in Ghana are responsible for monitoring teaching and learning in their schools and are directly accountable to the district directorates (Baffour-awuah 2011).

The reforms emanating from the Education Act of 2008 (Act 778) resulted in the increased involvement of non-state actors at both district and school levels (Bogaert et al. 2012). These include FBOs that play a major role in the provision of school infrastructure and management (Casely-Hayford 2011). It is worth highlighting, however, that from the perspective of the GES, FBOs have no institutional legitimacy to intervene in education service delivery, including with regards to the recruitment of teachers at school level (Casely-Hayford 2011). Consequently, at the district level, FBOs have little power to improve education outcomes. However, they seem to wield some influence over headteachers and teachers at the school level, and over other non-state actors at the school level, such as PTAs, especially in the schools they establish.

Other key actors at the community level include SMCs,[5] PTAs,[6] and local traditional authorities. PTAs and SMCs are tasked with working alongside headteachers to ensure effective school management and improvement,

[4] The district is zoned into circuits. There are also inspectors at the regional level.

[5] Membership of the SMCs includes parents, teachers (including the headteacher), a representative from the traditional authority, a representative from the old students' association, a male assembly member, and a female representative.

[6] The PTAs are made up of parents and teachers (including the head of the school).

including defining how financial allocations will be used, improving learning outcomes, and monitoring teacher attendance. Teacher unions are indirectly involved in the implementation of education decentralization, and they have a strong and effective voice, stemming from their large membership numbers and the electoral importance of their constituency to political actors (Casely-Hayford 2011). Teacher unions such as the Ghana National Association of Teachers, National Association of Graduate Teachers, and Concerned Teachers Association, have representatives at the national, regional, district, zonal, and school levels (Casely-Hayford 2004).

Ghana has put in place many of the governance measures that experts perceive as critical for the promotion of higher levels of educational performance, particularly in terms of decentralisation (Pritchett, 2013). These reforms in the governance of the education sector in Ghana have enabled the entry of a myriad of sub-national actors with particular interests and ideas into the domain of education. Given wider problems with political manipulation, local capture, and deficits in state capacity associated with decentralized service delivery in Ghana, it is essential to examine the extent to which the formal institutional reforms actually play out at the district and school levels, particularly in terms of promoting improved teacher accountability and associated performance outcomes in education (Crawford 2009; Crook 2017; Crook and Manor 1998).

The Politics of Education in Ghana: A District- and School-level Analysis

To establish a clear view of how politics shapes education sector governance at the district and school levels in Ghana, we identified differing levels of performance within contexts that were otherwise similar in terms of their levels of development, geographical features (e.g. urban–rural balance), and ethnic composition. We focused on two districts within the Central region of Ghana that are amongst the poorest districts in Ghana, and are similar in most respects other than their educational outcomes, referred to here as AK and TM. In each we randomly selected two schools to examine variation in performance in more depth, referred to here as AK Schools A and B, and TM Schools A and B.

Table 3.1 provides comparative performance statistics of the education system in the two districts. District-level figures conceal considerable school-level variation, however. While the two schools selected in TM for the case study recorded overall Basic Education Certificate Examination (BECE) pass rates of 88 per cent (TM School A) and 80 per cent (TM School B), those selected in AK recorded 33 per cent (AK School A) and 27 per cent (AK School B) for the 2013–14 academic year.

Table 3.1 Comparative educational statistics for two districts in Ghana

Indicators	District AK	District TM
District league table 2014 (DLT) ranking[7]	173 out of 216 13th out of 20	180 out of 216 14th out of 20
Number of schools	312	419
Enrolment of pupils	35,381	21,887
Number of teachers	1,132	875
Percentage of untrained teachers	49%	44.6%
Teachers engaged in primary schools	470	444
Pupil–teacher ratio	20.1	21.1
Pupil–trained teacher ratio	31.1	55.1
Average BECE pass rate for the four core subjects (2012–13)	53%	59%
Teacher attendance on average per term for the year	50%	79%

Source: Authors' construction from District League Table 2014 report and Education Management Information System.

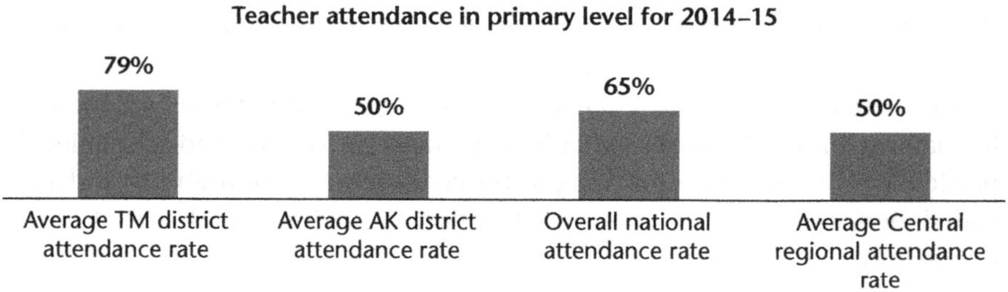

Figure 3.2 Teacher attendance at primary school level, Ghana
Source: CDD-Ghana field data, 2015.

Schools in TM district had a better record of teacher attendance than in AK district. Indeed, schools in the Central region of Ghana have a lower record of teacher attendance, with an average of about 50 per cent, compared with a national average of 65 per cent (see Figure 3.2). Set against this, TM's ability to ensure relatively high levels of teacher attendance is notable; given the evidence that teacher attendance is critical to achieving improved learning outcomes (see Chapter 1), we would expect to see further improvements in TM in the coming years.

As noted above, teacher attendance in TM district was reported at an average of 79 per cent in the 2014–15 academic year. In TM Schools A and B attendance was 80 per cent and 75 per cent respectively, well above the national average and the Central regional average of 65 per cent and 50 per cent respectively (see Figure 3.3).

[7] Note that the District League Table ranking is based on a composite of six indicators (health, education, security, governance, rural water, and sanitation). Although data suggests that TM is higher achieving than AK in terms of education, in other respects AK outperforms TM.

In AK district, on the other hand, teacher attendance on average per term for the year was 50 per cent, similar to the regional average, but below the national average of 65 per cent. Average attendance was the same in AK School A and AK School B in the district during the 2014–15 academic year (see Figure 3.4).

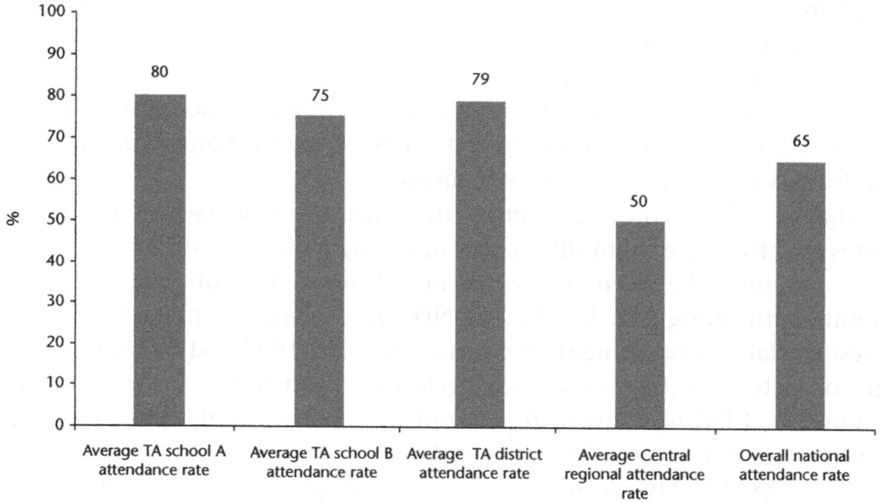

Figure 3.3 Teacher attendance at primary school level in TM district, Ghana
Source: CDD-Ghana field data, 2015.

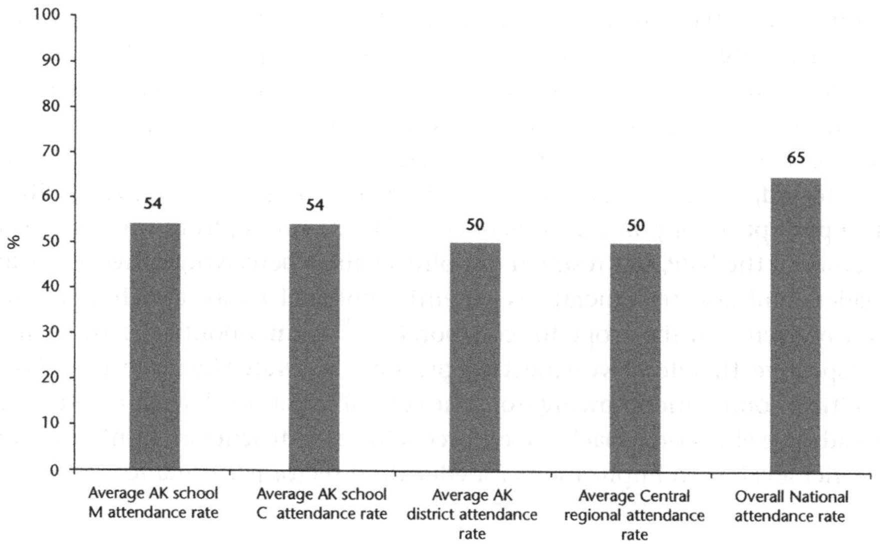

Figure 3.4 Teacher attendance at primary school level in AK district, Ghana
Source: CDD-Ghana field data, 2015.

Comparing teacher attendance rates across the two districts, we found that schools in TM district outperformed those of AK, the Central regional, and national averages. We also found similar patterns of better performance at the school level in this regard.

Given the clear variation in teacher attendance and educational outcomes described above, a key question for us is whether this variation can be explained by differences in the dynamics of the political settlement at the sub-district level. This means examining the ways in which sub-national politics and institutional dynamics shape the implementation of local governance reforms intended to secure higher levels of teacher accountability and performance. From this perspective, it is interesting to compare the levels of political competition across the two districts.

Analysis of election results since the return to democracy in 1992 indicates that there are slight differences in voting patterns, with a higher level of competition between the two main parties in AK compared with the higher-performing TM. In TM, the NDC has secured a majority in every presidential and parliamentary election between 1992 and 2012. The margin of victory in the presidential elections ranged from 34 per cent at its highest in 1996 to a low of 6 per cent in 2000, while the margin in the parliamentary elections ranged from 17 per cent in 1996 to 11 per cent in 2012. In AK, NDC has secured a majority in all presidential and parliamentary elections since 1992, with the important exception of 2004, when the NPP won with a majority of 8 per cent in the presidential election and 11 per cent in the parliamentary election. Despite the NDC winning both presidential and parliamentary elections in 2008 and 2012 in AK, with a higher margin of 23 per cent and 18 per cent, respectively, than in TM, AK has a higher level of political competition amongst political elites.[8] In this sense, AK more closely reflects the Central region's reputation as a 'swing' region than TM. A crucial difference between the two districts, in this regard, is the level of inter- and intra-party competition between elites. The perception of political insecurity in AK, stemming from the historical victory of the NPP, has resulted in political elites perceiving other political leaders and also bureaucrats as potential political rivals, and has significantly decreased the scope for collaboration.[9] From a political settlements perspective, therefore, we expect the pressures generated by intense levels of political competition flowing from the central to the local levels could have an adverse effect on capacity to enforce reforms in teacher accountability at district level, with implications for education sector performance.

[8] Interview data (2015). [9] Interview data (2015).

The Politics of Tackling Teacher Absenteeism in Ghana: The Role of Coalitions

This section explores why the variation in educational quality exists between AK and TM districts, focusing on the challenge of teacher accountability and performance. By comparing how the challenge of teacher absenteeism is dealt with across the two districts, we arrive at an understanding of how the political settlement—and in particular, political competition and the importance of district-level 'development coalitions'—impacts on the delivery of teaching at the frontline.

Significance of Political Competition

The differing levels of inter- and intra-party competition across the two districts significantly influenced the ability of political leaders and bureaucrats to address teacher absenteeism coherently. In AK, intense intra- and inter-party competition between the main political actors undermined the ability to promote teacher accountability and decrease absenteeism. The DCE in AK who, at the time of research, had served for two years of a four-year mandate, aspired to elected office in competition with the existing MP and other actors and party activists. Within the bureaucracy, the DCE perceived the DED and other highly trained bureaucrats as threats to his political ambitions, and as being aligned with the political opposition; he thus often refused to commit the resources of the District Assembly to support the budgets of decentralized institutions at the sub-national level.[10] Because of his political ambitions, the local MP, who belongs to his political party, was also perceived as a direct political rival to the DCE. As a result, the DCE was incentivized to undermine the local MP, in order to increase his chances of gaining the party candidature during the next election, and the MP was similarly engaged in efforts to undermine the DA and the DCE's role in promoting teacher accountability and district-level development as a whole. Indeed, mistrust between the MP, DCE, and DED in AK resulted in the appointment of trainee teachers who had loyalty towards either the MP or the DCE. These teachers were often difficult to control, decreasing the ability to reduce absenteeism. The competition between these political actors also resulted in the need to create visible projects within the districts to show or garner support, rather than antagonize non-performing teachers, which could have had implications for the political ambitions or the fulfilment of the political mandates of the MP and DCEs. The DCE tried to undermine the MP for the constituency by presenting local

[10] Interview data (2015).

government projects, such as the construction of schools, teachers' quarters, and other facilities, as his personal contribution to the constituency. One of the political actors in AK explained the over-emphasis on visible infrastructure projects in the light of intense political competition as follows:

> When it comes to infrastructure, we [the DCE and the DA] have been providing them classroom blocks and teachers quarters among other things since 2011. I have been able to put up about six teachers' quarters, some were abandoned and we have completed them. We have six classroom unit blocks and KGs [kindergarten blocks] among many others. The District Assembly also supports the activities of DEOC financially and the District Assembly [under the leadership of the DCE] is involved in organizing 'my first day at school programmes' [to welcome new students into schools in the district].

The DCE perceived such projects as more effective at promoting his political ambitions, at the expense of 'invisible' projects aimed at promoting improved accountability and higher performance. The determination of the DCE to unseat the sitting MP also led to covert scheming in internal party elections, including underhand dealings to control the hierarchy of the party at the grassroots level, through handouts to influential political party executives, scheming to get favourable executives elected at the grassroots level of the ruling party. This strategy also led to the appointment of influential community leaders and stakeholders as members of the DEOC and as government appointees to the DA.

In TM, on the other hand, less intense inter- and intra-party competition shaped the relations between the MP, the DCE, and officials of the DED, leading to far greater coherence in the application of strategies to address teacher absenteeism. The MP was the longest serving of the three officials, and the DCE and the DED deferred decisions to the MP. The DED aligned closely with officials of the ruling party in the constituency, working with key political officials to promote and achieve the political goals of the ruling government and party in the constituency. The MP was kept informed of all meetings and events, participating personally or through intermediaries to ensure strong political leadership in the constituency, and to ensure the party, rather than individual actors, were identified with projects and service provision.

As a result, key political actors controlled internal political machinery and minimized the potential for internal political competition with its ramifications for policy implementation. The MP and DCE collaborated to provide job opportunities for party loyalists through an elaborate patronage system. Using proceeds and resources of cocoa allocated from government through the district assemblies, as well as collaboration with owners of commercial plantations in the constituency, the MP channelled resources to party loyalists and key political actors in the constituency to consolidate his position, both within and across the political spectrum. The MP also aligned with key political actors and bureaucrats at the district level by channelling national- and regional-level funded programmes to the constituency. This enabled the MP to align intra-party interests to promote the district, rather than undermining the DCE.

In TM, the MP and DCE were also willing to sponsor potential teacher trainees, especially those belonging to the ruling party, for short-term training programmes under the Untrained Teacher Training Diploma in Basic Education programme. This government-funded distance-learning in-service programme is aimed at addressing geographical disparities in teacher allocation and improving the quality of education at the basic school level in Ghana (GES 2011; Sofo, Thompson, and Kanton 2015). The primary reason for training these party activists was to build a cadre of party-friendly teachers in the district, who could populate the classrooms in the district's deprived communities where regular GES teachers refused to accept postings. In addition, a political alliance between the MP, DCE, and officials at the DED at the district level ensured the appointment of party loyalists and activists through the National Youth Employment Programme. The teachers employed on this programme, who were mainly untrained personnel, filled the classrooms in the districts where the regular teachers were absent to attend distance-learning and sandwich programmes held at the two teacher education universities in the region, the Universities of Cape Coast, and Education in Winneba, respectively. The lower rates of teacher absenteeism that this ensured increased contact hours between tutors and pupils and ultimately improved school performance, as a DA official described:

> . . . this [arrangement to appoint teachers from communities in the district] is improving teaching and learning. To our surprise, this district never scores 0 per cent [BECE] as compared to the previous [period] when we [some of the schools in the district] were getting 0 per cent, 14 per cent, 17 per cent, 18 per cent in schools. But this year, because of the strategies we [the DA, MP, and DED] have put in place, performances have improved. Children are going to second cycle institutions [after successfully passing the BECE], so teaching and learning in the district has improved.

While this arrangement may raise questions about the politicization of education provision, in practice it enabled the political actors, the DAs and DED, to ensure adequate provision of teachers in school at all times, rather than relying on the regular teachers posted from the GES or the centrally appointed National Service Scheme personnel, whose appointment the political actors had little or no control over.

The Roles of District-level 'Developmental Coalitions'

The level of political competition at the district level had implications for relations between political actors and bureaucrats charged with the responsibility of implementing education policies, and their ability to enforce sanctions on absentee teachers. In the context of TM, the limited nature of political competition enabled the emergence of 'developmental' coalitions at the district level, which shaped the higher performance identified in that district, particularly in terms of the lower levels of absenteeism. There was evidence of the emergence of a developmental coalition between community-, school-, and district-level actors in education, which was able to circumvent the problems emanating from conditions of competitive clientelism, incoherent district- and school-level governance arrangements, and vested interests at the local level. In particular, an alliance was forged not only between the key political and bureaucratic actors involved in governing education at the district level, most notably the members of the education committee at the DA, the DEOC, and DED, but also with the teacher unions in the district.

This coalition was critical in overcoming opposition to policies from teachers and other local-level politically powerful stakeholders and promoting the enforcement of accountability mechanisms from the district to the school levels. The coalition helped to develop a range of context-specific approaches to the problem, which had proved to be critical constraints to higher levels of accountability and performance. For example, the DED in higher-performing TM had put in place several formal and informal arrangements to improve supervision and address teacher absenteeism and performance that went beyond the national policy framework on teacher attendance and absenteeism. These included deductions from teachers' salaries for unsanctioned absences, embargoing teacher salaries without challenge from teacher unions[11] or DA politicians,[12] and initiating community monitoring and reporting on absentee teachers. A bureaucrat in TM summarized some of the measures the DED had put in place:

> When teachers complete the college of education, instead of serving for three years, they quickly apply to upgrade themselves at the universities in the region. Unfortunately, the schedule for the university academic calendars for those courses conflicts with the GES timetable, and so they would even leave the classroom to pursue their programme without informing the District Education Directorate. We decided to embargo their salaries and invite them to the district office to arrange with the potential interim replacement during their absence from the classroom. First, the teacher is encouraged to prepare lesson notes ahead of time to reduce the workload on whoever is coming to replace them in the classroom. Second, we encourage the absentee teachers to arrange with people in the community who are qualified and have applied for recruitment in the Ghana Education

[11] In other districts, where there are no developmental coalitions, teacher unions sometimes choose to protect members' interests over those of students.

[12] For political actors at the DA, teachers constitute a significant voting bloc.

> Service . . . They are not trained teachers, but have completed university and are not employed . . . So such people can hold the fort in the absence of the teacher.

In TM there was also evidence of improved collaboration between political officials at the DA, DED officials, and teacher unions, which facilitated enforcement of sanctions for teachers who absented themselves from school without official permission. The main teachers' union in the district, the Ghana National Association of Teachers, often held dialogues with headteachers, PTAs, FBO representatives, and traditional authorities to devise mechanisms to monitor teacher attendance and develop strategies to replace absentee teachers without formal recruitment. Collaboration between education stakeholders was further entrenched in TM, where the political and administrative officials of the DA informally co-opted key executives of the teacher unions into the DEOC and relevant committees in education at the DA. DA officials also provided financial and logistical support to the activities of the teacher unions at the district. This collaboration between political, bureaucratic, and union executives at the district level resulted in the creation of a strong district-level coalition to promote teacher attendance and promote greater accountability amongst teachers.

In the lower-performing district AK, by contrast, competition between the government-appointed DCE and the directors of the DED resulted in an incoherent application of sanctions for absentee teachers. Rooted in competition between the MP and DCE, political officials at the DA did not effectively collaborate with the bureaucratic officials of the DED to implement a joint action plan to promote teacher accountability. Officials at the DA and the DED focused on their own initiatives and ideas to reduce teacher absenteeism, such as building teachers' quarters in politically important localities, without reference to local demands or needs. Meanwhile, the DED did not wholly support and enforce recommendations of the DEOC and the DA and its DCE, such as in relation to sanctioning absentee teachers in schools in the district. At the same time, the DA, which had a general mandate for oversight of education, often declined to allocate and release budgetary resources to support DED initiatives for improving teacher accountability.

The absence of an effective coalition between political officials at the DA and the bureaucratic heads at the DED in the low-performing district, AK, resulted in teacher unions undermining the capacity of DEDs to enforce sanctions against absentee teachers. Indeed, executives of the teacher unions seemed to benefit from the disharmony between political and bureaucratic elites in the district; this discordant relationship sometimes resulted in absentee teachers being promoted or transferred to another school or district without recourse to local school governance structures, rather than being sanctioned in accordance with existing GES regulations.

Community-level Dynamics

The emergence of 'developmental' coalitions in education at the district level, underscored by the sub-national political settlement, was mirrored at the community level. Key actors within community-level 'developmental' coalitions included circuit supervisors and headteachers, comprising a vertical axis of accountability, and PTAs, FBOs, and traditional authorities, supplying a horizontal axis of accountability (see Chapter 1). Actors in this coalition possessed differing levels of power and political influence at the community level.

Due to the alignment of political interests between key political actors at the district and community levels, Circuit Supervisors and headteachers in the higher-performing TM district schools liaised effectively with community-level political party officials, who also doubled as SMC officials. These 'politically salient stakeholders' (Levy and Walton 2013) were able to use their connections with both political and bureaucratic actors at the district level, namely the DAs and DEDs, to create strong incentives and pressures amongst headteachers and teachers to reduce absenteeism and drive up teacher and student performance at the school level.

In addition to liaising with SMCs to promote accountability amongst teachers, circuit supervisors in TM also devised mechanisms to benefit from the intra-party alignment at the district and community levels by tapping into the powerful influence and networks of the traditional authorities, PTAs, and FBOs within their jurisdictions, who controlled politically salient blocs of voters in their localities. The membership of the PTA, FBOs, and traditional authorities in TM mainly comprised retired district education officials[13] and former assembly members with strong political party connections,[14] and political party constituency and polling station executives. They could thus leverage their power and influence over key political actors in the district, such as the MP, DCE, and executives of the ruling party, amongst others, to exert pressure on school-level officials to generate positive incentives for teacher accountability.

In the poorly performing schools in AK, on the other hand, the political misalignment between the MP, DCE, and grassroots activists of the ruling party at the district level affected the ways in which vertical and horizontal structures promoted or undermined teacher accountability at the community and school levels. Partisan PTA and SMC members often accused headteachers and teachers of promoting opposition party interests in the constituency by

[13] They were former directors and assistant directors of education, former teachers, and local managers of the FBO schools, amongst others.

[14] This included former members of the education sub-committee of the MMDA, retired public servants, and representatives of the traditional council.

undermining efforts to monitor and sanction teachers, and contestation over the power to sanction or enforce sanctions on absentee teachers was common.

Conclusion

This chapter emphasizes the extent to which teacher accountability in Ghana's education sector is shaped by the dynamics of the country's political settlement, from the national level through districts, to schools themselves. A key finding was that while Ghana's competitive clientelist settlement generates a high degree of policy incoherence and politicization within the sector, the drivers of improved performance and accountability do not flow from the national to the local level, but instead need to be (re)generated at the level of districts and schools. Ghana's decentralization reforms in the domain of education have to some extent opened up space for manoeuvre amongst key stakeholders at both district and school levels and, when political conditions are conducive, this can result in the emergence of some forms of 'developmental coalitions', as was observed in the relatively high-performing TM district.

In TM, teacher accountability reforms were successfully implemented at the district and school levels thanks to a functioning and resourceful District Education Organising Committee, strong technocratic leadership of the District Education Directorate, a well-supervised cadre of circuit supervisors, active and functioning PTAs and SMCs, and (some) progressive teacher unions. In addition, and more importantly, the ways in which these different actors could be brought together into a coherent developmental coalition accounted for their interaction in ways that promoted effective teacher accountability. Such coalitions addressed teacher absenteeism through local and often informal solutions and governance arrangements, which needed to be recognized in order to improve teacher accountability. These developmental coalitions could then provide a critical basis to offset the collective action problems that characterize the education sector in Ghana, with its often incoherent reforms and governance arrangements, both of which are nested within, and flow from, the country's competitive clientelistic political settlement.

Critical for the emergence of such coalitions is an alignment between political and bureaucratic elites, something which the high-levels of inter- and intra-party competition undermined in the case of AK. Although more research is required to unearth the underlying drivers of these incoherent relations between actors and institutions at the sub-national level in the low-performing district, we hypothesize that higher levels of political competition faced by and within the then-ruling political party in AK may be reducing the level of collective action amongst district-level elites, as compared with the relatively more 'dominant' position enjoyed by elites in TM.

References

Abdulai, A.-G., and S. Hickey. 2016. 'The Politics of Development under Competitive Clientelism: Insights from Ghana's Education Sector'. *African Affairs*, 115(458): 44–72.

Antwi, M. 1992. *Education, Society and Development in Ghana*. Accra: Unimax.

Baffour-Awuah, P. 2011. 'Supervision of Instruction in Public Primary Schools in Ghana: Teachers' and Headteachers' Perspectives'. PhD thesis. Perth: Murdoch University.

Bogaert, S. E. B., M. Goutali, P. Saraf, and J. White. 2012. 'Transparency in Primary Schools Enhancing School-based Management in Ghana'. Report for Transparency International Workshop in Development Practice. New York: School of International and Public Affairs, Columbia University.

Booth, D., R. Crook, E. Gyimah-Boadi, T. Killick, R. Luckham, and N. Boateng. 2005. 'Drivers of Change in Ghana, Overview Report'. Report to Department for International Development (DFID). London: Overseas Development Institute.

Carbone, G. 2012. 'Do New Democracies Deliver Social Welfare? Political Regimes and Health Policy in Ghana and Cameroon'. *Democratization*, 19(2): 157–83.

Casely-Hayford, L. 2000. 'Education, Culture and Development in Northern Ghana: Micro Realities and Macro Context; Implications for Policy and Practice'. PhD thesis. Brighton: University of Sussex.

Casely-Hayford, L. 2004. 'A Social Appraisal of the Education Strategic Plan for Ghana'. Associates for Change Working Document 1. Unpublished.

Casely-Hayford, L. 2011. 'The Political Economy Analysis of the Education Sector in Ghana: The Implications for STAR-Ghana'. Report for STAR-Ghana. Accra: Strengthening Transparency Accountability and Responsiveness Ghana.

Casely-Hayford, L., R. Palmer, C. Ayamdoo, and N. M. Thompson. 2007. 'Aid and Donor Partnerships in Ghana's Education Sector, 1987–2007: A Critical Review of the Literature and Progress'. Working Paper. University of Cambridge, Research Consortium on Education Outcomes and Poverty (RECOUP).

Crawford, G. 2009. '"Making Democracy a Reality"? The Politics of Decentralisation and the Limits to Local Democracy in Ghana'. *Journal of Contemporary African Studies*, 27(1): 57–83.

Crook, R. C. 2017. 'Democratic Decentralisation, Clientelism and Local Taxation in Ghana'. *Institute of Development Studies Bulletin*, 48(2): 15–30.

Crook, R. C., and J. Manor. 1998. *Democracy and Decentralisation in South Asia and West Africa: Participation, Accountability and Performance*. Cambridge: Cambridge University Press.

Darvas, P., and D. Balwanz. 2014. 'Basic Education Beyond the Millennium Development Goals in Ghana'. World Bank Study. Washington, DC: World Bank.

GES (Ghana Education Service). 2011. *Director-General's Annual Report to GES Council*. Accra: Ghana Education Service.

Inkoom, A. 2012. 'Implementation of Initiatives to Reform the Quality of Education in Rural Ghanaian Junior High Schools'. PhD thesis. Perth: Edith Cowan University.

Kosack, S. 2009. 'Realising Education for All: Defining and Using the Political Will to Invest in Primary Education'. *Comparative Education*, 45(4): 495–523.

Lenhardt, A., and A. Rocha Menocal with J. Engel. 2015. 'Ghana, the Rising Star: Progress in Political Voice, Health and Education'. ODI Development Progress Case Study Report. London: Overseas Development Institute.

Levy, B., and M. Walton. 2013. 'Institutions, Incentives and Service Provision: Bringing Politics Back In'. ESID Working Paper 18. Manchester: Effective States and Inclusive Development Research Centre, The University of Manchester.

Little, A. W. 2010. Access to Basic Education in Ghana: Politics, Policies and Progress. CREATE Pathways to Access, Research Monograph 42. Brighton: Consortium for Research on Educational Access, Transitions and Equity, The University of Sussex.

Mankoe, J. 2006. *Educational Administration and Management in Ghana* (revised ed.). Kumasi: Payless Publication Ltd.

Mohan, G., and K. P. Asante. 2015. 'Transnational Capital and the Political Settlement of Ghana's Oil Economy'. ESID Working Paper 49. Manchester: Effective States and Inclusive Development Research Centre, The University of Manchester.

Oduro, F., M. Awal, and M. A. Ashon. 2014. 'A Dynamic Mapping of the Political Settlement in Ghana'. ESID Working Paper 28. Manchester: Effective States and Inclusive Development Research Centre, The University of Manchester.

Prempeh, H. K. 2011. 'Political Economic Analysis of Ghana for STAR-Ghana'. Accra: Strengthening Transparency Accountability and Responsiveness Ghana.

Pritchett, L. 2013. *The Rebirth of Education: Schooling Ain't Learning*. Washington, DC: Center for Global Development Books.

Rose, P. 2014. 'Education for All Global Monitoring Report 2014: Teaching and Learning: Achieving Quality for All', https://reliefweb.int/report/world/education-all-global-monitoring-report-2014-teaching-and-learning-achieving-quality-all, accessed 4 Apr. 2018.

Sofo, S., E. Thompson, and T. L. Kanton. 2015. 'Untrained Teachers Diploma in Basic Education Program in Ghana: Teacher Trainees' and Lecturers' Perspectives'. *American International Journal of Contemporary Research*, (5)6: 7–13.

Stasavage, D. 2005. 'Democracy and Education Spending in Africa'. *American Journal of Political Science*, 49(2): 343–58.

Tagoe, M. 2011. 'Lifelong Learning and the Attainment of the Education-related Millennium Development Goals 2 and 3 in Ghana. Is There a Critical Nexus?'. *International Journal of Lifelong Education*, 30(1): 19–35.

Whitfield, L. 2011. 'Competitive Clientelism, Easy Financing and Weak Capitalist: The Contemporary Political Settlement in Ghana'. DIIS Working Paper 27. Copenhagen: Danish Institute for International Studies.

Whitfield, L., O. Therkildsen, L. Buur, and A. Mette Kjaer. 2015. *The Politics of African Industrial Policy: A Comparative Perspective*. Cambridge: Cambridge University Press.

World Bank. 2004. 'Books, Buildings and Learning Outcomes: An Impact Evaluation of World Bank Support to Basic Education in Ghana'. Washington, DC: World Bank.

World Bank. 2010. 'Education in Ghana: Improving Equity, Efficiency and Accountability of Education Service Delivery. Africa Education Country Status Report'. Washington, DC: World Bank.

4

The Politics of Learning Reforms in Bangladesh

Naomi Hossain, Mirza M. Hassan, Muhammad Ashikur Rahman, Khondoker Shakhawat Ali, and Md. Sajidul Islam

Introduction

Why has Bangladesh failed to raise quality in basic education after it successfully expanded school provision? The country successfully eliminated gender disparities and raised enrolments at primary and lower secondary in the 1990s, expanding provision with innovative schemes and non-formal non-governmental provision (Hossain 2007; Chowdhury et al. 2002, 2003). An elite consensus about the need for mass education to stimulate national development in a labour-rich, resource-poor economy generated the political will, resources, and administrative capacity for rapid expansion of provision (Hossain, Subrahmanian, and Kabeer 2002). Primary education statistics are still cited as evidence of Bangladesh's 'surprising' human development achievements (Asadullah, Savoia, and Mahmud 2014). But by the early 2000s, concerns about quality were widespread, partly as the rapid expansion appeared to push average standards down (CAMPE 2005; Ahmed et al. 2007). Rates of completion were low, of grade repetition high, and learning attainments lagged behind expected levels; teacher capacity was below par, and children received woefully inadequate instruction time (CAMPE 2005, 2009; DPE 2014b).

If politics helped to explain the successful expansionary reforms, can politics also explain why Bangladesh has been slower to address the persistent problem of quality in basic education? This chapter explores this question through a power domains approach, analysing the influence of the political settlement on the design and uptake of education reforms in the 2000s, the extent to which they prioritized efforts to improve quality, and how effectively those efforts transmitted through to the governance of schools and the delivery of education on the frontline. Through review of reform design and sector performance documents, key informant interviews, and comparative primary research into how efforts to increase teacher motivations for performance played out in four schools, the chapter documents how the elite consensus on basic education in Bangladesh runs out when it comes to raising education standards.

The analysis concludes that this outcome reflects how competitive pressures in Bangladesh's clientelistic political settlement have until recently been aligned with expansionary, rather than quality-focused, reforms: elites have competed to build more schools with more teachers, children, and textbooks in them, rather than promote reforms to raise the standard of general education. This partly reflects the holding power of teachers within the political settlement: this ensures that on both sides of the political divide, reformers tread carefully around their interests, offering more training, better remuneration packages, and new entitlements, rather than disciplinary reforms designed to hold them to account for their performance. The centralized administration and its weak incentives to enforce unpopular reforms ensure discretion at the frontline of educational provision within schools. In the absence of system-wide pressures to deliver higher-quality education, teacher performance depends ultimately on their inherent motivations and the quality of school-level governance, which leads to highly variable outcomes in practice. These motivations have arguably been undermined by the declining status of the teaching profession as a whole, the result of broader sectoral and social change, contributing to great political sensitivities regarding the treatment of public school teachers in Bangladesh. This was clearly demonstrated by the nationalization of registered non-government primary schools in 2014 in response to teacher protests about pay and conditions.

If teachers may be expected to resist reforms that demand greater accountability and scrutinize performance, the literature suggests business interests, and the governance and personnel needs of the state itself, may have countervailing incentives to improve the education system. But in Bangladesh, there have been few signs that even large employers view the quality of public schooling as a matter of concern (cf. Doner and Schneider 2016). Nonetheless, the political equilibrium that has kept tough learning reforms off the basic education agenda in the past decades may now be shifting. In the past decade, concerns about quality have galvanized initiatives to monitor education performance more closely from the centre. While these efforts have yet to bear fruit in terms of improvements in learning attainments, they are a sign that the state is taking the challenge of learning seriously enough to track it, despite the potentially embarrassing effects. Moves such as the introduction of publicly available National Student Assessments, school censuses and Annual Sector Performance

Reviews, which are clearly intended to strengthen the state's capacity to improve learning across the system, are consistent with the longer time-horizons of more dominant party systems. This stronger capacity to monitor may reflect the ways in which the political settlement in Bangladesh has, since 2009, been less competitive and increasingly dominated by the Awami League, which has placed a strong emphasis on promoting development, in part to legitimize its project of securing political dominance. It remains too soon to be sure, but signs from the education sector at least indicate that a somewhat more developmentalist and programmatic—as distinct from short-term and clientelistic—approach to education policy may be in sight, even if the results have yet to show up in the form of improvements in classroom interactions and learning outcomes.

The Problem of Education Quality in Bangladesh

The primary education system in Bangladesh is large and complex, with 18.7 million children enrolled at primary level in 127,000 schools of 24 different types. Some 80 per cent of all children attend schools managed by the central government, and almost 70 per cent of the half million-strong primary school teaching force, 57 per cent of whom are women, are in the government system. Almost 8 million children from poor families receive cash stipends, and over 3 million receive school meals. All of this was achieved with an annual budget of only US$8 billion (2014), and although primary education comprises 10 per cent of all public expenditure, it comes to less than 2 per cent of GDP.[1]

By some indicators, educational performance improved over the 2000s. In terms of completion and repetition, this improvement has been comparatively fast: the primary completion rate rose nearly 25 percentage points between 2010 and 2013, and now stands at 81 per cent (DPE 2014b). The repetition rate improved from 50 per cent in 2008 to only 7 in 2013, dropping further to 6 per cent in 2016 (DPE 2017). Improvements in learning attainments have been slower: 75 per cent of grade 3 students performed at or above grade level in Bangla in 2013, up from 68 per cent in 2011, but with little improvement amongst grade 5 learners. In mathematics, 43 per cent of grade 3 students and 75 per cent of grade 5 students were behind expected grade-level learning outcomes in both years. The most recent National Student Assessment found, furthermore, that attainments had worsened slightly, a finding explained in the National Student Assessment 2015, due to the lagged nature of education reforms, as 'assessment instruments [are] aligned with the new curriculum but

[1] Information from the 2013 school census, also DPE (2014b), MOPME (n.d.).

classroom practice in many respects continues to be tied to the old curriculum' (DPE 2016, 22). Despite this depressing performance, 99 per cent of the more than 2.5 million students who took the Primary Education Completion Examination in 2013 and in 2015 passed (DPE 2014b, 2017).

Low performance is a feature of the South Asia region. One study noted that, with the exception of (far higher-performing) Sri Lanka, the region was not part of international student learning assessments, and attainment indicators were extremely low everywhere. In India, fewer than half of grade 5 students passed basic reading comprehension tests in 2011, while 43 per cent of grade 8 students could not do simple division. It was only by grade 4 or 5 that most students recognized two-digit numbers (supposedly taught in grade 2). One national assessment found that not even half of all grade 6 students were able to identify a number between five and eight. While rural Pakistani students performed somewhat better than their Indian counterparts on comparable arithmetic questions, regional studies showed up variations, with most students in Punjab unable to perform simple arithmetic until late into their primary school careers. In Sindh, most students could do basic addition, but subtraction was a challenge for around half.[2]

Within Bangladesh, official assessments have attributed these problems to a weak organizational framework; poor physical environment in schools; short contact hours, due to the shift system; lack of support materials and inadequate numbers of trained teachers; and traditional classroom teaching and learning practices (DPE 2014b). Teacher capacity has been a key concern. In 2008, only one-fifth of teachers were trained in the core curriculum, and 40 per cent of women and nearly 60 per cent of men teachers had no subject training (CAMPE 2009). Although subject training has been shown to make a difference, experience only affects student learning when teachers have worked for more than twenty years; then students tend to do *worse*, suggesting teacher motivations actually decline over time (DPE 2014c). Lesson observation studies suggest pedagogical skill has been limited and rote learning from textbooks routine (FMRP 2006).

Student backgrounds matter, but school-level factors may matter more. CAMPE (2009) argued that performance depended on students' socio-economic background (including whether they could afford private tuition). However, DPE (2014c) found that most variation in educational outcomes in publicly funded schools was due to differences between schools, rather than students (also World Bank 2013). This indication of frontline discretion (Lipsky 1980) gains support from our four-school comparative case analysis, which found that variations in the governance regimes at the school level

[2] These figures are from assessments cited in Dundar et al. (2014).

explained differences in teacher motivation and performance, perceived quality, and educational outcomes.

Discretion with respect to the time devoted to teaching and learning helps explain variation across schools. One study found only 67 per cent of government primary school (GPS) students were present during unannounced visits, and only 45 per cent in publicly funded *ebtedayee* madrassahs (FMRP 2006). Lesson observation found teachers out of the classroom on average 14 per cent and students off-task 12 per cent of the time (FMRP 2006, 177). The need for more time to achieve basic competencies was underlined by one study that found the average Bangladeshi student has to get through much of secondary school to achieve a primary school education (Asadullah and Chaudhury 2013), suggesting children are simply not getting enough learning time in primary.

Time-on-task is low for several reasons. Scheduled hours are low, and children in grades 1 and 2 in double-shift schools get only 520 hours per year on average (DPE 2014b), compared with an international average of 900–1,000. Unplanned closures mean schools operate between 42 and 78 per cent of planned school days (Tietjen, Rahman, and Spaulding 2004), although that situation may be improving (DPE 2014b; FMRP 2006). Teachers are frequently absent (Chaudhury et al. 2004), although rarely on unauthorized leave (FMRP 2006; CAMPE 2009). Teachers are often late, end class early, or use classroom time for other activities. So while pedagogy remains a problem, a critical determinant of education quality is the quantity of instruction time (DPE 2014c, 62; see also Rose, Lane, and Rahman 2014). In the classroom, students learn little from the many teachers who have no subject or pedagogical training, or who are demotivated and busy with private income activities (World Bank 2013).

Political Settlement and Education Policy

Elite Consensus on Mass Education across Political Settlements

An elite consensus on the need to expand basic education provision in Bangladesh was inspired by a vision of transforming the country's sole wealth—its human resources—into an income-earning asset, in the style of the East Asian 'tiger economies' (Hossain 2017). Consistency across political regimes on the directions of economic and social development was rooted in aid dependence (Sobhan 1982), but contending elites shared a belief in mass basic education as the foundation for national development (Hossain 2010a). Policies of expanding access have typically 'gone with the grain' of competitive clientelistic pressures on state and political actors. They have enabled politicians to provide resources and services to constituents, and sources of political capital, patronage, and rents to local elites, contractors, teachers, and other interest groups. And because of the significance of the national curriculum in imparting versions of nationalist identity, each incoming government has also had a strong incentive to expand provision, competing to reach a larger portion of the new generation. In addition, governments have had to compete with the highly visible role of NGOs such as BRAC providing schools for rural girls and the poor. It is no coincidence that government schools and education-related services (such as the Primary Education Stipend Programme) grew in parallel with NGO innovations in non-formal schooling (Hossain et al. 2002).

Judged in terms of its share of public spending, the political will to educate has plateaued with the achievement of near-universal primary education by the 2000s. Public spending on education has lost its share of the total, and remains static at an internationally and regionally low level of around 2 per cent of GDP (Islam 2010). But in real terms, spending rose 30 per cent between 2001 and 2005 alone (Al-Samarrai 2007). Spending remains concentrated on teachers' pay and benefits, and tightly controlled from the centre, however (see Rose et al. 2014). But because poor children attend public schools, the incidence of recurrent spending on primary education has been broadly pro-poor (Steer, Rabbani, and Parker 2014).

The thrust of basic education policy has closely tracked the changing political settlement since 1971. On independence from Pakistan, the nationalist party the Awami League and its left-leaning allies installed a 'socialistic', secular, statist programme of economic and social development, nationalizing 26,000 community primary schools and declaring that education would be compulsory, secular, and modernized—the last a reference to madrassahs/ Islamic schools. But, shortly after establishing this new mandate to educate the population, Bangladesh entered into a period of clientelistic military rule that lasted 15 years. The dominant elite coalitions during this period broadly accommodated Islamist political and social elites with latitude and financing for madrassahs, and with strong links with teacher unions. To earn the regime external and popular legitimacy, public administration was decentralized and state ideology Islamicized, both of which influenced education policies. Attempts to consolidate power during this period entailed political compromises with powerful social actors—for instance, in the 1990 Compulsory Primary Education Act. The Act aimed to appease student groups aggrieved by protracted authoritarian rule, but it was too late: student groups led the movement that toppled the regime later that year. However, the Act had other effects, reversing privatization and the Islamization of public education, and establishing free universal primary education as a goal and policy of the state.

Since the return to multiparty democracy in 1991, the political settlement has mainly presented as 'elitist competitive clientelist' (Levy and Walton 2013) with respect to the balance of power. This means that whichever elite faction happened to be in power was vulnerable to being displaced by the other, and also that ruling elites were under growing pressure from local-level factions on whom they relied to maintain themselves in power; this has tended to reduce the time-horizons of ruling elites and increase the incentives to use public resources and services to secure political loyalty (Hassan 2013). Since 1991, the emphasis on nationalization and Islamic education has oscillated. Across governments of both parties, however, there has been a growing emphasis on expanding access, through building schools, pro-poor conditional transfers, recruiting teachers, and using the curriculum to instil partisan versions of national identity. All governments have used public finance to expand the formal *ebtedayee* (primary madrassah) system, but it remains under-resourced compared with the mainstream GPSs. Nonetheless, this 'holy alliance' of support to madrassahs and to poor girls' education helped expand the system rapidly (Asadullah and Chaudhury 2009), as did the space for the non-formal schools of non-governmental organizations (Chowdhury et al. 2003). Enrolment rates of girls rose sharply on the return to democracy, as did recruitment of teachers (particularly women). It is notable that the democratic period has been closely associated with the feminization of public education.

Demand for Skills: Weak Support from Business

In Bangladesh, the average attainment from basic education is low, and public education does not equip graduates for the most ordinary interactions in work and life (World Bank 2013). Business and industrial elites appear to have at best mixed incentives to coordinate action to raise the quality of basic education. This may reflect the fact that in Bangladesh's flagship readymade garment (RMG) industry, labour has been transformed into considerable export wealth at, to date, very low overall levels of education. At the industry level, there has been less interest in raising average skill levels than in keeping wages low, and major employers view middle management, not assembly line workers, as where the key skills deficit lies. This situation may change as Bangladesh's main export industries are forced to raise productivity gains to stay competitive with rising domestic wages, political troubles at home, and new competitors (Saxena and Salze-Lozac'h 2010; Kathuria and Malouche 2015), and as a tighter rural labour market (Zhang et al. 2013) reduces the reserve army of labour. But to date, business interests in improved education quality have been muted.

Teachers and Schools in the Political Settlement

Despite the ebb and flow of secularism and statism, the emphasis on expansion has remained steady. This has brought growth in teacher numbers, and their associations now unite the interests of half a million organized middle-class voters with clout in the national policy space. Teacher interests in Bangladesh are prominent on the education agenda, and substantially protected against performance accountability, in a similar way to the dynamics observed in certain regions of Ghana. Some 90 per cent of education spending goes on teachers, and education accounted for 29 per cent of all directly employed government employees (400,000) in 2010. The strongest sign of their political significance is that a further 344,000 teachers employed in the nominally independent registered non-government primary schools (RNGPS) (BBS 2011) were recently made fully fledged government employees of newly nationalized primary schools.

State policy officially acknowledges sensitivities around teachers' declining social position (GoB 2010). Teachers are comparatively poorly paid (Asadullah 2006), and have 'low levels of teacher job satisfaction and motivation' (Haq and Islam 2005, 21; also Rahman, Shahriar, and Anam 2014; World Bank 2013). Teachers are more likely than not to be women, and the gender of the profession brings its own status issues. Yet teachers continue to be central to the vital business of the state, providing 500,000 polling officers during general elections (IRI 2008); it is believed that political parties view teachers as important allies, particularly because of their role in staffing polling stations during general elections. However, there is no evidence that teachers manipulate electoral procedures or results on any significant scale, nor that occupational, as opposed to partisan, considerations would matter in any such manipulation. Teachers have customarily fronted public health and other government campaigns (Mahmud 2002). Over and above its role in imparting the 'three Rs', the school is at the interface between state and society, developing basic citizenship skills, for example, communicating with officialdom, and imparting identities and knowledge of rights and responsibilities (Hossain 2010b).

Party Political Competitive and Local Clientelistic Pressures

One way in which party political competition connects public education to the political settlement is through the use of the curriculum to transmit competing partisan visions of nationhood and identity. Despite some variations, the policy recommendations of successive Education Commissions have typically been secondary to issues of national identity, which is the one issue over which the main political parties compete (Chowdhury and Kabir 2014, 3). Competition over the content of national history teaching is politically contentious, with each incoming regime rewriting textbooks with their version of history (Rosser 2003, 144).

The expanding school system created opportunities for local elites to earn rents, often through building or repair contracts, or through access to jobs (to a limited extent, as government school teacher recruitment is mainly centrally controlled and generally well-governed). School patronage is itself an important source of political capital, as an obvious means of demonstrating benevolence, raising social status, and building a profile. School management committee (SMC) membership is an established perk/responsibility of local councillors, and even MPs. While some forms of local political competition can have a benign influence on school management and teacher performance, others have been shown to paralyse local provision (FMRP 2007).

Education Policy Reforms

Recent Reforms: PEDP3

The Third Primary Education Development Programme (PEDP3) was an ambitious five-year (2011–15) sector-wide programme that aimed to establish efficiency, inclusion, and equity in primary education through action on learning outcomes, participation, reducing disparities, decentralization, effective use of budget allocations, and programme planning and management (DPE 2011b). In key respects, PEDP3 maintained the focus on institutional changes and quality reforms started under previous reforms, so that many of the reforms examined here had been underway for over a decade. PEDP3 marked a stronger emphasis on teacher-training investments, including increasing the professional certification of teachers, and widening access and increasing equity, as the poorest and most marginalized groups remained stubbornly hard to reach (Cameron 2010; Hossain and Zeitlyn 2010).

The two reforms that most directly addressed the issue of quality focused on learning outcomes, and decentralization and effectiveness (see Table 4.1). Recognizing the central need for effective teachers, reform efforts were combined in a bid to equip teachers with better knowledge and skills and increase their motivations and accountability. Competitive pressures driving the ongoing expansion were also expected to raise quality, by reducing student–teacher ratios. Under PEDP3, more teachers were set to be properly trained in subjects and pedagogy on recruitment, and then provided with regular in-work and refresher training. Professional certification now comes with the Diploma in Education qualification, gradually to be extended to all qualified teachers. The professionalization of the teaching corps was also to be enhanced through the development of teacher support networks and demand-based training programmes.

Two matters of direct relevance to teacher performance—headteacher training, and community mobilization (including SMC training)—were dropped from PEDP3 priorities. The current core feature of decentralization programming, the School-Level Improvement Plans were rolled out after a shaky start. By 2013, these funds were still only reaching two-thirds of schools (DPE 2014b). However, minimum quality standards under PEDP3 showed progress,

Table 4.1 PEDP3 components and key reforms in Bangladesh

Component	Key reforms
Learning outcomes	• fresh pedagogies • [holding] teachers accountable for each child's learning • revised curriculum and textbooks • classroom and school-based assessment • teacher pre-induction training upgraded to Diploma in Education
Participation and disparities	• one year pre-primary education through GPS • equivalency of formal and non-formal education • broadening the concept and mainstreaming inclusive education • providing education in emergencies and disasters • improving communications • reducing overcrowded classrooms through needs-based infrastructure development • providing sanitation and water to schools on a needs basis • providing school health and school feeding programmes • providing stipends to the poorest children
Decentralization and effectiveness	• school-level leadership development • field offices strengthened • increased decentralization of school management • mainstreaming school and *upazila* grants initiative • strengthening capacity at central-level institutions. • strengthening grade 5 examination, annual school census, and National Student Assessment systems • strengthening systems for teacher recruitment, deployment, and promotion
Planning and management	• strengthening results-based management • formalizing public–private partnerships • assuring adequate sector finance

Source: DPE (2011b).

including the timely delivery of textbooks, a rising proportion of teachers meeting the minimum professional qualification, in-service subject and sub-cluster training, and in student–teacher ratios (DPE 2014b).

Across the board, reforms were sensitive to teacher status and interests, and sought to raise performance without sanctioning failure. However, efforts to build teacher capacity were to be matched by new school and student assessment systems, and gathering other performance data, such as school censuses; these would enable monitoring, and provide the database for accountability with respect to learning outcomes. These efforts are more consistent with the learning reforms of a dominant political power, unconcerned about any possible short-term political effects of such new information sources, and may reflect the changing political settlement in Bangladesh.

National Level

The primary education sector is multi-stakeholder, with a few formal actors supporting the Ministry of Primary and Mass Education, and pressure groups (teachers' associations or unions) and civil society groups playing an informal role.

The PEDP3 steering committee, PEDP3 surveillance unit, and programme support office were designed to be inter-ministerial fora for deliberation over primary education policy. In theory, these were powerful entities; in practice, they were largely defunct. Some informants credited the inactivity of these committees to a lack of ownership amongst ministers and senior officials over the content of PEDP3, possibly reflecting the weak political support from the centre for systemic improvements in quality. Political governance was dominated by the powerful Prime Minister's Office (PMO), so that accountability relations between parliament and the ministry were weak. Parliamentary debates on governance and quality of education generally have limited effect, and MPs have little incentive to act, since education quality has to date been absent from electoral politics. Despite efforts by civil society groups to articulate demand for higher education standards, parent concerns about school quality appear to be chiefly expressed in exit from the system; hence the recent growth of the private sector.[3] Neither middle-class parents nor civil society activists have generated the political interest necessary to champion systemic learning reforms, nor have they succeeded in winning either major political party to their cause.

The more than a dozen national teachers' associations—the groups that represent teacher interests, frequently divided by party affiliation and official status—by contrast, present a formidable platform for the articulation of teachers' collective demands. Recent successful claims have included nationalizing RNGPS schools, so that all public school teachers' salaries, rank, and status are now part of the government system. It is notable that this costly and dramatic reform was undertaken during the lifetime of PEDP3, but not as part of the plan, or with reference to other stakeholders in the system. This highlights the extent to which education policy can be held hostage to the interests of groups with holding power within a competitive and clientelistic system.

Field Administration

The politicization of education policy also contributes to the policy incoherence or 'misalignment' in the education system (World Bank 2017). Interviews conducted with local government officials at multiple levels in the system make it clear that throughout the field administration, education officials lack the

[3] While numbers of government primary schools and students stayed static between 2010 and 2013 (remaining at just under 38,000 schools and increasing from 9.9 to 10.5 million students), 'kindergarten' schools, which provide the main competition from the private sector, increased from 4,418 to 14,100 over the same period, while student numbers almost doubled, from 535,000 to 981,000 (DPE 2011a, 2014a).

resources and authority with which to implement and monitor education reforms oriented towards improving teacher performance. Informal pressures from local and national actors divert bureaucratic attention away from a focus on learning throughout the system. Informal relations influence systemic accountability failures from the directorate responsible for policy implementation down to the *upazila* (sub-district) education office. Primary research conducted for this study on the district and *upazila* levels of the education system, as well as with the ancillary institutions tasked with delivering PEDP3 reforms, confirmed the World Bank's analysis of a system in which the allocation of resources and incentives is a poor fit with reforms targeting quality and learning (World Bank 2013). Officially at the helm of sub-national education administration, district primary education officers in practice lack the resources and authority for any effective monitoring of policy implementation at the *upazila*, let alone school, level. They frequently face informal pressures from political elites, mainly MPs, and senior officials, including from other ministries, over the transfer, deployment, and management of teachers. This is so despite the generally strong, merit-based system for teacher recruitment. At the *upazila* level, resource constraints, insufficient staff, excessive workloads, and lack of motivation amongst *upazila* education and assistant education officers weaken school monitoring. The latter are supposed to mentor primary school teachers on pedagogy, but mostly lack the training and knowledge themselves, spend too little time in schools, or are under-motivated by a lack of career development prospects.

Teacher-training reforms are supposed to be delivered via primary training institutes (PTIs). Interviews and observations indicate that these generally lack organizational skill, teaching proficiency, and capacity, as well as adequate physical infrastructure. Group rivalries and litigation over recruitment ensure that recruitment is neither meritocratic nor quality-focused. Instructors receive little on-the-job training, pedagogical knowledge is particularly weak, and specialized subject trainers are not recruited.[4] Provision in the training curriculum for trainee teachers to spend time teaching in schools with supervision from PTI instructors rarely happens. Not only do trainee teachers get little pedagogical, subject-based, or practical training, but cheating in examinations is also rife.

Reforms at the School Level

A comparative analysis of four schools was used to trace the effects of the political settlement and state capacity through to the implementation of learning reforms. Contrasting two pairs of comparatively high- and low-performing

[4] The recruitment policy dictates that all candidates must have bachelors- or masters-in-education degrees; this prevents recruitment of candidates with advanced degrees as specialized subject instructors.

institutions, one each in a lower-income rural (Narsingdi) and a higher-income urban (Mymensingh town) community setting, allowed us to control as far as possible for the influence of factors associated with politics and governance, rather than socio-economic contexts and the background of students. Case studies traced teacher-training and accountability reforms as implemented by headteachers and SMCs, examining outcomes against how local communities, education officials, and teachers themselves perceived the learning environment and student performance, and compared to key performance indicators from each school.

The school-level analysis supported the analysis of the field administration. In particular, it demonstrated that the competitive politicization that had supported the expansion of the system had not strengthened state capacities to deliver even the limited learning reforms adopted under PEDP3 directly into classrooms. The reforms were not universally absent or everywhere poorly implemented, but they were adopted with great discretion at the school level. Learning reforms had been adopted and implemented to the extent that the relationship between school authorities, the local elites involved in school governance, and the wider community aligned behind improved teacher and student performance. Where such informal relationships of accountability were absent or weak, the reforms had had limited effects on the teaching and learning in the community's school.

The school-level research found that teachers' subject knowledge and pedagogical skill varied significantly, even though teacher training is widely available and compulsory. In the 'good' schools, training was a regular matter, valued by the more capable teachers. In the good rural school, teachers were praised by school leaders for their successful efforts in explaining things to students, sometimes using pictures, interactive tools, and learner-centred activities; their successes had drawn children to enrol from less good nearby schools. Peer learning was encouraged, and teaching challenges discussed in weekly staff meetings. In the good urban school, teachers were strict about homework and memorizing lessons, but some were kind and affectionate, although children who failed to attend regular classes or extra coaching were fined. In the 'bad' schools, the situation was ad hoc, and teachers were criticized and mocked by their own students for not knowing their subjects. In the bad urban school, teachers were regularly present, but some were preoccupied with private tuition, including of outside students. Students who passed generally paid for extra tuition.

The role of the headteacher in setting a good example and motivating good teaching performance emerged clearly,[5] a finding that resonates across the country chapters. Headteachers in the good schools set clear goals and led

[5] See FMRP (2007) and Hossain and Tavakoli (2008).

by personal example, monitoring classroom performance, providing support and advice, and taking action against poor teacher performance or attendance. In the good rural school, the headteacher listened in to lessons to provide feedback later, personally collected textbooks to ensure her students got them on time, kept teacher attendance records, and marked them absent if they were late. The records had no real power (another list would go to the central office from which salary bills are made), but they did check tendencies to tardiness. In three of the schools, the headteacher revealed a vision and plan for achieving it, at least some of which was consistent with public policy. In the bad urban school, teachers were deployed and targets were reached, but public policy played little role. In the bad rural school, the headteacher had no discernible agenda and his demotivation infected teachers, pupils, and the community. He was said to arrive late, fall asleep in class, outsource his mathematics lessons in return for rights to conduct private tuition, and his teachers lacked direction, supervision, and motivation.

While teacher salaries are relatively low in Bangladesh (Asadullah 2006; World Bank 2013), teaching is a stable job with the status of public service. Yet teaching has few career prospects or pathways, with few chances for salary enhancement beyond the statutory increments. Private tuition was a factor in teacher performance, because it 'reduces the effort teachers put in in class', as one SMC member explained. Private tuition was particularly weakly governed in the worst schools, but managed with the aim of improving overall school and examination performance in the better schools. Half of all teachers are women, and unpaid care work also competes with many teachers' professional responsibilities. Students noted women teachers were often absent or late because of family matters. However, SMC and community members spoke forgivingly of women teachers' competing pressures, which suggests that a patriarchal benevolence to protect women's gender roles helps justify poor teaching performance.

Accountability with respect to teacher performance, specifically the minimal expectation that a trained teacher will show up on time and deliver full lessons to plan, requires that teacher performance can be examined and sanctioned. In practice, formal requirements to check on teacher attendance are delinked from teacher salaries, although teachers could in theory be disciplined, or lose salary or jobs if they are late or erratic. But teachers were only held accountable where they were being monitored by actors in a position to observe and authorized to act, in particular SMC members working with headteachers. When the SMC and headteacher shared a commitment to raising standards, they created a rule regime that raised teacher motivation and increased time-on-task, within the limits of the resources available.

The good schools were backed in these informal teacher discipline regimes by the support of visiting education officials. Under the best circumstances, official visits were constructive, mutually satisfying professional exchanges. All ranks of local education officials had recently visited all four schools, and in the more accessible and better-performing schools, these were regular and serious matters. But in the worse-performing schools, the inspection was, at most, cursory.

Informal accountability pressures were more important. For the good schools, teacher attendance mattered, because it determined overall results; in both, the headteacher and the community wanted better results, and monitored teachers and teaching as a result. Shaming and public humiliation were common sanctions against teacher transgressions, and SMC members were known to issue public reprimands. One irate parent in the dysfunctional urban school said that after their abysmal showing in the scholarship exam, he told teachers that 'with madams like these, we should break their teeth'.[6] The daily nature of schooling means the public sees teachers all the time, and basic indicators of their performance—whether they show up, on time—are public knowledge. Mothers of children in the good urban school waited at the school throughout the short day, and complained of teacher lateness or slow starts, and of excessive 'official work' taking up teachers' time, observing and commenting on classroom practices. The headteacher asked mothers to report latecomer teachers to her. Parental scrutiny kept the head monitoring the teachers, and the teachers alert. Yet whether the desire to earn the respect of the wider community actually motivates teachers to turn up and teach depends on other factors. The teacher might be looking to transfer, or have a private tuition practice in town, and have no need to maintain a good local reputation. For established local teachers, reputation matters because of status, and is useful branding for those with the time, energy, and market for private tuition.

Like all realms of public life, teacher motivation was influenced by party politics. Local and even national political actors had shown interest in the performance of the four schools studied here. SMC membership yields social and political capital, and education projects create opportunities to distribute contracts or other advantages. Schools can also be sites of local democratic competition over performance, with different parties competing to show their rule is superior by improving schools. Local parties influenced each of the schools' governance. In the bad rural school, local powerholders from within the ruling party controlled the school for personal interests, and excluded the opposition from school management. People there were scared to speak up, despite the school's declining performance, possibly for fear of reprisals from local party loyalists. This suggests the opposite dynamic to that observed in

[6] It is not unusual for extremely poor performance by heads and teachers to be punished using 'unruly' means, such as public protests, threats of or actual violence (Hossain 2010a).

Ghana, where political dominance at district level enabled more constructive and developmental relationships to emerge. In the bad urban school, political conflict between different parties had paralysed governance, as the SMC chairmanship was unresolved. In the good urban school, politics intervened less in school governance. But in the good rural school, a local political settlement meant the SMC chair was from the ruling party and the secretary from the opposition, a settlement that harnessed the benefits of political competition for the performance of a local public service.

Conclusion

Bangladesh's successful early expansion of mass education was driven by an elite consensus on the need for basic human development as the basis for national development, and the expansionary pressures of competitive party politics. Teachers held significant holding power within the political settlement, as a large and organized public sector group—a power demonstrated in the costly and unplanned recent improvements in pay and conditions of hundreds of thousands of registered non-governmental school teachers. Teacher associations have blocked or impeded consideration of reforms that would demand more accountability and higher performance. National political competition over education provision has not, to date, increased the political salience of the learning crisis in Bangladesh, nor have business or state actors shown any interest in lobbying for or supporting such reforms, partly because their educational needs are satisfied by even low-quality schooling. However, at the local level, political competition can shape school performance. In some instances, local competition between party-affiliated local elites creates positive incentives for SMCs to institute systems for improving teacher performance and student attendance. In others, however, political competition focuses on rent-seeking and securing jobs for party loyalists, paralysing efforts to improve learning.

Efforts to improve learning under the PEDP3 were shaped in part by the legacies of past policies, including those of the previous government, and in particular by the momentum for expansion and its impacts on teacher accountability and performance. This includes the feminization of the labour force in the expansionary drive, and the implications of gender disadvantage, including women's responsibilities for unpaid care work for matters such as teacher capacity, performance management, and time-on-task. PEDP3 involved a closer focus on quality and learning than previous development plans, and most notably strengthened the scope for central (although not local) monitoring of performance, through a new system of learning assessments (monitoring Bengali and mathematics performance amongst students in grades 3 and 5), in addition to official school censuses and Annual Sector

Performance Reviews. These efforts to strengthen central monitoring are consistent with the kinds of far-sighted policies we would expect of developmental elites without significant competitive pressures to deflect. They may reflect the growing concentration of power in the Awami League government, in power from 2009 to 2018 (to date), and the importance of development performance as a means of legitimating its authority and maintaining positive transnational relations.

While the quality of education does feature on political and policy agendas, teachers' collective holding power means that reforms targeting their performance have favoured positive incentives, doing little to hold them accountable for what they do in the classroom. Some reforms do reach schools, particularly where they involve more training or support to teachers. But it is only in some types of 'good' school that the reforms are harnessed to improve learning to any significant degree. The findings and analysis are consistent with the domain diagnosis that policy is weakly transmitted from the centre, so that inter-school differences explain most variations in student performance. There is effective school-level managerial control over the primary resource in education provision, namely, teacher time. But for a good school to exercise this core managerial function depends on cooperation between its headteacher and the community, and on an alignment of goals and visions for the school.

So, Bangladesh features an education system which, while formally highly centralized, is in practice fairly decentralized and discretionary in whether and how it implements reforms. And because SMC membership is amongst the spoils of local politics, there are competitive pressures on schools to adopt—and adapt—reforms. Local political competition can induce raised standards and overall improved schools where the oversight is generally benign. In others, political competition involving party affiliations destroys and distracts from efforts to improve learning. Overall, effective teacher management is likely to arise where the institutional fit between the school and the community enables a disciplinary regime focused around the management of time, the primary resource in the system. In this regime, students and teachers are driven to make the most of the resources available, with the clear aim of learning more and doing better. Community and school need to coordinate to achieve this disciplinary regime, and it helps if they are supported by the external administration. But there is little substantive support from district levels, and a variable amount from *upazila*-level officials. There is little external support for this effort to govern teachers, and no functioning system of formal accountability to enforce it.

The political will to improve learning remains concentrated within the central state's development project, from which its education ministries and agencies, in sectoral partnerships with aid agencies and projects, aim to deliver results. It is here, in the results-focused space of international aid and human development, that Bangladesh has been successful in the past, and seeks to demonstrate now the 'Bangladesh model' of development (GED 2015). To the extent that this matters to a core developmental elite that comprises politicians, bureaucrats, and aid and civil society actors, there is now some urgency around the problem of education quality. To date, this seems to be reflected most notably in the National Student Assessment, a monitoring exercise which was sustained throughout the lifetime of the PEDP3 despite persistent—and embarrassing—official evidence that learning remains at an abysmally low level. These costly innovations to monitor sectoral performance and learning outcomes have strong potential for improving performance accountability at different levels of the system.

A likely source of imminent change will be social and economic development itself. A richer and more educated population, and perhaps eventually larger and more globally integrated firms which require higher-quality human capital, will demand better education—but may not look for it in public schools. Private tuition is so common as to already constitute a partial privatization of the system, and is estimated to make an important contribution to learning outcomes. The recent rapid growth in primary enrolment in private schools may have the potential to raise standards and encourage public schools to improve in competition with the private sector. But shifts of effective teaching to the private sector are unequalizing, and may not raise standards further. And as middle-class groups at present benefit disproportionately from their ability to pay for private learning, gaining credentials and exam passes that ease them into good professional jobs, they lack any strong incentive to support reforms targeting teacher performance in public schools.[7] Amongst those who do remain in the public school system, socio-economic change should also affect how schools are governed and managed towards raising standards. More educated parents will be better able in theory to monitor schools and teachers, and to support children's schoolwork and non-cognitive learning. This should lead to further improvements in the institutional fit between schools and communities, and more effective teacher management regimes using informal accountability across more schools.

References

Ahmed, M., A. Kazi Saleh, I. Khan Nurul, and A. Romij. 2007. 'Access to Education in Bangladesh: Country Analytic Review of Primary and Secondary Education'. Brighton and Dhaka: Consortium for Research on Educational Access, Transitions and Equity/Institute of Educational Development, BRAC University.

[7] Many thanks to an anonymous reviewer for this point.

Al-Samarrai, S. 2007. 'Financing Basic Education in Bangladesh'. CREATE Pathways to Access, Research Monograph 12. Brighton: Consortium for Research on Educational Access, Transitions and Equity, The University of Sussex.

Asadullah, M. Niaz. 2006. 'Pay Differences between Teachers and Other Occupations: Some Empirical Evidence from Bangladesh'. *Journal of Asian Economics*, 17(6): 1044–65.

Asadullah, M. Niaz, and N. Chaudhury. 2009. 'Holy Alliances: Public Subsidies, Islamic High Schools, and Female Schooling in Bangladesh'. *Education Economics*, 17(3): 377–94.

Asadullah, M. Niaz, and N. Chaudhury. 2013. 'Primary Schooling, Student Learning, and School Quality in Rural Bangladesh'. Working Paper 349. Center for Global Development.

Asadullah, M. Niaz, A. Savoia, and W. Mahmud. 2014. 'Paths to Development: Is There a Bangladesh Surprise?' *World Development*, 62: 138–54.

BBS (Bangladesh Bureau of Statistics). 2011. 'Report on Labour Force Survey 2010'. Dhaka: Bangladesh Bureau of Statistics, Statistics Division, Ministry of Planning.

Cameron, S. 2010. 'Access to and Exclusion from Primary Education in Slums of Dhaka, Bangladesh'. CREATE Pathways to Access, Research Monograph 45. Brighton: Consortium for Research on Educational Access, Transitions and Equity, The University of Sussex.

CAMPE (Campaign for Popular Education). 2005. 'Quality with Equity: The Primary Education Agenda'. Education Watch Report 2003–04. Dhaka: Campaign for Popular Education.

CAMPE. 2009. 'State of Primary Education in Bangladesh'. Education Watch Report 2008. Dhaka: Campaign for Popular Education.

Chaudhury, N., J. Hammer, M. Kremer, K. Muralidharan, and F. Rogers. 2004. 'Teacher and Health Care Provider Absence: A Multi-Country Study'. Washington, DC: World Bank DEC.

Chowdhury, A. Mushtaque, R., S. R. Nath, and R. K. Choudhury. 2002. 'Enrolment at Primary Level: Gender Difference Disappears in Bangladesh'. *International Journal of Educational Development*, 22(2): 191–203.

Chowdhury, A. Mushtaque, R., S. R. Nath, and R. K. Choudhury. 2003. 'Equity Gains in Bangladesh Primary Education'. *International Review of Education*, 49(6): 601–19.

Chowdhury, R., and A. Haq Kabir. 2014. 'Language Wars: English Education Policy and Practice in Bangladesh'. *Multilingual Education*, 4(1): 1–16.

Doner, R. F., and B. Ross Schneider. 2016. 'The Middle-Income Trap: More Politics than Economics'. *World Politics*, 68(4): 608–44.

DPE (Directorate of Primary Education). 2011a. 'Annual Primary School Census 2010'. Dhaka: Directorate of Primary Education, Ministry of Primary and Mass Education, Government of Bangladesh.

DPE. 2011b. 'Third Primary Education Development Programme (PEDP3): Main Document'. Dhaka: Directorate of Primary Education, Ministry of Primary and Mass Education, Government of Bangladesh.

DPE. 2014a. 'Annual Primary School Census 2013'. Dhaka: Monitoring and Evaluation Division, Directorate of Primary Education, Ministry of Primary and Mass Education, Government of Bangladesh.

DPE. 2014b. 'Bangladesh Primary Education Annual Sector Performance Report (ASPR) 2014'. Dhaka: Government of Bangladesh.

DPE. 2014c. 'National Student Assessment 2013 for Grades 3 and 5'. Dhaka: Monitoring and Evaluation Division, Directorate of Primary Education, Ministry of Primary and Mass Education, Government of Bangladesh.

DPE. 2016. 'National Student Assessment 2015 for Grades 3 and 5'. Dhaka: Directorate of Primary Education, Ministry of Primary and Mass Education, Government of Bangladesh.

DPE. 2017. 'Bangladesh Primary Education Annual Sector Performance Report (ASPR) 2017'. Annual Sector Performance Report. Dhaka: Directorate of Primary Education, Ministry of Primary and Mass Education, Government of Bangladesh.

Dundar, H., T. Béteille, M. Riboud, and A. Deolalikar. 2014. *Student Learning in South Asia: Challenges, Opportunities, and Policy Priorities*. Washington, DC: World Bank.

FMRP (Financial Management Reform Programme). 2006. 'Primary Education in Bangladesh. Social Sector Performance Surveys'. Dhaka: Financial Management Reform Programme, Ministry of Finance, Government of Bangladesh.

FMRP. 2007. 'Governance, Management and Performance in Health and Education Facilities in Bangladesh: Findings from the Social Sector Performance Qualitative Study'. Dhaka: Financial Management Reform Programme, Ministry of Finance, Government of Bangladesh.

GED (General Economics Division). 2015. '7th Five Year Plan 2016–2020 Accelerating Growth, Empowering Citizens'. Dhaka: General Economics Division, Bangladesh Planning Commission. Government of Bangladesh.

GoB (Government of Bangladesh). 2010. 'National Education Policy 2010'. Dhaka: Ministry of Education, Government of the People's Republic of Bangladesh.

Haq, N. M., and M. Sajidul Islam. 2005. 'Teachers' Motivation and Incentives in Bangladesh'. Institute of Education and Research, University of Dhaka, Bangladesh.

Hassan, M. 2013. 'Political Settlement Dynamics in a Limited-Access Order: The Case of Bangladesh'. ESID Working Paper 23. Manchester: Effective States and Inclusive Development Research Centre, The University of Manchester.

Hossain, A., and B. Zeitlyn. 2010. 'Poverty, Equity and Access to Education in Bangladesh'. CREATE Pathways to Access, Research Monograph 51. Brighton: Consortium for Research on Educational Access, Transitions and Equity, The University of Sussex.

Hossain, N. 2007. 'Expanding Access to Education in Bangladesh'. In *Ending Poverty in South Asia: Ideas That Work*. Edited by Narayan, D., and E. Glinskaya, 304–25. Washington, DC: World Bank.

Hossain, N. 2010a. 'Rude Accountability: Informal Pressures on Frontline Bureaucrats in Bangladesh'. *Development and Change*, 41(5): 907–28.

Hossain, N. 2010b. 'School Exclusion as Social Exclusion: The Practices and Effects of a Conditional Cash Transfer Programme for the Poor in Bangladesh'. *Journal of Development Studies*, 46(7): 1264–82.

Hossain, N. 2017. *The Aid Lab: Understanding Bangladesh's Unexpected Success*. Oxford: Oxford University Press.

Hossain, N., and H. Tavakoli. 2008. *School Choice in Bangladesh*. Dhaka: Oxford Policy Management Limited.

Hossain, N., R. Subrahmanian, and N. Kabeer. 2002. 'The Politics of Educational Expansion in Bangladesh'. IDS Working Paper 167. Brighton: Institute of Development Studies, University of Sussex.

IRI (International Republican Institute). 2008. 'Bangladesh Parliamentary Elections December 29 2008: Election Observation Mission Final Report'. Washington, DC: The International Republican Institute.

Islam, S. 2010. 'Access with Quality in Primary Education: Re-Inventing Inter Organizational Synergy'. *Bangladesh Education Journal*, 9(1): 5–27.

Kathuria, S., and M. Mezghenni Malouche. 2015. 'Toward New Sources of Competitiveness in Bangladesh: Key Insights of the Diagnostic Trade Integration Study'. Washington, DC: World Bank.

Levy, B., and M. Walton. 2013. 'Institutions, Incentives and Service Provision: Bringing Politics Back In'. ESID Working Paper 18. Manchester: Effective States and Inclusive Development Research Centre, The University of Manchester.

Lipsky, M. 1980. *Street-Level Bureaucracy: Dilemmas of the Individual in Public Service*. 2nd rev. ed. New York: Russell Sage Foundation.

Mahmud, W. 2002. 'National Budgets, Social Spending and Public Choice: The Case of Bangladesh'. IDS Working Paper 162. Brighton: Institute of Development Studies, University of Sussex.

MOPME (Ministry of Primary and Mass Education). n.d. 'Achievement in Primary Education in Past Five Years 2009–13'. Dhaka: Ministry of Primary and Mass Education, Government of Bangladesh.

Rahman, M. I., S. Shahriar, and S. Anam. 2014. 'A Study on the Disparity between the Job Satisfaction of Private and Public School Teachers in Bangladesh'. *Global Journal of Quantitative Science*, 1(1).

Rose, J., T. M. Lane, and T. Rahman. 2014. 'Bangladesh Governance in the Primary Education Sector: A Systematic Literature Review'. Bangladesh, Governance in Sectors Working Paper. Dhaka: World Bank.

Rosser, Y. C. 2003. 'Curriculum as Destiny: Forging National Identity in India, Pakistan, and Bangladesh'. PhD thesis. Austin, TX: University of Texas.

Saxena, S. B., and V. Salze-Lozac'h. 2010. 'Competitiveness in the Garment and Textiles Industry: Creating a Supportive Environment. A Case Study of Bangladesh'. The Asia Foundation Occasional Paper 1.

Sobhan, R. 1982. *The Crisis of External Dependence*. London: Zed Press.

Steer, L., F. Rabbani, and A. Parker. 2014. 'Primary Education Finance for Equity and Quality: An Analysis of Past Success and Future Options in Bangladesh'. Washington, DC: The Brookings Institution.

Tietjen, K., A. Rahman, and S. Spaulding. 2004. 'Bangladesh Educational Assessment. Time to Learn: Teachers' and Students' Use of Time in Government Primary Schools in Bangladesh'. Basic Education and Policy Supports (BEPS) Activity Creative Associates International.

World Bank. 2013. 'Seeding Fertile Ground: Education that Works for Bangladesh'. Education Sector Review 80613. Washington, DC: World Bank.

World Bank. 2017. 'World Development Report 2018: Learning to Realize Education's Promise'. Washington, DC: World Bank.

Zhang, X., S. Rashid, K. Ahmad, V. Mueller, H. Lim Lee, S. Lemma, S. Belal, and A. Ahmed. 2013. 'Rising Wages in Bangladesh'. IFPRI Discussion Paper 01249. Washington, DC: International Food Policy Research Institute.

5

The Downsides of Dominance

Education Quality Reforms and Rwanda's Political Settlement

Timothy P. Williams

Introduction

Two decades after a devastating civil war and the 1994 genocide, Rwanda's government has charted an audacious social and economic development project to transform the country into a market-driven, modernized society. Formal education has featured prominently in this project. Thanks in part to a fee-free basic education policy entitling children to 12 years of public education, enrolment in primary and secondary schools surged in the 2000s. But, while student numbers rose quickly, recent evidence has shown that little was being learned in these schools: a majority of primary students failed to meet reading and arithmetic standards (EDC 2016, 2017; Friedlander, Gasana, and Goldenberg 2014; USAID 2014), and dropout, repetition, completion, and transition rates stagnated or worsened over this period (MINEDUC 2015).

Perhaps no country better exemplifies a 'dominant developmental' political settlement than Rwanda. This implies a strong commitment to deliver development to its citizens. The political elite and political power are aligned with a single principle in the form of the ruling party, the Rwandan Patriotic Front (RPF), with its leader and the country's President, Paul Kagame. Dominant party regimes like Rwanda are known for governing through a high degree of control and top-down discipline. Dominant regimes have strong, shared, and centralized approaches to state building, and a political system relatively free of both rent extraction and genuine political competition.

The stability of a regime such as that in Rwanda allows the state to engage in longer-term planning (Hickey, Sen, and Bukenya 2015), with limited political space for meaningful pushback or alternative projects to arise. These conditions favour rapid transformation over more incremental approaches to policy development and implementation. In Rwanda, strategies for development under the RPF have focused on lifting the country out of poverty with attention to the factors believed to have precipitated conflict—namely, ethnic divisionism, resource scarcity, and limited opportunities for social mobility. The government is mandated, in other words, to deliver development inclusively, to all Rwandans.

Given the ruling party's commitment to delivering development, why has it not introduced reforms that have improved educational standards? This chapter explores the interaction between Rwanda's political settlement and the education policy domain, to shed light on its unexpected inability to improve learning. This failure is surprising because the Rwandan political elite has demonstrated both capacity and willingness to undertake and implement reforms that it has deemed necessary to deliver development in other sectors.

As Chapters 1 and 2 in this volume have summarized, the evidence suggests that both dominant and more competitive political systems have incentives to expand education provision; by contrast, getting the often more politically difficult reforms needed to improve teaching and learning outcomes appear to attract little political support, whether from citizens and politicians, business, or employers, and can be blocked by powerful organized teacher interests. Rwanda under the RPF appears to have been insulated against the kinds of political pressures that might block unpopular teacher-related reforms, and it has demonstrated state capacity to deliver when needed. So why have such reforms been a low priority on the education policy agenda? And how have quality-focused reforms been implemented?

To answer these questions, we drew from existing literature and policy reports, and 65 semi-structured interviews carried out over six months with members of government, civil society, development partners, local education officers, teachers and headteachers, school-based mentors, and members of parent–teacher committees. Local-level interviews were conducted around four schools, two each in an urban and rural district, selected on the basis that one in each district was relatively high- or low-performing. These were selected in order to help us understand how Rwanda's political settlement and the policy domain interacted to influence learning outcomes at the local level. Further details on methods are available elsewhere (Williams 2016a).

The remainder of this chapter is organized as follows. In the following section, we locate the education system within the broader political settlement. We then focus on reform efforts that the government has undertaken in recent years. Finally, we investigate how frontline education stakeholders have experienced and responded to these reforms at the local level. The chapter concludes with a brief discussion of how the particular dominant developmentalism in the

Rwandan political settlement has interacted with the education policy domain to keep learning reforms low on the policy agenda.

The Political Settlement and the Education Policy Domain

Since taking power, the RPF-led government has introduced a series of reforms aimed at social and economic transformation, with the goal of becoming a middle-income country by the year 2020 (MINECOFIN 2000). The government's development strategy aims were premised on distancing the country from a past marked by ethnic division, conflicts over scarce natural resources, social inequalities, and limited opportunities for social mobility. Education features prominently within these broader aims (MINEDUC 2003, 2010).

Elite commitment and state capacity in Rwanda centres on delivering development to its citizens. This point is outlined in government documents (Senate 2014) and was supported in our interviews with officials at every level of government. Officials explained that their personal commitments are guided by national development plans, rather than the prospect of individual gain. Their sentiment underscores one of the characteristics of the dominant developmental political settlement: that if the government moves 'fast enough', it can bring about the changes needed to distance itself from the past, while charting a sustainable and peaceful future for all Rwandans (Booth and Golooba-Mutebi 2012, 391).

There was a general agreement that during the time period in which our study was carried out (2015), the inner circle of power in the education sector consisted of the President of the Republic, the Cabinet, the Ministry of Education (MINEDUC), Ministry of Finance (MINECOFIN), the Ministry of Local Government (MINALOC), and the UK's Department for International Development (DFID). In the outer circle was the Rwandan Education Board (REB), Parliament, the United States Agency for International Development (USAID), and a consortium of NGOs called the Rwandan Education NGO Coordination Platform. The Office of the President was understood to play a critical function in establishing the priorities of the education sector. Ministers report directly to the President, who has the power to replace them without notice. The President can make key decisions that impact the priorities of the education sector, such as the expansion of the basic education system from nine to twelve years (Williams 2017). In practice, this initiative went through the formal institutional channels to become national policy, but the decision originated with the President. The Cabinet is the key decision-making entity. Cabinet members are appointed by the President and comprise different ministers. By law, no more than half of Cabinet members can be from the ruling party, that is, the RPF. Within the Cabinet, the Minister of Education holds overall responsibility for MINEDUC. However, each of MINEDUC's three ministers of state are also Cabinet members. They report directly to the President. MINALOC plays a crucial role through the country's decentralized system of governance. Within the education sector, it is responsible for the implementation of policy and the administration of schools. District- and sector-level education officers are technically members of MINALOC, even though their primary duties are in education. MINECOFIN also has a determining role in education priorities through its responsibilities for budget implementation, including ensuring the education sector and budget harmonize with the country's broader development aims, as outlined in the country's broader economic development and poverty reduction strategies (MINECOFIN 2013). MINECOFIN does not have a direct role in establishing priorities for the sector, but it funds the line items of the sector's budget. The final decision on priority targets rests with MINALOC, who can re-prioritize after receiving MINEDUC's ideas. DFID is also an influential actor within the education sector. DFID and the United Nations Children's Fund (UNICEF) are the co-chairs of the Education Sector Working Group. DFID funds a large proportion of the education sector budget, disbursing over £100 million between 2011 and 2015 with the aim of 'increased equitable access to quality education and improved learning outcomes' (British Council 2015, 6). Most of these funds are disbursed through direct education sector budget support. In 2015, DFID contributed £65 million, including £44m to sector budget support, £9 million for a Results-Based Aid programme linked to learning outcomes and primary school completion, and £12 million for a project called Innovations for Education, which funded 26 pilot projects developed by NGOs, universities, and civil society organizations aimed at improving education quality and learning.

Sector priorities are also established at the government's annual leadership retreat. Each year, high-level government officials meet to produce a series of resolutions. Resolutions often include items relevant to the education sector. For example, Honeyman (2015, 26) noted that the 2014 retreat led to a specific resolution concerning quality, which called for the establishment of 'a monitoring and evaluation system for tracking educational quality, and putting into place an education quality strategic plan with a baseline and desired targets'. The introduction of school feeding was another example of a resolution adopted at the retreat, and one that highlights their ad hoc nature. Schools were expected to start providing food for students, but as the policy had not been part of the budget for the 2014–15 fiscal year, schools had to pass on the cost of school feeding to students.

Understanding the significance of decision-making processes in and beyond the education sector is important for thinking about how policies are established and implemented. As we shall see in the next section, policy decisions may well align with the government's broader developmental ambitions. At the same time, the fact that these decisions often occur outside the strategic planning processes presents challenges for producing a coherent and focused system. The domains of power approach offers guidance for thinking about how these challenges affect policies that affect the quality of education.

Education Reform and Quality

The domains of power shaped policy priorities and outcomes. The government was oriented towards delivering development, but with a strong focus on tangible and visible outputs that could be offered as evidence to its citizens and outsiders of its commitment to inclusive development. National and local officials, including local education officers, sign performance contracts or *imihigo*, officially intended to enable a more active voice in decision-making processes, but which in practice ensure accountability primarily continues to flow upwards (Chemouni 2014). District and sector performance contracts include indicators concerning education quality, but focus on indicators that are measurable and comparable, such as the construction of classrooms or the building of latrines (Honeyman 2015). Performance outcomes that were more difficult to measure and improve, such as learning outcomes, were assigned lower priority. In this section, we focus on two interrelated areas of education policy and reforms that have had a big impact on education quality: language reform and teacher training. The language policy was introduced outside of strategic planning processes, and how this decision was implemented has had important effects for the ways in which teacher training has been carried out.

The Switch from French to English: Causes and Effects

Up until 2008, the language of instruction was French, owing to the country's Franco-Belgian colonial roots (King 2013). However, in 2009, the language was switched from French to English. We draw on interview data and the existing literature to explore the possible motivations and incentives for the language change, and its effects on efforts to raise the standard of learning.

One explanation offered for the 2008 switch to English traces this to the social and political demographic of the ruling party, and the legacy of the genocide (Samuelson 2013; Williams 2016b). The predominantly anglophone Tutsi political elite sought to distance itself and the country from its francophone roots and sever its ties to France, owing to its controversial role in the genocide. Many of the core members of the RPF themselves grew up in Uganda and studied English (Prunier 1995). The 2008 switch to English was thus consistent with an elite with predominantly anglophone backgrounds.

A second explanation for the switch to English is economic: that is, a strategy to facilitate regional integration, and a point of entry into the global market economy. The switch to English coincided with the country's entry into the British Commonwealth. Rwanda also recently joined the predominantly anglophone East African community. Thus, the language switch helped to foster strategic alliances and promote trade with its neighbours. As one policy expert we interviewed put it, the country's 'cultural alliances' and economic ambitions are aligned with the anglophone world. 'You don't go to China and speak French. Or Germany or Pakistan', the expert said. While no definitive account of the political motivations behind the language change may be possible, it is possible to explore the consequences for learning outcomes.

It is not an exaggeration to suggest that the language change presented a shock to primary education, to which the system was unprepared to respond. This can be better understood by reviewing education planning documents developed around that time. The language shift was announced in 2008. Yet, the 2008–12 Education Sector Strategic Plan—the document used to guide the priorities (and budget) of the sector—offers no indication of the language change. The switch was made so quickly that it has left the quality of the education system in a perpetual state of catch-up. Stakeholders ranging from teachers to senior members of MINEDUC explained how the language shift had made it difficult to maintain or improve quality. 'It was a matter of choice,' a senior MINEDUC official said of the policy. 'You go for access and you will compromise quality. When you then add English as a challenge, the problem of quality became a lot worse.'

The change has been an immense challenge for teachers in government schools. A study of over 600 primary and secondary school teachers found that almost half of all teachers had a competency of English considered to be either at 'elementary' or 'intermediate' stages (British Council 2015), and these figures were an improvement over the baseline study carried out two years previously (Simpson 2013). It is clear that the proportion of teachers using English at such a basic level presents challenges for the effective delivery of the curriculum (Abbott, Sapsford, and Rwirahira 2015).

Since the language change was introduced, the Ministry of Education and development partners have implemented many different responses. Most notably, the Rwanda Education Board (the implementation arm of MINEDUC) introduced a School-Based Mentorship (SBM) programme in 2012. The idea was to hire up to 1,000 English-speaking teachers from neighbouring anglophone countries to assist Rwandan teachers to improve their ability to carry out their own lessons in English. The SBM programme also included a pedagogy component, but interviewees noted that, in practice, it concentrated on improving English only. Their rationale was that pedagogy did not matter if teachers could not speak the language of instruction. The programme produced mixed results (Wilson 2013).

The switch to English may have made sense given the country's broader economic ambitions and the nature of its political settlement. On the other hand, the implementation of the policy seems to have plunged all actors in the education policy domain into a state of crisis, in which teachers instruct their students in a language they have little knowledge of themselves, while students struggle to learn because they have so little knowledge of the language.

Training of Primary School Teachers

During the period in which the fieldwork took place, teacher training was in a period of transition. In 2007, the Ministry of Education introduced the Teacher Development and Management Policy (MINEDUC 2007). The policy outlined the core priorities for how teacher training was to be done. The Teacher Service Commission, an entity within MINEDUC at the time, was responsible for overseeing the implementation of the teacher-training policy. But the key challenge to this teacher-training policy was timing. That it was published in 2007 meant it made no note of, or provision for, the switch to English announced the following year. In other words, almost as soon as the policy was introduced, it was inadequate to the challenges facing teachers. During the data gathering for our project, government-led in-service teacher training was also in a state of transition. The 2007 policy was still on the books, but was now largely irrelevant. A new Teacher Development and Management Policy had been developed, but had not yet been finalized. During this time, in-service training was still happening, but it was mostly offered by NGOs, rather than as part of an integrated system of continuous professional development.

This brings us to an important point concerning resource allocation and education quality. A hallmark of the government's development strategy was its decentralization policy (MINALOC 2001). Some scholars have argued that the policy has had the effect of extending the state's reach (Chemouni 2014). However, the stated intention of the policy was to empower local government and communities to use resources to meet locally identified needs. When it comes to education, the decentralization policy meant that funds were transferred directly to schools, so that parents and teachers could decide what was needed to improve their school (Transparency International 2013). Up until 2012, about 10 to 15 per cent of the funds transferred to schools were earmarked for schools to send their teachers for training.

The English language policy changed this. When the SBM programme was introduced, the decentralized funds that had been earmarked for in-service training were *recentralized* (i.e. REB withheld these funds) to finance it. This meant that virtually all government-financed in-service teacher training became English language training, a point which was confirmed by senior education sector officials, school administrators, and development partners.

Interviews with government and non-government stakeholders clearly highlighted a commitment towards improving education. National and local education officials said that a key need of the sector was more training for teachers to be effective. But therein was the challenge. It was difficult to implement in-service training when policy changes were introduced that occurred outside of MINEDUC's strategic planning processes. The language change immediately channelled NGO and government attention onto this issue. Available funds for teacher training were used for English training.

Frontline School Management and Performance

In this section, we explore how the domains of power converged to shape policy implementation and education quality in communities, through a comparative case study of one rural Southern Province district and one urban district in Kigali. Within each district, high- and low-performing schools were selected, in order to 'reveal major system weaknesses that become targets of opportunity for programme or system improvement' (Patton 1990, 177). Within each district, we collaborated with local education officials to identify the highest and lowest-performing schools, drawing on results from the 2014 Primary 6 national examination as an imperfect proxy for performance.

Urban District

In general, urban schools tend to perform better than rural on various learning metrics (USAID 2014). Urban households are generally wealthier and can make financial contributions to the running of the schools. The allure of urban areas enables schools to attract more qualified teachers, in part because of a higher top-up in salary, and because more economic opportunities are available for teachers. The urban student experience is different as well, characterized by shorter commutes and fewer daily responsibilities than rural children (NISR 2012). At the same time, the cost of living is more expensive in a place like Kigali. It was under these conditions that we investigated how schooling was experienced in the urban district.

At the district office, the offices of the mayor and vice mayor for social affairs had display cabinets of trophies, signifying their achievements in relation to the countrywide performance contracts. When asked how his district had been so successful over the years, the mayor attributed the gains to hard work and innovation. At the same time, the area was also a wealthy centre of commerce compared with other areas. Unlike its rural counterparts, it did not need to rely exclusively on the central government funds to pay its expenses, because it was able to generate revenue through its tax base. As the district mayor explained, 'Revenues come through taxes. We manage those taxes and revenues to pay our staff. This district has pressure to tax businesses so that it can get funds to pay its staff from the district to the cell level.' With the extra revenue, the district has been able to hire more district education staff members to provide oversight of, and support to, schools. This was not an option in the rural district.

According to local officials, school attendance in the urban district was a non-issue. 'I can say we have achieved education for all,' said a District Education Officer (DEO). The priority now, the official explained, was to improve quality, primarily through mobilizing the parent–teacher associations (PTAs) to participate in school development, build classrooms, and lower the student-to-teacher ratio. These commitments mirrored national-level education priorities.

District officials and education officers reported that they did not have a problem attracting qualified teachers. Urban schools were a desirable location for teachers. Their base salary was low, but they could get additional work on weekends and holidays, or continue their own professional development and training at nearby universities if they wished. There were other financial incentives for teachers working in urban primary government schools compared with their rural counterparts. In particular, families were expected to make PTA contributions to their children's school. A PTA contribution is an amount of money agreed upon by the parent–teacher committee (PTC) that parents are expected to pay for each of their children. Technically, the PTA contribution is not a fee and thus should not be the basis for exclusion from school (Williams, Abbott, and Mupenzi 2015). On the other hand, urban areas are wealthier, PTA contributions were higher, and teachers depended on the contribution. PTA contributions for primary school in the urban district were around 3,000 RWF (US$5) per child per term.

Another element of the district-level success in education was the number of private schools in the district. This presents something of a paradox in itself: the urban district was one of the highest-performing districts in the country, but the top nineteen performing primary schools within its jurisdiction were private. Many key informants acknowledged that government primary schools across the country—even in this particular urban district—have a reputation for poor quality. However, government secondary schools tend to be higher quality than their private counterparts, and are considered more prestigious, reflecting the fact that many originated in the colonial era (King 2013). The trend, then, was for better-off families to send their children to a private primary school, so that they could receive better training, particularly in English. Private primary school students who did well on their national examinations then had the opportunity to re-enter government education to attend a well-regarded government boarding school for their secondary studies. When asked about teacher training, the DEO said it was less of an urgent issue than for their rural counterparts. There was little mention of in-service training. According to local officials, the training that was happening was organized directly through REB, and mostly through the SBM programme.

HIGH-PERFORMING SCHOOL IN THE URBAN DISTRICT

The high-performing primary school in the urban district was technically a government-aided school. That is, the Catholic Church owned the property and built some of the original infrastructure. However, the school was otherwise government run, with administration and oversight handled by the district.

In separate meetings, both the headteacher and PTC members reported a productive collaboration. The PTC included members who themselves had been formally educated. Parents said this allowed them to draw from their experience to speak knowledgeably about school operations and offer their contributions to the decision-making and administration of the school, permitting accountability relations to work both ways. The PTC and headteacher worked together to manage the finances of the school. Though schooling is officially free, and children were reportedly not excluded for an inability to pay, the PTA contribution was considered by headteachers as an essential top-up to the otherwise low teacher salaries. According to the headteacher, the school did not have a mentor through the SBM programme, but it was not clear why. Perhaps because they were a top-performing school, a mentor was a less urgent need compared with other schools. In any case, the headteacher did not see the absence of a mentor as having any bearing on quality at the school.

Rwanda's double shifting policy meant that primary students attended either in the morning or the afternoon. However, officials at this primary school said that they kept Primary 6 students in school for both shifts, with the aim of a final push to improve students' national examination scores. This was not a national directive, nor was it official policy, but the school administrators saw it as a way to keep examination scores high. But as strongly as this particular primary school performed, nineteen private primary schools in this urban district ranked higher in the year-end national examinations. 'People say that we performed well on the exams,' said the headteacher. 'But we do not perform well like private schools.'

LOW-PERFORMING SCHOOL IN THE URBAN DISTRICT

The lowest-performing government primary school in the urban district was characterized by thorough dysfunction. In separate meetings, the PTC and the headteacher described one another as uncommitted and poorly functioning. The school was in a fairly well-off area, but the student population mainly comprised poor families. In recent years, as Kigali has expanded in size, the surrounding area has changed from suburban and poor to urban and well-off. Its proximity to Kigali made the area more desirable for wealthier families, and land prices increased. Teachers and school administrators suggested that less well-off families living in the area sold their land to wealthier ones moving in. Better-off families opted to send their children to private schools, rather than the government primary school. Lower enrolment rates meant the school received a lower total capitation grant through which to operate the school. The concern expressed by the headteacher and PTC was that the flight of better-off families also removed well-educated parents, who could have positively impacted school operations through participation in the PTC.

There was discord between the local school management through the PTC and the head- teacher. The headteacher blamed the parents for failing to be committed to their children's education. Members of the PTC, in turn, said they cooperated with the headteacher, but that there was not a sense of shared decision-making when it came to the administration of the school. In the PTC group discussion for this project, five parents and two teachers agreed to participate in our group discussion, but only one parent and two teachers ended up attending—perhaps a symptom of broader disharmony at the school, or of weaker engagement in school activities.

Individuals also noted that, while children at the school came from poor families, the boom in construction meant that temporary forms of employment had become available. Richer families needed manual labour. School administrators expressed concern that the availability of work had the potential to motivate students to work rather than study, or to discontinue their studies altogether. This could help to explain low examination performance.

Rural District

The rural district we worked with in the Southern Province was amongst the poorest in the country (NISR 2011). Like all districts in the country, and as emerged in interviews with district-level staff, its district-level goals were aligned with broader development strategies of the country. As the DEO put it, 'The priority of this district is national priorities'. According to local officials, district-specific needs were also established through consultation with stakeholders at the local levels.

District officials linked education priorities to the improvement of access and provision of infrastructure as their primary targets. About one-third of schools in the area were connected to electricity (MINEDUC 2015). District and sector officials pointed to the importance of improving educational quality, operationalized through performance contracts. Like most performance contracts we reviewed, the key focus was on achieving measurable and objective targets, such as the construction of classrooms. District, sector-, and school-level officials understood the training of teachers as a centralized affair, responsibilities for which lay with REB or the handful of NGOs operating in the area. The consensus was that teacher training happens through the SBM programme, which, as we saw above, primarily focused on improving English.

Households in the district principally relied on agricultural production for their livelihoods. Most were poor. Whereas PTA contributions in the urban district were expected, PTA contributions could not be enforced in the rural district. As the DEO said, 'When you talk about money everything [i.e. priorities and goals] can unravel... [expectation of PTA contributions] only happens in urban areas'. In effect, this meant there were fewer financial constraints for children from poor families. But the lack of an enforced PTA contribution—sometimes referred to as a 'teacher motivation'—could also limit the ability of schools to recruit and retain qualified teachers.

District officials pointed out that the recruitment and retention of qualified teachers remained an ongoing challenge. Teachers from outside the district were reluctant to migrate to a remote area for a low-paid teaching position. Interviewees said that teachers in urban areas could supplement their salary through additional work, along with PTA contributions that they could count on. For teachers in this district, economic opportunities were limited. 'That is why we have that problem of recruiting qualified teachers,' said the DEO. 'After a few days, they just leave.' Other district officials also noted this problem and said they had worked to address it. In 2011, a teacher-training college (TTC) was built in the area, and its first cohort of primary school teachers graduated in 2014. According to the district mayor, the rationale for building a local TTC was to improve the ability to train and hire teachers from the area, with the hopes of improving retention rates.

Another challenge was the recent introduction of 'district education units', a team of staff members to be in charge of primary education, secondary education, pre-primary, technical and vocational education and training (TVET), and school construction, respectively. However, funding for the units was intended to come out of district budgets and local revenue. While the urban district had the funds to fully staff all five posts of their education unit, the rural district had the capacity to fill just one post (in addition to the DEO) to date. As the DEO explained in a meeting at the district office:

> We are supposed to be four education staff in this office but we are only two staff—me and my colleague [who works on primary education, pre-primary, and literacy]. There is someone else who is supposed to be in charge of secondary schools and TVET. There is someone who is supposed to be an engineer in charge of classroom construction. The district was told 'Here is that new organogram. Employ them from the financial capacity that you have'. [. . .] [But] if the district doesn't have salaries for those staff, it cannot employ them.

In effect, we may interpret this strategy as meaning that poorer districts receive poorer education and supervision than wealthier, urban districts. While this appears to be the case at the moment, both local and national education officials we met with noted that the establishment of district education units was a new endeavour, one which would take some time to fully fund and institutionalize.

HIGH-PERFORMING SCHOOL IN THE RURAL DISTRICT

The top-performing school in the rural district presented a paradox. The school was located in an extremely remote part of the district. The quickest way to reach the sector office and primary school was by motorcycle, and involved a journey of over two hours from the district office—itself a 90-minute drive from the nearest paved road—at a round-trip cost of about 10,000 RWF (US$15), that is, roughly one-quarter of a primary teacher's monthly salary. The executive secretary of the sector remarked that the forest, along with the bad road, served as an unfortunate barrier, and that few NGOs had operations in the area. Sector officials said that the area was too rural and too isolated to reach. Why then did the primary school outperform some other schools located in closer proximity to key infrastructure, such as decent roads, marketplaces, and the district office—amenities that could presumably attract more qualified teachers?

That the school was secluded appeared to have had a buffering effect on teachers. Teachers had few other non-farm options to make money aside from teaching; transport was too time-intensive and expensive to travel elsewhere on weekends for further study, and so teachers focused on teaching, supplementing their own income with extra tutorials on weekends and during holidays for children from households that could afford it. Another key to the school's success was the reportedly strong collaboration between the PTC and the headteacher. They worked together to decide how capitation funds should be used to improve the school. When students did well in examinations, the PTC members organized an event to recognize the achievements of teachers and students. The headteacher spent a lot of time supervising teachers at school, in part because the sector and district offices were too far to travel to.

The school also organized events aimed at making their education relevant to the local context. Students were trained in cultivation, noted the headteacher, generating a new source of revenue for the school. The school also owned several cows, whose milk went to students who arrived at school hungry or undernourished. This is an example of the school exercising its autonomy to establish creative measures to improve the welfare of students. While the school did comparatively well, a number of challenges were reported. For example, the PTC comprised committed members, but many were uneducated themselves. According to school officials, parents were often unable to give helpful ideas in meetings with teachers, and so sat in silence, while the headteacher and teachers made decisions at meetings.

LOW-PERFORMING SCHOOL IN THE RURAL DISTRICT

The lowest-performing primary school in the district was located near some main roads and markets. The commitment of the headteacher at the school appeared different to that of the high-performing school. The headteacher seemed rushed and eager to finish the interview because he had a private matter to attend to in another town. The Sector Education Officer and executive secretary of the sector also lived in Kigali and Butare, respectively. One of the key obstacles to effectiveness in the school was the interaction between the PTC and the headteacher. PTC members indicated they were not involved in the decision-making process through which the capitation grant money was spent, and that the headteacher did not want to involve them in the decision-making. The way finances were being used was unclear, and they did not know how much money the school was receiving. Members did not imply that misuse of funds was occurring, but suggested that the headteacher did not communicate with the PTC because he was not clear about how to best use the allocated resources. They said that if the school hired an accountant, it might help the school to operate more effectively.

PTC members and the headteacher also pointed to what they felt was a lack of commitment on the part of parents. They said that parents allowed their children to come to school without notebooks, and that some failed to follow up if their child missed a class. But teacher commitment was also questioned. According to the PTC, teachers did not always attend their in-service training, and could be found walking down the road or at a bar when they should have been at school or in training. The PTC stated that this lack of commitment on the part of teachers may have influenced the commitment of families and their children.

Discussion and Conclusions

Rwanda's political elite have staked their claim to viability on a longer-term investment in the development of the country, one which is relatively free from the problems of rent-seeking common to other types of political settlements (Levy and Walton 2013). Rwanda's developmental and dominant leader framework plays a central role in establishing its focus on governance and accountability. Yet the analysis here identifies some potential downsides to top-down, executive-led policymaking within the education policy domain. Education priorities were clearly political as well as developmental. Policy decisions were often not grounded in the realities of the education system and its local stakeholders. Some of the key policy decisions that impacted on quality, for example, the language policy, occurred outside the sector's strategic planning processes. That efforts to address education quality have been so limited in Rwanda is a surprise, given that a dominant developmentalist framework suggests a harmonization of priorities to achieve inclusive development and maintain power. What explains the failure to introduce effective learning reforms, for instance, in relation to teacher training?

Rwanda's political settlement has enabled the government to advance ideas and introduce transformative policies because the interests and incentives of the elite are aligned with developmental gains, rather than shorter-term rent-seeking behaviour (Booth and Golooba-Mutebi 2012). However, in the absence of significant pushback, this transformation did not always reflect the realities facing the country and the majority of its citizens (Scott 1998). Understanding these conditions may help to explain some of the challenges facing the education sector, particularly with regards to quality. As other chapters in this volume show, in more competitive systems, states may struggle to agree upon and implement major reforms and thus eventually negotiate a gradual approach. Rwanda's consensus-building approach opened itself up to the opposite problem: the strong political will of the country's principal and elite, coupled with a lack of real opposition or pushback, enabled it to introduce transformative educational policies in line with its developmental ambitions, but which may be at odds with the present-day realities of classroom learning.

Understanding Rwanda's political settlement helps us to analyse the role of individuals, institutions, and incentives that are at the core of the domains of power. The dominant developmentalist framework suggests that the country's elite has staked its claim to viability on its attempt to deliver development as quickly as possible. Accountability was high, and tolerance for corruption and underperformance low. Individuals failing to perform in accordance with the government's expectations were likely to be replaced. The government introduced new policies that were aligned with its developmental aims, but that did not always reflect the actual situation facing the education sector. These discontinuities prevented the education system from maturing and improving over time. The introduction of English did not occur within the strategic architecture of the education sector. If it had done, sector officials, schools, and development partners could have worked to ensure that the rollout of the new language was done in a way that could have better anticipated the profound changes that would need to happen. However, policies were introduced at such a pace and in such a way that stakeholders in the education sector were left operating in catch-up mode.

In terms of hierarchical forms of accountability and oversight, Levy and Walton (2013) suggest that multi-stakeholder reforms may only provide limited additional value where principal–agent issues are largely solved. However, district and school local-level work showed that centralized, top-down aspects of education quality were not working well, whereas some more bottom-up aspects were doing better (e.g. PTCs), especially where undertaken in concert with headteachers. Again, this may reflect the lack of political priority given to the quality of schooling by the RPF. School-level governance matters, but so too do matters of poverty and geography. This is particularly the case with headteachers and also with PTCs. The quality of the latter appeared to be strongly shaped by the socio-economic background of the households involved. The fact that better-off families opted to send their children to private primary schools before transferring to government schools for secondary education did not strengthen PTCs and is symptomatic of the low quality of government primary schools. Remoteness provided unexpected benefits, in terms of reducing the opportunities for teaching staff to be distracted by other opportunities.

Levy and Walton also suggest that there may be something about the nature of formal education that may make improvements to quality particularly challenging. In Rwanda, as elsewhere, many elites tend to be committed to expansionary education programmes (Levy and Walton 2013). School infrastructure is fairly easy to build, and it is popular (Hossain and Moore 2001). Examining the domains of power in Rwanda, we find that 'quality' needed to fit within the government's development ambitions and incentives. It needed to be easily measurable and comparable across sectors and districts. It also needed to be publicly visible to Rwandans and the development community that the government was fulfilling its promises to deliver development to all Rwandans. In many ways, this approach makes sense. Construction of classrooms was material proof that the government's commitment to development was legitimate. But, at the same time, the quality of teaching and learning within those classrooms remained poor.

One of the most vivid examples of how the dominant coalition contributed to deleterious learning outcomes was in-service teacher training. The decentralization policy was designed to give greater autonomy to local government and schools. Yet, teacher training was an exception. During the study, the approach to in-service training could be best characterized as a (re)centralized affair amidst a deconcentrated education sector. Community-level research confirmed that any in-service training that teachers received occurred almost exclusively through SBM—a programme that focuses on English. The centralized programme relieved local education officers from having to plan and organize training. Yet, the case could also be made that the teacher training meant a recentralization of a sense of duty to ensure that teachers were employing effective pedagogical practices in the classroom.

The present study also builds on existing studies of the education system in Rwanda, such as on the untoward effects of PTA contributions. PTCs agree upon an amount that all parents are expected to pay for their children to attend the school. In the urban district, students paid 3000 RWF per term to supplement teacher salaries. In poorer areas, however, schools did not ask for PTA allowances, because families could not afford them. It is reasonable to assume that PTA contributions and school location are factors that attract better-qualified teachers to wealthier areas. This may offer one explanation as to why urban government schools tend to have better learning outcomes than anywhere else in the country, even when controlling for other socio-economic factors (USAID 2014).

The nature of the political settlement–policy domain interaction in Rwanda has permitted the government to introduce many reforms to the education sector. Many of these reforms have been positive, particularly with regards to access. New classrooms and schools represented some of the most visible and popular commitments of the elite's promise to deliver development to ordinary Rwandans. But it was evident that this sense of urgency and elite commitment has yet to carry over to adopting reforms to improve learning (Williams 2018). Policy reforms focused on learning have not resulted in a coherent and sustained strategy. Until the ruling party sees poor quality education as a threat to its hold on power, thereby producing a sense of urgency leading to a sustained and effective strategy, the situation is unlikely to improve for the foreseeable future.

References

Abbott, P., R. Sapsford, and J. Rwirahira. 2015. 'Rwanda's Potential to Achieve the Millennium Development Goals for Education'. *International Journal of Educational Development*, 40: 117–25.

Booth, D., and F. Golooba-Mutebi. 2012. 'Developmental Patrimonialism? The Case of Rwanda'. *African Affairs*, 111(444): 379–403.

British Council. 2015. 'Endline Assessment of English Language Proficiency of School Teachers in Rwanda'. Kigali: British Council.

Chemouni, B. 2014. 'Explaining the Design of the Rwandan Decentralization: Elite Vulnerability and the Territorial Repartition of Power'. *Journal of Eastern African Studies*, 8(2): 246–62.

EDC (Education Development Center). 2016. 'National Fluency Assessment of Rwanda Schools: Midline Report'. Kigali: Education Development Center, USAID.

EDC. 2017. 'Literacy, Language, and Learning Initiative: National Fluency and Mathematics Assessment of Rwandan Schools Endline Report'. Kigali: Education Development Center, USAID, Rwandan Education Board.

Friedlander, E., J. Gasana, and C. Goldenberg. 2014. 'Literacy Boost Rwanda: Reading Assessment Report'. Stanford, CA: Stanford University Graduate School of Education, Rwanda Education Board, Save the Children.

Hickey, S., K. Sen, and B. Bukenya. 2015. 'Exploring the Politics of Inclusive Development: Towards a New Conceptual Approach'. In *The Politics of Inclusive Development: Interrogating the Evidence*. Edited by Hickey, S., K. Sen, and B. Bukenya, 3–32. Oxford: Oxford University Press.

Honeyman, C. A. 2015. 'Early Literacy Promotion in Rwanda: Opportunities and Obstacles'. Kigali: Save the Children; Ishya Consulting.

Hossain, N., and M. Moore. 2001. 'Arguing for the Poor: Elites and Poverty in Developing Countries'. IDS Working Paper 148. Brighton: Institute of Development Studies, University of Sussex.

King, E. 2013. *From Classrooms to Conflict in Rwanda*. Cambridge: Cambridge University Press.

Levy, B., and M. Walton. 2013. 'Institutions, Incentives and Service Provision: Bringing Politics Back In'. ESID Working Paper 18. Manchester: Effective States and Inclusive Development Research Centre, The University of Manchester.

MINALOC. 2001. 'National Decentralization Policy'. Kigali: Ministry of Local Government and Social Affairs, Government of Rwanda.

MINECOFIN. 2000. 'Rwanda Vision 2020'. Kigali: Ministry of Finance and Economic Planning, Government of Rwanda.

MINECOFIN. 2013. 'Economic Development and Poverty Reduction Strategy 2013–2018 (EDPRS-2)'. Kigali: Ministry of Finance and Economic Planning, Government of Rwanda.

MINEDUC. 2003. 'Education Sector Policy'. Kigali: Ministry of Education, Government of Rwanda.

MINEDUC. 2007. 'Teacher Development and Management Policy in Rwanda'. Kigali: Ministry of Education, Government of Rwanda.

MINEDUC. 2010. 'Education Sector Strategic Plan 2010–2015'. Kigali: Ministry of Education, Government of Rwanda.

MINEDUC. 2015. '2014 Education Statistics'. Kigali: Ministry of Education, Government of Rwanda.

NISR (National Institute of Statistics Rwanda). 2011. 'The Third Integrated Household Living Conditions Survey (EICV3)'. Kigali: National Institute of Statistics Rwanda.

NISR. 2012. 'The Fourth Integrated Household Living Conditions Survey (EICV4)'. Kigali: National Institute of Statistics Rwanda.

Patton, M. Q. 1990. *Qualitative Evaluation and Research Methods* (2nd ed.). Newbury Park, CA: Sage.

Prunier, G. 1995. *The Rwanda Crisis: History of a Genocide*. New York: Columbia University Press.

Samuelson, B. 2013. 'Rwanda Switches to English: Conflict, Identity and Language-in-Education Policy'. In *Language Policies in Education: Critical Issues*. Edited by Tollefson J. W., 211–32. New York and Abingdon: Routledge.

Scott, J. C. 1998. *Seeing Like a State: How Certain Schemes to Improve the Human Condition Have Failed*. New Haven, CT: Yale University Press.

Senate. 2014. 'The Constant Quest for Solutions through Dialogue and Consensus in Rwanda'. Kigali: Republic of Rwanda.

Simpson, J. 2013. 'Baseline Assessment of English Language Proficiency of School Teachers in Rwanda'. British Council.

Transparency International. 2013. 'Transparency and Accountability in the Management of Resources Allocated to the Nine Year Basic Education Program in Rwanda: A Citizen Report Card'. Kigali: Transparency International Rwanda, Results for Development Institute.

USAID (United States Agency for International Development). 2014. 'Rwanda National Reading and Mathematics Assessment'. Kigali: USAID Education Development Center.

Williams, T. P. 2016a. 'Oriented towards Action: The Political Economy of Primary Education in Rwanda'. ESID Working Paper 64. Manchester: Effective States and Inclusive Development Research Centre, The University of Manchester.

Williams, T. P. 2016b. 'Theorizing Children's Subjectivity. Investigations in Rural Rwanda'. *Childhood*, 23(3): 333–47.

Williams, T. P. 2017. 'The Political Economy of Primary Education: Lessons from Rwanda'. *World Development*, 96(C): 550–61.

Williams, T. P. 2018. 'The Things They Learned: Aspiration, Uncertainty, and Schooling in Rwanda's Developmental State'. *The Journal of Development Studies*, 1–16.

Williams, T. P., P. Abbott, and A. Mupenzi. 2015. '"Education at Our School Is Not Free": The Hidden Costs of Fee-free Schooling in Rwanda'. *Compare: A Journal of Comparative and International Education*, 45(6): 931–52.

Wilson, J. 2013. 'Teacher Development for English Medium Education in Rwandan Schools: A Discussion Paper'. Kigali: Department for International Development, Centre for British Teachers (CfBT) Education Trust.

6

Political Transformation and Education Sector Performance in South Africa

Brian Levy, Robert Cameron, Ursula Hoadley, and Vinothan Naidoo

Introduction

With the political miracle of South Africa's first democratic election in April 1994, the country seemed transformed, almost overnight, from an exclusionary polity serving the interests only of a small minority, to an inclusionary state committed to providing a better life for all. This transformation makes South Africa an ideal setting for exploring how a political settlement influences policymaking and implementation in the education sector.

Notwithstanding the 1994 'miracle', the legacy of apartheid left the country saddled with amongst the highest levels of inequality in the world.[1] The longer-term sustainability of democracy depended on moving the economy in a more inclusive direction—and this, in turn, depended on transforming basic education from a system geared to the reproduction of subservience amongst the majority of the country's population, to one that builds skills, citizenship, and enhanced economic prospects for entrants into the labour market from historically poor communities.

As a middle-income country, South Africa had available relatively abundant fiscal resources to channel into education. It also had in place the knowledge, institutions, and track record of a relatively high-performing public education system—albeit one that, historically, was heavily skewed in favour of only a minority of its people. And the country's bureaucracy seemingly had the capability to use the available money effectively to address the challenge of

[1] Levy, Hirsch, and Woolard (2015) contrast South Africa's pattern of inequality with those of four other middle-income countries (Brazil, Mexico, Thailand, and Turkey).

providing a quality education for all. But, for all of these strengths, achievements in educational quality have proven elusive. Why?

This chapter synthesizes the results of a multi-level (national, provincial, and school) and multi-methods research project on how political and institutional constraints have influenced education policymaking and implementation in South Africa, and how the constraints might be alleviated. The methodology of the South Africa research programme is closely aligned with the 'domains of power' framework laid out by Hickey and Hossain in Chapter 2 of this book, extending the approach to sub-national levels. The detailed South Africa research findings are available in a companion volume to this one (Levy et al. 2018a).

Figure 6.1 illustrates the logic of the multi-level research design. The central idea is that policy and implementation outcomes are shaped at each level by the interplay between the actors/groups seeking to influence the outcome, and the institutions ('rules of the game') which shape how the actors interact with one another. Action at each level is nested within a set of incentives and constraints shaped in part by the higher level; and each level shapes, in part, the incentives and constraints which prevail at lower levels. In this chapter we explore some of the links between politics and institutions, and some aspects of South Africa's national-level policymaking; we go on to analyse how the divergent political and institutional legacies of the Western Cape and Eastern Cape provinces shaped the capabilities of their education bureaucracies; and explore the independent role of the school level in shaping educational outcomes. First we set the stage, with an overview of how South Africa's educational outcomes have evolved over the past quarter-century.

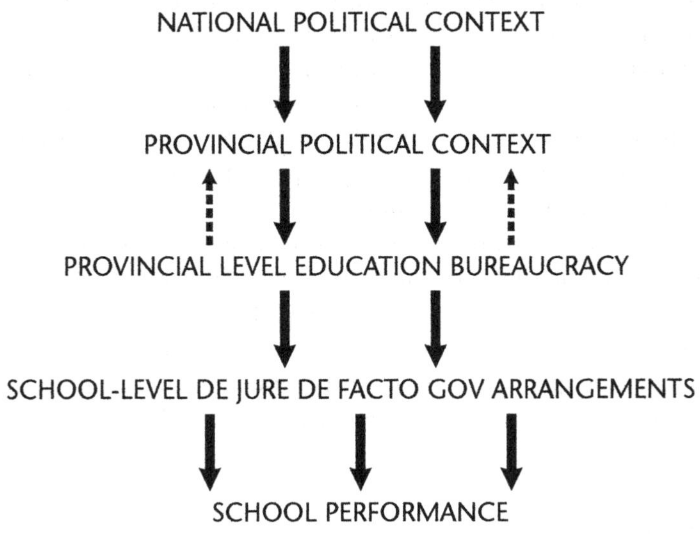

Figure 6.1 The governance of education in South Africa—a multi-level framework

Education Outcomes: South Africa's Quality Challenge

Unsurprisingly, apartheid South Africa was characterized by extreme racial disparities in access to, and expenditure on, education; in 1969, spending per white child was 20 times the amount per black child, and access was also hugely unequal. By the mid-2000s, as Crouch and Hoadley (2018) detail, financing and access had been transformed. Between 1990 and 2005, the share of public spending going to the richest 20 per cent of children fell from 28 per cent to 13 per cent, and the share going to the poorest 20 per cent rose from 19 per cent to 25 per cent. In 1990, the average per child expenditure in the Western Cape (the province with the highest proportion of non-African children) was 80 per cent above the national average; by 2005, the disparity had fallen to below 10 per cent. By the mid-2000s, there was universal access to primary education, and access to secondary education was on a par with other middle-income countries, and rising. When it came to outcomes, however, the apartheid legacy proved to be more resistant to change.

Table 6.1 uses the results of the multi-country Trends in International Mathematics and Science Study (TIMSS), and the Progress in International Reading Literacy Study (PIRLS), to contrast South Africa's educational outcomes across its socio-economic distribution with those of some other countries. As the table shows:

- At all points along the distributional spectrum, South Africa's results are well below those of high-income and global high performers, such as Australia and Singapore; they also are below those of the more directly comparable middle-income countries of Chile and Turkey, although above low-income Egypt and (depending on the year used for comparison) Ghana.
- Strikingly, South Africa's results at the top of the distribution largely follow the above overall pattern, contrary to the usual perception that public schools catering to South African elites are equivalent in quality to those of high-income countries.
- As of 2015–16, the inequality of outcomes between schools serving the upper and lower ends of South Africa's socio-economic distribution continues to be stark (although it appears to have declined over time)—but, strikingly, turns out to be comparable to that of Turkey and Egypt.
- There is some evidence, especially when TIMSS data for 2003 are also considered,[2] of improvements in the South African outcomes, especially at the lower ends of the distribution. However, it is important to underscore that results are well below those of the middle-income country comparators.

[2] But note that South Africa's 2003 TIMSS data (and all data for other countries) are for 8th grade; the 2011 and 2015 tests were administered to 9th graders.

Table 6.1 Distribution of educational outcomes—within and across countries

Country/year	Test scores at multiple percentiles of the score distribution, TIMSS (grade 8) and PIRLS (grade 4), various years					Inequality ratio
	5th percentile	25th percentile	50th percentile	75th percentile	95th percentile	
TIMSS (mathematics and science, generally 8th grade)						
Singapore 2003	455	556	614	662	723	0.44
Australia 2003	368	450	506	561	634	0.53
South Africa 2015 (9th grade)	***242***	***311***	***364***	***426***	***529***	***0.79***
South Africa 2011 (9th grade)	***229***	***295***	***343***	***398***	***516***	***0.84***
South Africa 2003 (8th grade)	***117***	***191***	***248***	***316***	***484***	***1.48***
Chile 2015	297	372	427	482	560	0.62
Turkey 2015	289	385	454	531	634	0.76
Ghana 2003	130	213	274	337	430	1.09
PIRLS (reading, 4th grade)						
Singapore	432	528	570	633	695	0.38
South Africa	***147***	***246***	***311***	***390***	***498***	***0.70***
Chile	356	442	489	550	614	0.42
Egypt	112	246	319	420	520	0.78

Notes: (i) For 2011 and 2015, South Africa administered TIMSS to 9th graders.
(ii) Inequality ratio is defined as (score at 95th percentile minus score at 5th percentile)/score at 50th.
Source: Crouch and Hoadley (2018).

Table 6.2 Some educational outcomes in Southern and Eastern Africa, 2007

	50th percentile (median)	25th percentile	75th percentile
South Africa	483	424	548
Kenya	548	509	610
Kenya (Nairobi)	585	535	662
Western Cape	560	496	636
Gauteng	548	483	610
Eastern Cape	454	408	509

Note: Achievement in grade 6 mathematics and home language by province, 2007.
Source: SACMEQ data files (2007); Republic of South Africa (RSA), Department for Basic Education (2010).

Table 6.2 uses the results of the 2007 Southern African Consortium on Monitoring Education Quality (SACMEQ) tests, to contrast South Africa's outcomes with those of Kenya. As the table shows, Kenya has better performance at all three points along the distributional spectrum, notwithstanding the fact that its per capita income (and per child spending on education) is one-fifth that of South Africa's. The table also provides provincial-level scores for the Western and Eastern Cape, the two provinces on which later sections in this chapter focus (Gauteng is included as a comparator). The Western Cape was the best-performing SACMEQ province, and the Eastern Cape the worst. But, at the lower ends of the distributional spectrum, even the Western Cape scores below Kenya. Some possible reasons for the Kenya–Western Cape disparity are explored later.

The National Level: Political Settlements and Policymaking

National-level political decision-making in the 1990s shaped the subsequent development of South Africa's education sector in two distinct ways. As part of the process of forging a political settlement, some overarching parameters framed how the sector would operate going forward. Subsequently, political drivers emanating from the agreed political settlement significantly influenced the process and content of national-level policy decisions.

Following the typology outlined in Chapter 2 of this book (and a related framework laid out in Levy 2014), the political settlement that has prevailed in South Africa since the end of apartheid rule can be characterized in terms of the configuration of political power by the relative dominance of the ruling African National Congress (ANC), which won almost 63 per cent of the national vote in the first democratic elections in 1994; and in institutional terms by a history of state building over the course of the twentieth century that bequeathed the elected ANC relatively strong institutions, which operated (at least to some extent) along impersonal lines. As we discuss later, the ANC is constituted by a broad range of actors, and characterized by a good deal of internal dissent and negotiation around policy agendas, but since 1994 it has been electorally dominant nationally. Likewise, although the leadership of President Zuma (2009–18) raised serious concerns with regards to the issue of 'elite capture', the country's institutions have proven to be largely resilient, restraining efforts to undermine rules-based governance. However, given the country's size, its racialized history of state formation, and the fragmentation of governance institutions during the apartheid years, it makes sense to consider whether different types of sub-national political settlements exist. We explore this issue in subsequent sections through a comparative analysis of the different political and institutional conditions that prevail in the Western and Eastern Capes, respectively. This section focuses on the national level.

One further common (if somewhat oversimplified, but adequate for present purposes) way of describing South Africa's political settlement is as an agreement between two nationalisms—Afrikaner nationalism and African nationalism.[3]

[3] Mbeki (2009) and Macdonald (2006) are amongst the commentators who interpret the settlement through a 'rival nationalisms' lens. Large-scale organized business (disproportionately

Throughout the political transition, how South Africa's education sector was to be transformed was a central concern of South Africa's leaders, negotiated in parallel with the broader political settlement. It is no coincidence that the South African Schools Act (SASA) was promulgated in 1996, the same year in which the country's final constitution was formally approved.

For black South Africans, an immediate concern was equalization of access, and a redress of the stark financing inequities; for white South Africans, a central concern was agreement on a system of governance that could sustain the quality of the public[4] schools, which historically had served the white minority.

The governance arrangements for education incorporated within SASA were responsive to the concerns of the main protagonists who negotiated the political settlement. The apartheid era education system comprised 19 separate education departments, divided along racial, political, and geographic lines. An immediate and broadly agreed-upon task was to transform this morass into a unified, non-racial system. But this needed to be done in a way that could respond to the country's political complexity. In part for this political reason, SASA made provision for substantial delegation of the education system:

- Responsibility for policymaking, for resourcing the system, and for setting the overall regulatory framework was retained at the national level.
- Responsibility for implementation, including direct oversight of schools, was delegated to the country's nine provinces, which differed substantially from one another, both politically and institutionally.
- Responsibilities at school level (including the recruitment of the school principal and senior teachers) were assigned to school governing bodies (SGBs), in which parents were required to be in the majority.

With the overarching parameters of the system in place, attention turned to policy. National-level policies were shaped by a collision between the idealistic visions of South Africa's new, ANC-aligned education sector technocrats, and the political complexities of the ANC's governing 'alliance'. The technocrats had scanned education sectors worldwide to identify 'best practices'; the

anglophone) also played a key role in facilitating negotiations. Powerful ethnic factions (the Afrikaner Weerstandbeweging; the Freedom Front; the Inkatha Freedom Party) came close to derailing the settlement. The ANC itself was something of an umbrella; its negotiations team included influential leaders of the South African Communist Party, the Congress of South African Trade Unions (COSATU), and the United Democratic Front, a galvanizing umbrella organization for non-violent civic resistance within South Africa. For detailed histories of how South Africa's political settlement was achieved, see Mandela (1994); Sparks (1996); Marais (1998); Welsh (2009). For a structural perspective, see Seekings and Nattrass (2005).

[4] In South Africa, public education dominates, both historically and to the present day; as of 2015, over 95 per cent of school-going children were enrolled in the public system.

result was a far-reaching agenda of sectoral reforms, described in detail by Crouch and Hoadley (2018). While much was achieved, the gap between initial visions and what actually played out on the ground sometimes turned out to be wide. The reasons had much to do with political dynamics within the ANC.

With its long history (dating back to 1912) as a broad-based, nationalist political movement, the ANC was in practice an umbrella organization, straddling a wide variety of interests. Upon assuming the reins of power in 1994, it confronted the challenge of mediating amongst diverse stakeholders:

- As a mass political movement, with a long history of political struggle against oppression, the ANC had a deeply rooted commitment to address South Africa's profound challenges of poverty, and of racial and class inequality.
- It formally incorporated as members of the 'ruling alliance' both the South African Communist Party and COSATU.
- Since the earliest days of its founding, it had also voiced the aspiration of African (and other black) 'petty bourgeois' and other groups seeking economic empowerment.[5]

These varied interests have co-existed uneasily with one another. Over the past two decades, the result has been something of a race between consolidation of a high-performing 'developmental state' at one end of the spectrum of possible outcomes and, at the other, an accelerating slide into more personalized and patronage-oriented approaches to governance.

In the first two decades of democracy, the ANC's labour market policies were broadly favourable to the interests of its alliance partner, COSATU (Seekings and Nattrass 2015). Between 1994 and 2007, real average wages of unionized workers (both white-collar and blue-collar) rose, even as real wages of their non-unionized counterparts fell. Over the period, the employment profile of union members changed radically. As of 1994, unskilled and semi-skilled workers accounted for 60 per cent of the members of COSATU-affiliated unions; by 2008, their share of COSATU membership had fallen to 22 per cent. Correspondingly, the share in COSATU membership of skilled and professional employees had risen to 59 per cent of the total; these employees were predominantly in the public sector, with the South African Democratic Teachers Union (SADTU) now one of COSATU's largest affiliated unions.

The (narrowly conceived) interests of SADTU's unionized workforce had a powerful impact in shaping employee relations within the education sector.

[5] For an in-depth review of the history of elite, neo-patrimonial influences in the ANC, see Lodge (2014).

As Cameron and Naidoo (2018) detail, technocrats within the education sector repeatedly tried to introduce new tools for performance management, as one way of addressing the quality challenges. However, these tools collided with the narrowly conceived interests of SADTU's members. The result was that the ambitious initial proposals were heavily watered down.

Cameron and Naidoo describe in depth the evolution of a 2007 proposal to introduce occupation-specific, performance-related pay. The effort was initiated in the wake of an almost month-long strike by over 700,000 public employees over pay and other conditions of service. The intention was to enhance the attractiveness of a teaching career and expand salary progression, to reward good performance, and to introduce incentives for experienced and capable teachers to remain in the classroom. An initial proposal was introduced at the Education Labour Relations Council (ELRC), set up as part of the complex corporatist arrangements for managing labour relations as part of South Africa's new political dispensation. The proposals included:

- a career path in which pay increases were not automatic, but based on performance, qualifications, scope of work, and experience;
- provision for a specialist career path for teachers who wanted to remain in the classroom, and an accelerated career progression based on performance;
- inclusion of learner performance as a basis for assessing the performance of educators;
- performance agreements for principals and deputy principals; and
- a pay progression based on performance (1 per cent increase for satisfactory; 3 per cent for good; and 6 per cent for outstanding), with external moderation of assessments of 'good' and 'outstanding'.

To sweeten the deal, the initiative also proposed a broad salary increase to all teachers, and an increase in the starting salary of newly qualified teachers. SADTU strongly opposed the proposals.

An agreement was finally reached after almost two years of contentious negotiation, punctuated by work stoppages protesting the proposed arrangements—but only after a closed-door intervention by the ANC's top political leadership, outside of the formal negotiation process. In the final agreement, most of the performance-related elements were stripped out. Instead of a pay progression based on performance, educators were given an across-the-board increase of 3 per cent, plus an additional increase for teachers at the lowest end of the qualifications scale. Evidently, the ambitions of technocrats to strengthen the performance orientation of the education system were no match for the strong constituency interests that had to be mediated politically within the ANC's ruling alliance.

The Provincial Level: Divergent Contexts, Divergent Bureaucratic Capabilities

South Africa's provinces are where responsibility lies for the operation of the education sector—for employing teachers, providing essential school infrastructure, spending the resources allocated for public education, and for managing the system more broadly. This section summarizes and synthesizes analyses of education sector management in two provinces—the Western Cape (Cameron and Levy 2018) and the Eastern Cape (Kota et al. 2018).

In 2013, South Africa's Department of Policy Monitoring and Evaluation, located in the office of the Presidency, released the results of a Management Performance Assessment Tool (MPAT) conducted in over 100 national and provincial government departments. As Table 6.3 shows, as of 2012–13, the Western Cape Education Department (WCED) was rated as the best managed of the country's nine provinces (Gauteng was rated second). The Eastern Cape Department of Education (ECDoE) was rated the weakest (with the Northern Cape rated second weakest).

Consistent with the analytical framework illustrated in Figure 6.1, this section explains the performance differences in terms of the contextual differences with regards to the interplay of politics and institutions within each province. Applying at a sub-national level the typology laid out in Chapter 2 of this volume, the Western Cape and Eastern Cape turn out to be paradigmatic provincial-level examples of two distinct patterns.

The Western Cape emerges as a classic example of a 'competitive' political order, governed largely by 'impersonal' rules of the game.

Table 6.3 MPAT assessments of South Africa's education departments *(selected provinces 2012–13; distribution of scores, by level for assessed key performance areas)*[6]

	Level 1	Level 2	Level 3	Level 4
Western Cape	0	21	34	45
Gauteng	14	21	31	34
National average, all provinces	24	31	31	15
Northern Cape	28	41	28	3
Eastern Cape	59	17	17	7

Source: South Africa, The Presidency 2012.

[6] For each key performance area, the MPAT rates performance according to four levels: Level 1—non-compliance with legal/regulatory requirements; Level 2—partial compliance with legal/regulatory requirements; Level 3—full compliance with legal/regulatory requirement; Level 4—full compliance, and doing this smartly.

Table 6.4 Two divergent contexts in South Africa

	1. Socio-economic	2. Political	3. Inherited institutions
Western Cape	Diverse—both ethnically and by economic class	- elites dispersed across multiple political parties, with two broad groupings - competitive elections	Inheritance of relatively 'impersonal' bureaucracy
Eastern Cape	Homogenous—disproportionately poor and Xhosa-speaking	- ANC electorally dominant - deep intra-party fragmentation	Inheritance of patronage Bantustan bureaucracies

Source: Levy et al. (2018b).

The Eastern Cape, by contrast, emerges as a paradigmatic example of a personalized, clientelist, and fragmented political order, operating under the umbrella of a de facto dominant political party.

Table 6.4 groups some contextual differences between the two provinces into three categories—socio-economic, political, and institutional. The discussion that follows explores how these variables influence bureaucratic behaviour and performance, distinguishing between demand-side and supply-side influences.[7]

Demand-side Pressures for Performance

By demand-side pressures, we mean the mechanisms through which exogenous socio-economic and political variables influence the *effectiveness* of citizens' demands on bureaucrats and politicians for decent public services. A first mechanism comprises the well-recognized[8] relationship between social class and effective demand, with middle-class citizens generally better positioned than their low-income counterparts to exercise voice effectively in response to poor quality services (and mismanagement and corruption, more broadly).

Economically, the Western Cape was (and remains) amongst the wealthiest of South Africa's nine provinces; as of 1996, its per capita income was 50 per cent higher than for the country as a whole. The Eastern Cape, by contrast, was the poorest province in the country; its per capita income hovers at around 50–60 per cent of the national average. These differences in average income between the two provinces translate into far-reaching differences in class composition.[9]

[7] This discussion is taken directly from Levy, Cameron, and Naidoo (2018b).

[8] For some analyses of the role of a rising middle class in pressing for greater public sector accountability, see Lipset (1959), Moore (1966), Huntington (1968), Acemoglu and Robinson, (2006), Fukuyama (2014).

[9] These differences in social class composition would, of course, be magnified (or diminished) if the provinces also differed in their (intra-province) patterns of relative inequality. But the limited available evidence on provincial-level Gini coefficients suggests that these differences are relatively small.

Table 6.5 Distribution of social classes in South Africa, 2014

	South Africa (all)%	Western Cape%	Eastern Cape%
Elite	4	5	2
'Middle' class	20	35	13
Vulnerable	14	15	10
Transient poor	13	20	5
Chronic poor	49	25	70
TOTAL	100%	100%	100%

Note: The distribution is based on an empirical analysis of four waves of panel data collected between 2008 and 2014 by South Africa's National Income Dynamics Study.

Source: Schotte et al. (2017).

Table 6.5 reports some findings from Schotte, Zizzamia, and Leibbrandt's (2017) disaggregation of South Africa's income distribution into five distinct social classes; 49 per cent of South Africa's total population is classified as 'chronically poor'.[10] In the Eastern Cape, the share of the population which is 'chronically poor' rises to 70 per cent. In the Western Cape, it is 25 per cent. The 'modal' social class in the Western Cape is the middle class (35 per cent of the total population), with the 'vulnerable' and 'transient poor' accounting for a further 35 per cent. Insofar as there is a positive correlation between economic status and voice, then solely on the basis of these differences in class composition, non-elite citizens in the Western Cape generally are likely to be better positioned to pressure for better public services than are their Eastern Cape counterparts.

A second demand-side mechanism works via the electoral process. Here the key proposition is that citizens will be better positioned to exert demand-side pressure for services in settings where elections are competitive than in those where politicians can take the support (or acquiescence) of citizens for granted, independent of how well they govern and in a context where political institutions operate more along impersonal than personalized norms.[11] For reasons which are rooted in part in demography, and in part in history, the differences between the two provinces in electoral competitiveness have been stark.

[10] The high proportion of the population who are 'chronically poor' is not an artefact of where the benchmark is set. For one thing, over half of the income of this group comes from social grants (pensions, child support, and disability), set at less than $100 per month. For another, South Africa's 'chronically poor' are notably poor when benchmarked against other middle-income countries. As Levy et al. (2015) detail, in the year 2000, the poorest 40 per cent of South Africans accounted for only 5.5 per cent of expenditure, a starkly lower share than for the comparator countries (all of which have similar per capita incomes)—Brazil (8.1 per cent), Mexico (11.4 per cent), Turkey (15.1 per cent), and Thailand (17.1 per cent). As of 2010, the South African share had risen to 6.9 per cent, still below the comparators.

[11] Acemoglu and Robinson (2006). Khemani (2016) in chapter 5 reviews the literature on the impact of democratic political engagement on development outcomes.

In the Eastern Cape, 86 per cent of the 1996 population of 6.1 million was black African, almost all Xhosa-speaking. (For South Africa as a whole, the 1996 black African share of the total was 77 per cent.) In the Western Cape, by contrast, the largest ethnic subgroup of the population was (in the South African lexicon) 'coloured'. In 1996, this group comprised 54 per cent of the 4.1 million people in the province; black Africans comprised only 21 per cent. By 2011, population in the Western Cape had risen to 5.8 million (with the increase driven in significant part by migration from the Eastern Cape), with the black African and 'coloured' shares now comprising 33 per cent and 49 per cent, respectively.

The Western Cape's relatively high ethnic diversity provided a platform for closely contested elections. To be sure, the province had been a major locus of opposition to apartheid and, as elsewhere in the country, most 'non-white' anti-apartheid activists identified strongly with the ANC. But the distinctive ethnic characteristics of the Western Cape implied that, amongst at least part of the population, loyalty to the ANC was not necessarily unequivocal. Insofar as the ANC was perceived to frame the basis for its allegiance in narrowly 'African nationalist' terms, rather than an inclusive non-racialism, there was ample scope for shifting allegiances, and thus voting patterns, away from the ANC and towards the opposition Democratic Alliance (DA), and other political parties.[12]

The result was a highly competitive provincial politics, with multiple competing political parties, and hotly contested elections. Over the course of the first two decades of democracy, seven different political parties/coalitions have controlled the province. In these contested elections, non-elite swing voters (in the 'middle', 'vulnerable', and 'transient poor' classes) became politically central. Indeed, contestation amongst rival political parties for the allegiance of this demographic and economic middle has been heated.

In the Eastern Cape, by contrast, the ANC dominated electorally. In 1994 it won 84 per cent of the vote in the province; this percentage declined subsequently, but as of 2015 had not fallen below 70 per cent. The electoral dominance of the ANC can be explained in part by the interaction between the province's ethnic homogeneity and its distinctive historical legacy. A disproportionate number of the leaders of the struggle for liberation from apartheid—including Nelson Mandela, Oliver Tambo, Thabo Mbeki, Winnie

[12] The DA elite comprised those in the upper tiers of business, the professions, and the bureaucracy within the province. Cohesion did not come naturally amongst these elite subgroups. At the dawn of democracy, there was a clear split between those with historical allegiance to the apartheid National Party, and those aligned with more liberal (but not revolutionary) 'white' opposition parties. Over subsequent decades, these two factions largely merged—and were joined by smaller, independent (non-ANC) parties, whose allegiance was generally not 'white', and who historically had been very active in the struggle against apartheid.

Madikizela Mandela, Chris Hani, and Walter Sisulu—were Xhosa-speaking sons and daughters of the province. This proud history translated into strong electoral loyalty to the ANC on the part of the numerically preponderant Xhosa-speaking voters. The result was that for the first two decades of democracy, electoral competition did not serve as a significant source of pressure on the ANC to improve public services.

Politics, Institutional Inheritances, and the Supply of Services

We turn now to the two 'supply-side' causal mechanisms through which politics and institutions influence bureaucratic behaviour: the role of inherited institutional legacies and patterns of intra-elite contestation within a governing political party.

As Keefer and Khemani (2005) explore, in choosing how to seek the allegiance of non-elites, political leaders confront a fundamental choice. One option is 'programmatic'—leaders might try to win legitimacy by promising a specific programme of public action, and then utilize the public bureaucracy to deliver on these promises. Alternatively, they could seek to win support through personalized patronage and clientelistic vertical networks that link elite and 'intermediate class'[13] powerbrokers with local communities. A key determinant of how political leaders choose between these two mechanisms is whether their promises to provide broad-based services (rather than targeted patronage) are perceived to be credible by voters. This is where inherited institutional legacies come into play.

The Western Cape inherited a bureaucracy that could straightforwardly respond to the relatively strong effective demand of citizens for services. During the apartheid era, alongside the 'white' political and bureaucratic structures, the apartheid government had established a parallel 'parliament' and bureaucracy, the ('coloured') House of Representatives (HoR). The 'white' civil service and the HoR bureaucracy together were responsible for the provision of services (including education services) to the large majority of the Western Cape population.[14] As numerous studies of organizational culture have shown,[15] both South Africa's 'white' public service and the HoR bureaucracy were steeped in traditional public administration, albeit with an apartheid bent. This inherited legacy of a relatively capable bureaucracy meant that

[13] The term is used in this way in Khan and Jomo's (2000) analysis of rent networks in South Asia.

[14] Africans living in urban townships were under the control of the Department of Education and Training (DET). In the Western Cape, Africans were a minority and the number of DET schools in the province was relatively small. There were also no Bantustans in the province. This meant that the province had to deal with only a modestly sized 'deadweight' of the most dysfunctional, control-oriented part of the apartheid state (Fiske and Ladd 2004).

[15] McLennan and Fitzgerald (1992); Schwella (2000).

voters were likely to perceive politicians' promises to provide public services as credible, adding to the impetus for political competition to be oriented around competing programmatic platforms, rather than patronage.

Indeed, as Cameron and Levy (2018) detail, throughout the democratic era, the WCED has consistently had a relatively strong professional orientation amongst both the administrative bureaucracy and teaching staff. Turnover amongst the senior bureaucratic officials was low, insulating the bureaucracy to a significant degree from the cycles of political change, including the rapid turnover of the provincial-cabinet-level appointments of political heads (i.e. the provincial ministers of education). The WCED had consistently worked to implement the ongoing stream of results-oriented systems reform initiatives which emanated from the national level, and has complemented them with a variety of more home-grown initiatives to strengthen performance, all implemented especially vigorously under the DA administration, which has governed the province since 2009. These include sophisticated computerized tools for managing budgets, staffing, and procurement, school improvement plans (SIPs) for each of the province's 1,500 schools, online tracking systems for monitoring the progress of individual learners through the WCED system, and (on a quarterly basis), the progress of schools in implementing their SIPs.

The institutional legacy of the Eastern Cape was very different from that of its Western Cape counterpart. Two-thirds of the Eastern Cape's total 2015 population of 6.9 million people reside in areas which formerly had been part of either the Transkei or Ciskei 'Bantustan' polities created by the apartheid government. Both the Transkei and Ciskei had nominally been independent (recognized as such only by South Africa's apartheid government). Both had large-scale bureaucratic apparatuses, which were moulded together to comprise the major[16] part of the post-apartheid provincial bureaucracy.

The two Bantustans had been organized along personalized, patronage lines.[17] These patronage patterns carried forward into the workings of the Eastern Cape province via two distinct mechanisms. As per Keefer and Khemani (2005), one mechanism worked through the credibility of political promises: the weakness of the bureaucracy at the outset of the democratic era meant that, even under the best of circumstances, persuading citizens that promises to provide decent services would be credible would be an uphill challenge. But the circumstances prevailing in the province were especially unpropitious. This brings us to the second supply-side influence on

[16] Along with the two Bantustan bureaucracies, the third part of the Eastern Cape bureaucracy comprised some portions of the apartheid era Cape provincial bureaucracy—though the head office, and senior staff had been located in Cape Town, and most transferred into the Western Cape's bureaucracy.

[17] Streek and Wickstead (1981).

bureaucratic behaviour—the role of intra-elite contestation within a governing political party.

In the wake of the dissolution of the Transkei and Ciskei Bantustans, a large majority of their political and bureaucratic elites (and also many ordinary citizens) joined the ANC—not out of conviction, but out of convenience. Further, the (non-Bantustan) Eastern Cape ANC was itself hardly an ideologically unified party. In its early years, the ANC (both within the Eastern Cape and nationally) reflected the aspirations of a mission-educated aspirant African middle class, which was increasingly being constrained by racially discriminatory policies.[18] In the decades prior to democracy, parts of the party had become increasingly militant; both Govan Mbeki (Thabo Mbeki's father) and Chris Hani (chief of staff of the armed wing of the ANC in exile) were stalwarts of the South African Communist Party. The result was that the Eastern Cape ANC was less a disciplined, programmatically oriented political organization than an overall umbrella, beneath which inter-elite contestation was endemic. This continuing contestation afforded the ANC's provincial leadership neither the authority nor the longer-term time-horizon needed to translate electoral dominance into a commitment to better service provision.[19]

In sum, the Eastern Cape was especially poorly positioned vis-à-vis each of the causal mechanisms linking context to bureaucratic operation and performance. The middle class was weak. Elections were uncompetitive. The bureaucratic legacy was dismal. The wide diversity of ideologies and motivations resulted in ongoing internecine struggles within the Eastern Cape ANC's leadership. Patronage, not programmatic commitments to improve services, became the default mechanism for maintaining the political allegiance of non-elites.

The result was an ECDoE bedevilled by divergent and competing regional interests, organizational cultures, and patronage ties that consistently defied centralized control. As Kota et al. (2018) detail, subsequent to 1994 the ECDoE has experienced repeated leadership turnover, and a general flouting of centralized authority. Provincial ministers of education and their senior officials belonged to divergent subgroups of the party, with some officials outranking the ministers within the ANC, making vertical accountability difficult. The obstacles to enforcing management control and sustaining leadership continuity in the ECDoE have contributed to chronic weaknesses in both financial and personnel management. In March 2011, the national government intervened, and temporarily took over administration of the ECDoE. But this

[18] Lodge (2014); Southall (2014).

[19] In the terminology of Kelsall and vom Hau (2017), the Eastern Cape ANC was a multipolar, rather than unipolar, political party.

did not stem the crisis. Provincial politics proved too powerful. After a few years, intervention was scaled back, having had only a limited impact.

Is Bureaucracy Destiny? Educational Outcomes and School-level Governance

As the previous section has detailed, in the Western Cape political and institutional context (plus effective leadership) have come together in a way that has resulted in a well-functioning education department. The same factors have conspired to produce the opposite result vis-à-vis the ECDoE. But is bureaucracy destiny?

To be sure, a well-functioning education bureaucracy makes it possible to perform well many tasks that contribute to the quality of an education system. The allocation of scarce public funds across the system; the assignment of personnel to the places where they are most needed; building the capabilities of teachers and other employees who work within the system; monitoring and managing the results achieved by staff; the construction and management of infrastructure; and the provision of furniture, textbooks, and other teaching materials—all are quintessentially bureaucratic tasks. But, as noted earlier, the SASA also delegated substantial decision-making authority to SGBs. Might this horizontal governance dimension independently influence outcomes in ways which complicate the relationship between bureaucratic quality and educational outcomes?

Organizational theory suggests that the latter might be the case—that in sectors such as education, where service provision is diffused across a large number of frontline providers, delegation of authority potentially creates opportunities for customization, for improving local-level motivation, and for utilizing local-level information in ways that improve performance.[20] The ways in which horizontal governance might plausibly add value would be different in settings where bureaucracy is strong, from settings where it is weak:

- Where bureaucracy is strong (as in the Western Cape), can horizontal governance *complement* hierarchy via its particular strengths at the local level?
- Where bureaucracy is weak (as in the Eastern Cape), can horizontal governance function as a potential *substitute* by also taking on, reasonably effectively, some tasks which might otherwise have been done bureaucratically?

[20] Key contributions to the literature on the value added of frontline autonomy include Sah and Stiglitz (1986), Aghion and Tirole (1997), Wilson (1989), Lipsky (2010), and Scott (1998).

This section explores the above questions. It reviews some robust statistical comparisons of the relationship between bureaucratic quality and educational outcomes across multiple locales (including the Western Cape). It then provides an overview of findings from school-level case study analyses of how micro-governance dynamics influenced performance in some Western and Eastern Cape schools.

Assessing the Determinants of Educational Outcomes

As Table 6.2 signalled, the Western Cape achieved the highest scores amongst South Africa's provinces in the 2007 SACMEQ standardized test—but its scores were generally similar to Kenya's (a much poorer locale, with less than a fifth of the per pupil public resources available for education), indeed somewhat below Kenya at the lower end of the socio-economic distribution. Given the evident robustness of the Western Cape bureaucracy, and the well-known unevenness of Kenya's public management systems, it is highly unlikely that the performance gap can be explained by superior hierarchical management on the part of Kenya.

Outcomes, of course, depend on multiple influences. Consequently, as part of the overall research effort, the qualitative country-, provincial-, and school-level analyses were complemented by a robust statistical study, conducted by Wills, Shepherd, and Kotze (2018). Their econometric strategy was to isolate a 'Western Cape effect' on educational outcomes (in the form of the coefficient of a dummy variable for the province) once other influences were controlled for—home background, socio-economic status, teacher qualifications, other teacher/classroom characteristics, plus a subset of governance indicators.[21] With these controls, the coefficient of the Western Cape dummy variable can be interpreted as being, in significant part, a 'management effect'. Wills et al. (2018) comprehensively describe the data, the research methods, and the econometric findings. Table 6.6 reports a small subset of their results. As the table shows, relative to both Gauteng and the Eastern Cape, this Western Cape effect is significant and positive.

However, relative to Kenya,[22] the Western Cape effect is negative—even after controlling for a wide variety of influences. At the broadest level, this residual effect could be attributed to governance. Viewed through the narrow

[21] Each of these is a composite measure, built on very detailed student-, parent-, and school-specific information collected in the SACMEQ survey. Wills et al. (2018) detail each of the underlying data points, including average scores for each, in each of the locales they analyse.

[22] The comparison is specifically with results for Kenya's Nairobi and Central provinces. As Wills et al. (2018) detail, these provinces are reasonably similar in their socio-economic status (SES) demographic to the Western Cape. The statistical procedures break down when SES differences across the populations are too large.

Table 6.6 Grade 6 mathematics SACMEQ scores—the 'Western Cape' effect (coefficient on Western Cape dummy variable)

	1	2
Comparison country/region:		
Kenya (Nairobi and Central)	−0.373**	−0.434**
Eastern Cape	0.488***	0.890***
Gauteng	0.299***	0.408***
Controls:		
home background	X	X
socio-economic status	X	X
teacher test scores	X	X
teacher/classroom characteristics	X	X
parents contribute to school building and teaching materials		X

Notes: Teacher and classroom characteristics include: teacher education, teacher age, teacher experience, weekly teaching time (hours), textbook availability, class size, pupil–teacher ratio, frequency and discussion of homework, and frequency of classroom assessment. Standard errors clustered at the school level are shown in parentheses.
***significance at 1 per cent level **significance at 5 per cent level *significance at 10 per cent level.
Source: Wills et al. (2018).

prism of hierarchical governance, the Western Cape is relatively strong. Thus the results could be interpreted as pointing to the possibility that it is in the 'softer' side of the governance of education—perhaps motivation on the part of teachers and other stakeholders, perhaps the patterns of participatory, horizontal governance—that Kenya has an advantage.[23]

A closer look at the results for the Eastern Cape offers an intriguing added pointer as to the relevance of the softer side of governance. As Table 6.6 shows, the inclusion of 'parental contribution to school building and teaching materials' as an explanatory variable has a large effect on the magnitude of the 'Western Cape effect' on educational outcomes. Why? In the SACMEQ data series, 57 per cent of Eastern Cape parents (but only 13 per cent of Western Cape parents) assist with school building—and 65 per cent (but only 18 per cent in the Western Cape) with school maintenance. Plausibly, parental participation serves as a partial institutional substitute for weaknesses in the Eastern Cape bureaucracy—with the true proportions of the costs imposed on Eastern Cape children by weaknesses in the ECDoE only evident once the parental role is accounted for.

[23] Levy et al. (2018a) appendix 10A explore the historical roots of Kenya's 'soft governance' advantage. Here what can be noted is that a distinguishing feature of Kenya's education system comprises its strong roots in the country's *harambee* ('self-help') movement in the wake of independence.

In sum, the econometric results suggest that bureaucracy need not be destiny—that there are other dimensions of the governance of education systems, which can be, as in the Eastern Cape, partial institutional substitutes for relatively weak hierarchical bureaucratic capability, or (as seems likely in Kenya) complements, adding to the overall efficacy of the system. The findings of the school-level case studies offer added insight into these softer sides of governance.

School-level Governance Dynamics

School-level governance research in the Western Cape (Hoadley et al. 2018) and Eastern Cape (Levy and Shumane 2018) used process-tracing methodologies (George and Bennett 2005) to explore the causal mechanisms through which interactions between school leadership and other stakeholders inside and outside the school influenced educational outcomes. The research focused on eight schools, four in each province, all in poor communities, and with variations in performance, both across schools and over time. All eight schools had gone through a change in principal over the relevant period, making for the three distinct governance 'episodes' illustrated in Figure 6.2: an initial period; a transitional period and associated process of selection of a new principal; and a later period. This sub-section provides an overview of some key findings.[24]

Table 6.7 summarizes some of the main findings from the case studies vis-à-vis the influence on performance of hierarchical and horizontal governance in each school. The table distinguishes between two facets of hierarchical governance: hierarchical influence exerted by the relevant provincial department, and leadership by the school principal. In none of the Eastern Cape case studies was there any evidence that the ECDoE offered more than very modest help in fostering a performance orientation at the school level. The Western Cape's WCED, by contrast, played a more proactive role—but there are some paradoxical findings, which are best considered jointly in the discussion that follows of the role of the school principal.

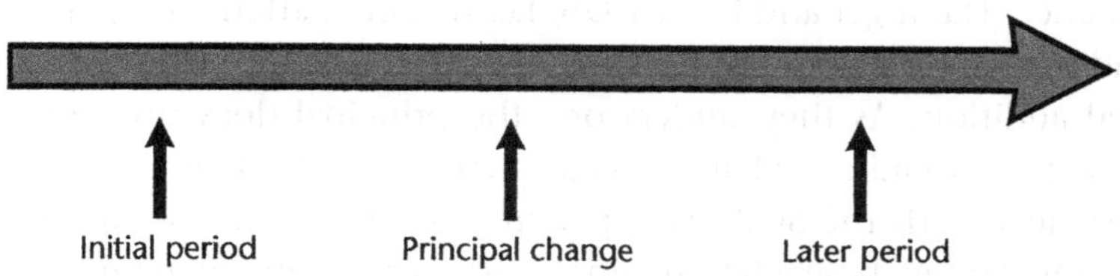

Figure 6.2 Governance 'episodes' in South African schools

[24] A fuller account of the school-level case studies can be found in Levy et al. (2018a).

Table 6.7 Governance and performance in the case study schools in South Africa

	Eastern Cape	Western Cape
I: INFLUENCE OF HIERARCHICAL GOVERNANCE		
Role of provincial bureaucracy	– Protects dysfunctional status quo in two schools. – Offers modest support for school principals seeking turnaround in later period in two schools.	WCED buttresses authority of charismatic principals in initial period in two schools, but performance declined when the principals left.
Role of school-level leaders	How authority is exercised by school leaders consistently has a strong influence on governance and performance in all periods in all schools.	
	Highly respected principal drives relatively strong performance in early initial period in one school.	Charismatic principals drive strong performance orientation in initial period in two schools.
II: INFLUENCE OF HORIZONTAL GOVERNANCE		
Positive influence	– Sustained performance-oriented multi-stakeholder governance in one school. – Stakeholder-initiated turnaround in two schools.	– Stakeholder-supported turnaround in one school.
Negative influence	– Ongoing capture in one school. – Capture during earlier period in two schools.	– Ongoing capture in one school. – Capture in latter period in one school. – Conflictual principal succession disrupts performance in one school.

Source: Levy (2018).

As the table also summarizes, there were substantial variations in the influence of horizontal governance. In some schools, for some periods of time, its influence was positive. In others, a variety of school-level stakeholders were complicit in the capture of school-level resources for more narrowly personalized purposes. The efficacy of horizontal governance turned out to be strongly associated with the approach to leadership of the school principal, with some striking interactions between the initial period (Figure 6.2) and later period patterns.

The centrality of the school principal has been identified in global research on school-level governance as an important proximate determinant of school performance (Hallinger and Heck 1996; Leithwood, Patten, and Jantzi 2010). The findings in the school-level case studies are consistent with this, but with a crucial addition. As they underscore, the principal does not function in isolation, but is embedded in a dense network of horizontal interactions with teachers, with the SGB, with parents, and with the community more broadly. Over time, these relationships—and how the principal nurtures them (or fails to nurture them)—are key underlying determinants of school-level educational outcomes. The interactions between leadership and governance in the initial period (Figure 6.2) had a strong influence both on school performance, and on the governance dynamics in the subsequent period. Three distinct patterns of 'initial period' leadership were evident.

A first pattern, evident in the initial period in three schools, comprised strong top-down leadership by a charismatic, committed, results-oriented principal. This leadership style yielded good results in the initial period, but with performance in all three schools subsequently declining—with the declines pointing to the limitations of this 'heroic' style of leadership. Although in the short term, the determined efforts of a strong principal can yield success, at some point the time comes for succession. If succession turns out badly (as happened in the two Western Cape schools), or if the principal loses authority for some other reason (as happened in the Eastern Cape example), then this successful performance is likely to be reversed. Charismatic personalized leadership without institution-building risks leaving behind an institutional vacuum, conflict, and a collapse of school performance.

In a second contrasting pattern, evident in four schools, governance was more participatory—with the clearest illustration coming from a school in the Eastern Cape. The institutional culture of the school, established by its founding principal, was one where all stakeholders—teachers, the SGB, the extended community—felt included; even with the ECDoE, which was carefully kept at arm's length, relationships remained cordial. This pattern of collaborative governance was underpinned by impersonal rules, collectively developed, collectively owned, and largely self-imposed. The school's inclusive culture supported a smooth process of principal succession. The successor principal, an internal candidate from within the teaching staff, had been mentored by the previous principal, enjoyed the support of the SGB, and, once appointed, continued along the path that had been established. Indeed, this was the only one of the eight case study schools that consistently sustained a relatively[25] strong performance.

Another variant of participatory governance was more bottom-up. One of the Eastern Cape case study schools had long been characterized by sustained, neglectful, and predatory leadership on the part of an often-absent principal. The number of pupils had fallen from close to 1,000 in the early 1990s to a low of 341 in 2011. After over a decade of ongoing dysfunction, a group of parents and some SGB members met, and jointly reached the view that the principal needed to be replaced. At the group's urging, the SGB took their decision to the ECDoE district office. After failing to win support from the bureaucracy, the parent community staged a protest, preventing the principal from

[25] Both the trend in numbers of students, and area feedback (and visual observation during fieldwork) identify the school as a relatively strong performer locally. But given the vast disparities between average performance in the Eastern and Western Cape, there is no basis for extrapolating this relative success into absolutely strong performance in relation to schools in low-income areas in both provinces.

accessing the school, and forcing the appointment of a replacement, with whom they worked closely to turn around the school. By 2015, four years after the intervention by parents, the number of pupils in the school had risen to 547, up by 70 per cent from the trough.

The third broad governance pattern was one of weak/captured leadership. In two cases (one in each province), this dysfunctional leadership was linked directly to the predatory preferences of 'strong' principals, who inculcated a culture of self-seeking and inattention to learning throughout their schools. In two other schools (both in the Eastern Cape), leadership was relatively weak; in one of the two, there was a low-level equilibrium of capture, with the principal, teachers, and the SGB working in cahoots with one another; in the other, the stakeholders were mired in endemic conflict.

A noteworthy implication of this last governance pattern is that there is no necessary one-to-one relationship between a particular configuration of school-level governance, and success or failure. Andrews, Pritchett, and Woolcock (2012) make a related point in underscoring that seeming compliance with external conceptions of 'good governance' can be a reflection of 'isomorphic mimicry'—of an effort to win validation from external actors, even as the way in which the relevant rules of the game are applied—and may in fact reproduce a low-level equilibrium.

What shapes the outcome for a specific school at a specific point in time is less the form of governance than the dynamics amongst stakeholders, specifically the relative balance between developmental and predatory influences. These stakeholder dynamics are not pre-ordained by either the broader local context or the strength of the education bureaucracy. They turn out to be contingent and cumulative, with individual agency by stakeholders playing a significant role. This raises the possibility that proactive interventions could potentially tilt the balance of threat-trumping interactions in some fraction of schools away from predatory and towards more developmental actors, with a positive impact on educational outcomes.

Before concluding our discussion of the school-level case studies, one final empirical finding is worthy of note. Going into the research, the expectation was that the largest teachers' union, SADTU, would play a significant role in shaping school-level dynamics, using its power to influence appointments, and to assert control more generally. We also expected to see evidence of political parties using the power of appointment for patronage purposes. While we did find a few instances of these problems, in general we found that, in both provinces, hyper-local school-level dynamics were decisive, and that, generally, these were only loosely linked to these broader forces. Though surprising, this finding is consistent with the observation of a seasoned scholar/practitioner of South African education, Nick Taylor (quoted in Jansen 2015) that:

> When I entered the National Education Evaluation Unit in South Africa's Department of Basic Education, I thought SADTU was a huge problem... But the more I got into the data... I began to realize that there is a bigger problem. The biggest problem is the poor management in many parts of the system. Where management is weak, unions do what they do...

Conclusion

As this chapter has shown, politics and institutions have had a substantial influence on education sector policymaking and implementation in South Africa, and thus on the country's educational outcomes. The pathways through which these influences have been felt are multiple and circuitous. Only for the broadest, foundational policies (e.g. universal access; intergovernmental delegation of authority) is it plausible to map causality directly from South Africa's early 1990s political settlement. Rather, the South Africa research suggests that contextually grounded explanations require a careful exploration of the distinctive features of the relevant policy domain (e.g. commitment to performance management), the relevant sector (e.g. education, where service provision is diffused across a large number of frontline providers), and the relevant locale (e.g. the Western and Eastern Cape provinces, and individual schools, each with distinctive dynamics).

For all of the evident complexity, the conclusion need not be the nihilistic one that every setting is unique, and thus that there is little to be learned in one context that is useful for policymaking and implementation in another. To illustrate, this concluding section suggests how the research findings might contribute to the long-standing debate amongst education sector scholars and practitioners as to what should be the right balance between hierarchical and horizontal approaches to the governance and accountability of the sector.

A central question explored by the research concerned the determinants of the capability of bureaucratic hierarchies. The results suggest that such capability is embedded in a complex system, comprising a variety of interdependent economic, demographic, political, and institutional variables/drivers. These interdependencies can result in a variety of distinct equilibria for bureaucracies, which can be difficult to change. In the Western Cape, the drivers were aligned in a way that sustained relatively strong bureaucratic capability. By contrast, in the Eastern Cape, the drivers were configured in a way that, in the absence of far-reaching broader political and institutional reforms, made the likelihood of bureaucratic improvement remote.

For horizontal governance, the SASA granted significant responsibility to SGBs. But its contribution potentially varies significantly between settings where hierarchy is strong, and settings where it is weak. In settings such as the Western Cape, where hierarchy is strong, the relevant questions concern the role of horizontal governance as a *complement*—providing support for tasks where there are inherent limitations to the efficacy of hierarchy. Conversely, in settings such as the Eastern Cape where hierarchy is weak, might horizontal governance plausibly be (at least in part) an institutional *substitute*—with local-, school- and community-level actors taking on, reasonably effectively, some tasks which might otherwise have been carried out bureaucratically? Both roles were evident in the school-level case studies; but so was capture, with the outcome dependent on the relative weight of developmental and predatory influences.

Insofar as stronger horizontal governance can indeed improve educational outcomes (either as complement or as substitute) how can it be strengthened? There is strikingly little to be learned on this score from within South Africa. Despite the central role given to SGBs in the 1996 South African Schools Act, there have been few efforts aimed at strengthening their performance. But there have been systematic evaluations in other developing countries of the impact of efforts to improve horizontal governance.

Bruns, Filmer, and Patrinos (2011) offer rich detail on dozens of carefully evaluated horizontal reforms, including reforms to improve school-based management, to enhance information transparency, and to make teachers more accountable for performance. They find considerable variations in impact; some interventions turn out to make a significant positive difference, others have been ineffective. The school-level case studies summarized in this chapter suggest that the success of such efforts depends not so much on 'capacity building' (which is technically straightforward) or on the specific accountability mechanisms introduced (World Bank 2003), but on power: whether intervention is able to tilt the balance between developmental and predatory school-level forces in favour of the former.

Indeed, the research findings laid out in this chapter suggest that, in the final analysis, stakeholder dynamics (that is, politics and power) are key to governance reform of both the hierarchical and horizontal variety. For hierarchical governance, incremental reforms to improve public management may perhaps make some modest difference, but far-reaching improvements in bureaucratic performance will be dependent on difficult-to-achieve supportive political circumstances. For horizontal reforms, the Eastern Cape school-level case studies suggest that, insofar as stakeholder dynamics at school level are hyper-local, there may be scope for interventions (either by government or by non-governmental organizations) that tilt the balance in at least some schools in a developmental direction.

Those seeking a 'magic bullet'—one right way to turn schools around—will doubtless be frustrated by the conclusion that there are multiple possible governance entry points for improving educational outcomes, and that the efficacy of any of them depends as much on politics and power as on the technocratic expertise of reformers. But there is an alternative interpretation, namely that uncovering institutional diversity and its political drivers expands opportunity, clarifying what might work across different settings, and thereby adding to possibilities for improving educational outcomes, even in contexts where governance is difficult.

References

Acemoglu, D., and J. Robinson. 2006. *Economic Origins of Dictatorship and Democracy*. New York: Cambridge University Press.

Aghion, P., and J. Tirole. 1997. 'Formal and Real Authority in Organizations'. *Journal of Political Economy*, 105(1): 1–29.

Andrews, M., L. Pritchett, and M. Woolcock. 2012. 'Escaping Capability Traps through Problem-Driven Iterative Adaptation'. Working Paper 299. Washington, DC: Center for Global Development.

Bruns, B., D. Filmer, and H. Patrinos. 2011. 'Making Schools Work: New Evidence on Accountability Reforms'. Washington, DC: World Bank.

Cameron, R., and B. Levy. 2018. 'Provincial Governance of Education—The Western Cape Experience'. In *The Politics and Governance of Basic Education: A Tale of Two South African Provinces*. Edited by Levy, B., R. Cameron, U. Hoadley, and V. Naidoo. Chapter 4. Oxford: Oxford University Press.

Cameron, R., and V. Naidoo. 2018. 'Education Policymaking at National Level—The Politics of Multiple Principals'. In *The Politics and Governance of Basic Education: A Tale of Two South African Provinces*. Edited by Levy, B., R. Cameron, U. Hoadley, and V. Naidoo. Chapter 3. Oxford: Oxford University Press.

Crouch, L., and U. Hoadley. 2018. 'The Transformation of South Africa's System of Basic Education' Principals'. In *The Politics and Governance of Basic Education: A Tale of Two South African Provinces*. Edited by Levy, B., R. Cameron, U. Hoadley, and V. Naidoo. Chapter 2. Oxford: Oxford University Press.

Fiske, E. B., and H. F. Ladd. 2004. *Education Reform in Post-Apartheid South Africa*. Washington, DC: Brookings Institution Press.

Fukuyama, F. 2014. *Political Order and Political Decay*. New York: Farrar, Straus, and Giroux.

George, A., and A. Bennett. 2005. *Case Studies and Theory Development in the Social Sciences*. Cambridge, MA: MIT Press.

Hallinger, P., and R. H. Heck. 1996. 'Reassessing the Principal's Role in School Effectiveness: A Review of Empirical Research, 1980–1995'. *Educational Administration Quarterly*, 32(1): 5–44.

Hoadley, U., B. Levy, L. Shumane, and S. Wilburn. 2018. 'Case Studies of School-Level Governance Dynamics in the Western Cape'. In *The Politics and Governance of Basic Education: A Tale of Two South African Provinces*. Edited by Levy, B., R. Cameron, U. Hoadley, and V. Naidoo. Chapter 8. Oxford: Oxford University Press.

Huntington, S. 1968. *Political Order in Changing Societies*. New Haven, CT: Yale University Press.

Jansen, L. 2015. 'SADTU Exploits Culture of Chaos'. IOL News. 19 August 2015.

Keefer, P., and S. Khemani. 2005. 'Democracy, Public Expenditures and the Poor: Understanding Political Incentives for Providing Public Services'. *World Bank Research Observer*, 20(1): 1–27.

Kelsall, T., and M. vom Hau. 2017. 'Beyond Institutions: A Political Settlements Approach to Development'. University of Manchester. (Mimeo).

Khan, M., and Jomo, K. S. 2000. *Rents, Rent-seeking and Economic Development: Theory and Evidence in Asia*. New York: Cambridge University Press.

Khemani, S. 2016. 'Making Politics Work for Development. A World Bank Policy Research Report'. Washington, DC: International Bank for Reconstruction and Development.

Kota, Z., M. Hendricks, E. Matambo, and V. Naidoo. 2018. 'Provincial Governance of Education—The Eastern Cape Experience'. In *The Politics and Governance of Basic Education: A Tale of Two South African Provinces*. Edited by Levy, B., R. Cameron, U. Hoadley, and V. Naidoo. Chapter 5. Oxford: Oxford University Press.

Leithwood, K., S. Patten, and D. Jantzi. 2010. 'Testing a Conception of How School Leadership Influences Student Learning'. *Educational Administration Quarterly*, 44(4): 455–7.

Levy, B. 2014. *Working with the Grain: Integrating Governance and Growth in Development Strategies*. New York: Oxford University Press.

Levy, B. 2018. 'All for Education—Meeting the Governance Challenge'. In *The Politics and Governance of Basic Education: A Tale of Two South African Provinces*. Edited by Levy, B., R. Cameron, U. Hoadley, and V. Naidoo. Chapter 10. Oxford: Oxford University Press.

Levy, B. and Shumane, L. 2018. 'Case Studies of School-Level Governance Dynamics in the Eastern Cape'. In *The Politics and Governance of Basic Education: A Tale of Two South African Provinces*. Edited by Levy, B., R. Cameron, U. Hoadley, and V. Naidoo. Chapter 9. Oxford: Oxford University Press.

Levy, B., R. Cameron, U. Hoadley, and V. Naidoo (eds.). 2018a. *The Politics and Governance of Basic Education: A Tale of Two South African Provinces*. Oxford: Oxford University Press.

Levy, B., R. Cameron, and V. Naidoo. 2018b. 'Context and Capability: A Tale of Two Bureaucracies'. In *The Politics and Governance of Basic Education: A Tale of Two South African Provinces*. Edited by Levy, B., R. Cameron, U. Hoadley, and V. Naidoo. Chapter 7. Oxford: Oxford University Press.

Levy, B., A. Hirsch, and I. Woolard. 2015. 'Governance and Inequality: Benchmarking and Interpreting South Africa's Evolving Political Settlement'. ESID Working Paper 51. Manchester: Effective States and Inclusive Development Research Centre, The University of Manchester.

Lipset, S. 1959. 'Some Social Requisites of Democracy: Economic Development and Political Legitimacy'. *American Political Science Review*, 53(1): 69–105.

Lipsky, M. 2010. *Street-level Bureaucracy: Dilemmas of the Individual in Public Service*. New York: Russell Sage Foundation.

Lodge, T. 2014. 'Neo-Patrimonial Politics in the ANC'. *African Affairs*, 113(450): 1–23.

MacDonald, M. 2006. *Why Race Matters in South Africa*. Cambridge, MA: Harvard University Press.

Mandela, N. 1994. *Long Walk to Freedom*. Johannesburg: Macdonald Purnell.

Marais, H. 1998. *South Africa: Limits to Change: The Political Economy of Transition*. London and Cape Town: Zed Books and University of Cape Town Press.

Mbeki, M. 2009. *Architects of Poverty: Why African Capitalism Needs Changing*. Johannesburg: Picador Africa.

McLennan, A., and P. Fitzgerald. (eds.). 1992. *The Mount Grace Papers: The New Public Administration Initiative and the Mount Grace Consultation*. Johannesburg: Public and Development Management Programme, University of Witwatersrand.

Moore, B. 1966. *The Social Origins of Dictatorship and Democracy*. Boston, MA: Beacon Press.

Sah, R. K., and J. E. Stiglitz. 1986. 'The Architecture of Economic Systems: Hierarchies and Polyarchies'. *American Economic Review*, 76(4): 716–27.

Schotte, S., R. Zizzamia, and M. Leibbrandt. 2017. 'Social Stratification, Life Chances and Vulnerability to Poverty in South Africa'. SALDRU Working Paper 208. Southern Africa Labour and Development Research Unit, University of Cape Town.

Schwella, E. 2000. 'Paradigms: Context and Competencies'. In *The State of Public and Development Management in South Africa. The Mount Grace II Papers*. Edited by Theron, F., and E. Schwella, 33–43. Stellenbosch: University of Stellenbosch.

Scott, J. 1998. *Seeing Like a State*. New Haven, CT: Yale University Press.

Seekings, J., and N. Nattrass. 2005. *Race, Class and Inequality in South Africa*. New Haven, CT: Yale University Press.

Seekings, J., and N. Nattrass. 2015. *Policy, Politics and Poverty in South Africa*. New York: Palgrave Macmillan.

South Africa, The Presidency. 2012. 'Management Performance Assessment Tool (MPAT). Report on Results of Assessment Process for 2011/2012'. Pretoria: Department of Performance Monitoring and Evaluation.

Southall, R. 2014. 'From Liberation Movement to Party Machine? The ANC in South Africa'. *Journal of Contemporary African Studies*, 32(3): 331–48.

Sparks, A. 1996. *Tomorrow is Another Country: The Inside Story of South Africa's Road to Change*. Chicago, IL: University of Chicago Press.

Streek, B., and R. Wickstead. 1981. *Render unto Kaiser: A Transkei Dossier*. Johannesburg: Ravan Press.

Welsh, D. 2009. *The Rise and Fall of Apartheid*. Charlottesville, VA: University of Virginia Press.

Wills, G., D. Shepherd, and J. Kotze. 2018. 'Explaining the Western Cape Performance Paradox: An Econometric Analysis'. In *The Politics and Governance of Basic Education: A Tale of Two South African Provinces*. Edited by Levy, B., R. Cameron, U. Hoadley, and V. Naidoo. Chapter 6. Oxford: Oxford University Press.

Wilson, J. Q. 1989. *Bureaucracy: What Government Agencies Do and Why They Do It*. New York: Basic Books.

World Bank. 2003. 'Making Services Work for Poor People: World Development Report 2004'. Washington, DC: World Bank.

7

The Political Economy of Primary Education Reform in Cambodia

Tim Kelsall, Sothy Khieng, Chuong Chantha, and Tieng Tek Muy

Introduction

In August 2014, Cambodian students up and down the country sat for their grade 12 national exit exams. Unlike in previous years, elaborate measures had been taken to ensure that exam questions were not leaked by education officials, students were frisked for mobile phones, calculators, or other cheating aids by thousands of volunteers, and, in some cases, exam halls and papers were protected by armed Anti-Corruption Unit guards.[1] One student summed up the situation with the statement, 'It's damn strict this year' (Brehm 2014) (NE2,[2] TTCA). When the exams were graded, it transpired that of the 75,000 students who sat them, a mere 26 per cent had passed—a striking contrast to the 87 per cent that had passed the previous year (Ponniah and Heng 2014).[3] Dismal though they were, these results came as little surprise to experts on Cambodia's education, since they reflect a system which, while successful in building infrastructure and getting large numbers of children into school, has been less adept at delivering educational quality.

The exam reforms were the brainchild of Dr Hang Chuon Naron, a new Education Minister with the mandate to shake up the sector and deliver

[1] In fact, there was also a clampdown on cheating in 2002, which also saw a dramatic decline in the pass rate. However, subsequent years saw a return to cheating as normal (Brehm 2014).

[2] Interviews are referenced throughout this chapter according to the following codes: EA: Expatriate advisor; FG: Focus group; NGO: Non-governmental organization; IS: International scholar; NE: National expert; NM: National Ministry of Education Youth and Sport official; TTCA: Teacher Training College Province A.

[3] Following protests from higher education institutions, failing students were given a second chance to sit exams in October. However, regulations were again strictly enforced, and the failure rate was 82.06 per cent (Barron 2014a).

tangible results prior to the birth of the Association of South East Asian Nations (ASEAN) Economic Community in 2015, and to what were expected to be hard-fought general elections in 2018. He explained them as both a tool for diagnosing the ills of the sector, and as one part of a wide-ranging reform agenda (Barron 2014b). In this chapter, we delve into the politics of the reforms, applying a 'political settlements' and domains of power approach to explain, retrospectively, how Cambodia's political settlement has conditioned the emergence of an education system that focuses on quantity rather than quality, and, prospectively, to help us assess the prospects for reform.

We describe the contemporary Cambodian political settlement as weakly dominant and personalized (see also Chapter 2), though with some pockets of rule-governed behaviour. This provides a set of opportunities and constraints for education reformers. Weak dominance provides some potential to impose top-down reform on the sector and to persist with this over a relatively long time-horizon. However, personalization implies that bureaucratic sophistication will be low, and that changes in rules and regulations may be weakly adhered to. However, if we are to understand the trajectory of reform in detail, we must delve into the internal politics of the policy domain, its organizational culture, ideas, and interests, and assess the potential for the emergence of coalitions that can create pockets of effectiveness dedicated to improving quality.

The chapter is based on a review of secondary literature and official documents, one focus group with national NGOs and expatriate advisors, and twenty-five national-level interviews.[4] It begins by describing the politics of primary education up to 2013, incorporating a discussion of the commitment to quality, or lack thereof, and the political settlement and policy domain dynamics that underlie this. It then proceeds to the present period, examining, amongst other things, concerns around teacher quality and the government's new Teacher Policy Action Plan. It suggests that the odds are stacked against Cambodia successfully implementing far-reaching quality-enhancing reforms in the relatively short timeframe it has set itself; however, with persistent political will, and civil society and donor support, the chances of success over the longer term are better.

The Politics of Education Policy in Cambodia

Cambodia has had two basic types of political settlement since independence and several political regimes, each of which has provided a distinct flavour to its education policy. Whether dominant or competitive, however, all of these

[4] Fieldwork took place in 2014 and 2015, with the findings updated for the current period by means of a document review.

regimes and each of these settlements have been based on a personalized elite bargain with rather low bureaucratic capacity and complexity. Each has been interested in rapidly expanding access to education, and rather less interested in, or at least less able to promote, educational quality. Due to a combination of external and internal pressures, that is now beginning to change—but the predominantly personalized nature of Cambodia's political settlement means that reform champions still face an uphill struggle.

Sihanouk Dominant (1953–70)

The story starts in 1953, when Cambodia gained independence from France under the leadership of Prince Norodom Sihanouk. Driven by a vainglorious desire to mimic the greatness of Angkor, together with an attempt to earn popular legitimacy with a peasantry that associated education with an escape from rural poverty, Sihanouk quickly embarked on a massive expansion in educational provision. There were rapid moves to introduce universal primary education, universal secondary education, and a higher education system that was the envy of other states in the region (Ayres 2000). Sihanouk consistently interfered with the policies of the ministry, overriding its technocratic approach in favour of grand political gestures (Ayres 2000). The result was that 'schools were poorly constructed, teachers hastily trained, too many students were crammed into classrooms, and teaching facilities and materials were inadequate' (Ayres 2000, 63).

The failure of Sihanouk's educational and economic policies fuelled opposition to his regime, and in 1970 he was overthrown in a coup. For the next five years, civil war raged, and Cambodia cannot really be said to have had a 'political settlement' at all. In 1975, the Maoist Khmer Rouge overthrew the regime and imposed a new order under the name of Democratic Kampuchea.

Khmer Rouge Dominant (1975–9)

The Khmer Rouge, reacting in part to the excesses of Sihanoukism, had an entirely different educational vision. According to Pol Pot, its leader, 'there are no schools, faculties, or universities in the traditional sense... because we want to do away with all vestiges of the past' (Ayres 2000, 104). Teachers were forced to flee the country or were killed, school buildings were used as cattle sheds or go-downs, while whatever education that took place—much of it teaching revolutionary slogans through song and dance (Sloper 1999)—was entrusted to untrained 'base people' (Ayres 2000).[5]

[5] 'Base people' were defined by the Khmer Rouge as those who joined the 'Revolution', viz. the fight against the Republic, prior to 1975.

Kampuchean People's Revolutionary Party Dominant (1979–89)

By the time the Vietnamese-backed Kampuchean People's Revolutionary Party (KPRP) overthrew the Khmer Rouge in 1979, the education system was practically non-existent (NM5). The KPRP vigorously rebuilt it, but, once again, quality was not the main concern. According to Ayres, 'education was seen as a primary tool for state building and establishing legitimacy' (Ayres 2000, 135), and, in the eyes of Vietnamese advisors, that meant building a nation of 'new socialist workmen', by placing as many students as possible in schools as quickly as possible (Ayres 2000, 128). A key obstacle when it came to improving educational quality remained the nation's teaching corps, who were 'very poorly trained and poorly remunerated' (Ayres 2000, 143); teacher-training colleges were desperately short of materials, while many teachers at provincial teacher-training colleges were unfit to be teachers themselves (Ayres 2000, 143).

Moreover, these efforts were proceeding in a context of state building on a shoestring. When it came to power, the KPRP was bereft of Western support, and highly vulnerable to revanchist assaults from the Khmer Rouge and other rebel forces. The most urgent need was to establish a network of supporters, who would act as a bulwark against ongoing insurgency. Consequently, there was a drive to recruit functionaries to the new state. But with the formal economy in ruins, and formal revenue-raising powers weak, the new political settlement was built on the understanding that, in addition to their meagre salaries, new recruits could use their positions to extract rents. By controlling access to the most lucrative of these, while turning a blind eye to petty rent-scraping, the leadership was able to build a patronage-based state (Gottesman 2004). As in most patronage systems, loyalty was more important than competence—a trend compounded, no doubt, by the fact that many former, competent officials had either fled or been murdered by the Khmer Rouge. Consequently, most ministries were staffed by poorly qualified, underpaid staff, who understandably expended as much energy moonlighting or extracting rents as they did pursuing official government policies, establishing a legacy that Cambodia has yet to fully escape.

Competitive Power Sharing (1991–8)

In 1989, the Vietnamese withdrew from Cambodia, opening the door to a peace accord in 1991, multi-party elections in 1993, a power-sharing government, and increased involvement in the education sector by international donors (Sloper 1999). Initially, donors' experience was a frustrating one. National administrators had no idea of how to construct plans or budgets, and, according to one observer, 'it was common to see education ministry staff playing *boules* in the ministry yard, gossiping at their desks and departing early for lack of any clear idea of what to do in the office' (McNamara 2013, 24). Capacity, nevertheless, was gradually built, and the sector attracted substantial donor funds (McNamara 1999; Sloper 1999). It was less successful in attracting government money, languishing at around 10 per cent of total spending. And, while most donor attention went into trying to improve quality, the government focused its own resources on infrastructural expansion (McNamara 1999, 100–01).

The background to this was that the KPRP, renamed the Cambodian People's Party (CPP), now found itself in competition with a deadly enemy—the royalist party, *Front Uni National pour un Cambodge Indépendant Neutre Pacifique et Coopératif* (FUNCINPEC)—for control of the state, in which they both held offices, courtesy of the UN-brokered power-sharing arrangement. The size of the civil service ballooned, as each party attempted to appoint its own loyalists (McNamara 1999; Roberts 2001). A large portion of the resources reaching education went to populist measures, such as increasing teacher salaries and school infrastructure. Reports from the field mention 'attractive new buildings without equipment or competent teaching staff' (McNamara 1999, 101), a not uncommon feature of competitive clientelist regimes.

CPP Dominant, 1998–2013

After vanquishing FUNCINPEC in a bloody contest in 1997, and finally defeating the Khmer Rouge in 1998, Prime Minister Hun Sen was finally able to consolidate his political settlement (see Figure 7.1). It is based on a dominant coalition, comprising local tycoons (often awarded the honorific *oknha*), foreign investors, military men, selected technocrats, and international donors. Under its informal terms, technocrats and foreign investors have created the conditions for jobs and growth; business cronies and the military have made rents from concessions and contracts; and international donors have provided technical advice and supported the budget, particularly in the social sectors.

This settlement, it should be noted, is an evolution, not a displacement of, the state-building process initiated in the 1980s, the main difference being that Western and multilateral donors have grown in importance relative to the Vietnamese, and liberal democracy (despite de facto CPP dominance) has replaced state socialism as the official ideology. It is still based on a predominantly personalistic bargain between members of the elite and lower-level cadres, though with some pockets of bureaucratic effectiveness, especially in the economic ministries. The compliance of subordinate groups—and electoral victories—is secured through a mixture of ideology (the CPP takes credit for defeating the Khmer Rouge), patronage (a portion of the dominant coalition's rents is channelled to the masses in the form of roads, schools, etc.),

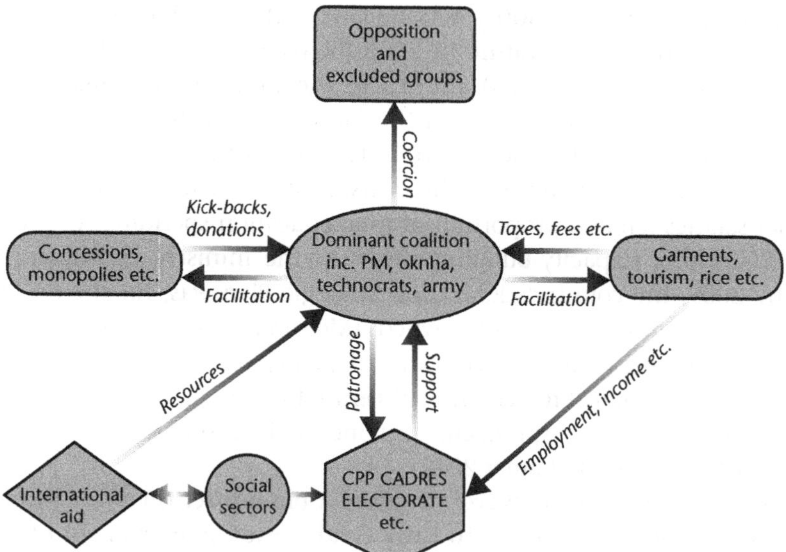

Figure 7.1 Cambodia's political settlement, 1998–2013

programmatic policy (as with some of the donor-supported initiatives in education and health) and coercion (dissenters rapidly incur the wrath of the security forces) (Craig and Pak 2011; Hughes and Conway 2003; Hughes and Un 2011; Kelsall and Heng 2014; Kelsall and Heng 2016; Pak 2011; Un 2005). But the patronage-based nature of the state has not been radically overhauled.

In the introduction to this chapter we described the settlement as 'weakly dominant'. Evidence for this is that, despite the CPP's consistent ability to win elections and the undoubted pre-eminence of Hun Sen within his own party, the Prime Minister has always taken great care to balance CPP factions. Until recently it has been rare for ministers or other high-ranking officials to be sacked, or even reshuffled, and in areas such as land-grabbing and forest exploitation, the Prime Minister seems to tolerate behaviour that he recognizes is not ideal. The Prime Minister, himself a former Khmer Rouge commander, was politically schooled in an era when the Khmer Rouge fatally weakened itself in intra-party factional struggle and paranoid purges, and his unwillingness to discipline other high-ranking members of the elite stems perhaps from this.

The CPP-dominated settlement coincided with a period of increasing alignment between the party's desire for popular legitimacy, and donor efforts to expand education access under the Education for All initiative and the Millennium Development Goals. As such, the revenue situation in education improved markedly after 2000, with more funds channelled to the sector under the government's Priority Action Plan (reaching a high of 19 per cent of budgeted recurrent expenditure in 2006 [Benveniste, Marshall, and Araujo 2008, 4, 60]).[6] Between 2000 and 2014, the number of primary schools increased from 5,468 to 6,993, and the number of teachers from 45,152 to 55,958 (MoEYS 2014; UNESCO 2010).[7] The amount of training received by teachers increased steadily over the years, as did teacher salaries (although teacher salaries fell as a proportion of total education spending) (Benveniste et al. 2008, 67). Capacity-building efforts in the ministry continued, such that by 2009, the country's Education Strategic Plan was, for the first time, said to be genuinely 'nationally owned' (McNamara 2013). There were also numerous schemes to improve educational quality, for example the Education Quality Improvement Project, student-centred learning, cluster schools, the Child Friendly School Approach, and life skills curriculum development (Benveniste et al. 2008; Reimer 2012).

These schemes failed, however, to make a big impact on overall learning outcomes. For example, the 2010 Early Grade Reading Assessment of grades 1–6 found that 33 per cent of children could not read, and that 47 per cent of those who could had difficulty comprehending what they had read. A recent impact evaluation found that grade 9 schoolchildren performed no better in maths and vocabulary than children who were not in school (cited in Tandon and Fukao 2015, 1). The aforementioned grade 12 exam results show that problems continue throughout the system, and, indeed, many investors in Cambodia complain of a poorly educated workforce seriously deficient in generic employment skills (Barron 2014b; Madhur 2014).

One possible explanation is that quality-focused initiatives have received little political commitment. Ayres, writing in 2000, claimed that the Prime Minister was, apparently, 'unconcerned about the finer details of educational quality and relevance' (Ayres 2000, 190), while a long-term observer writes, 'National leader initiatives . . . are driven by political motives, uninformed by the technical considerations underlying the effectiveness of the institutions of a modern state' (McNamara 1999, 101).

Disentangling the degree to which this can be attributed to Cambodia's political settlement type, and the extent to which it is more to do with sui generis features of Cambodian history, is not an easy matter. One could argue that the CPP's dominance should have provided the political leadership with the space to plan a more rational education policy, in which the demands of access and quality were better balanced; and that its failure to do so is thus a

[6] The actual spend may have been lower (IS1).

[7] Note that owing to 'a surge in demand', the expansion in secondary education, which started from a very low base, has been even more rapid than that for primary education (Benveniste et al. 2008).

result of misguided ideas about education, or personal failings on the part of its leaders. At the same time, the CPP has only ever been weakly dominant, constrained by relatively strong factions within its own party, and fearful of a resurgent opposition, meaning that the desire to cater to popular aspirations around access is understandable. Moreover, the predominantly personalized nature of the settlement would have made implementing a learning agenda challenging, even in the presence of a political desire to do so. The government consequently put more energy into outcomes that were easily achievable and earned the most political capital (NM5). In this, it was aided and abetted by donors, for whom expanding access was at least as important as improving quality, at least in the first decade of the twenty-first century.[8]

Improving school infrastructure and access arguably paid political dividends in the short term. On the campaign trail, Hun Sen was known to fly around the country by helicopter, describing the CPP as a 'superpower' when it came to building schools (Ayres 2000, 180). In addition to donor money, many were built with political contributions from well-connected businessmen, and bore the Prime Minister's name.[9] Between 1998 and 2013, the CPP recorded three successive election victories, the last one, in 2008, comfortable. But in the longer term, the disproportionate emphasis on access to education has created problems, by contributing to social changes that threaten to undermine CPP dominance. In 2013, the opposition Cambodian National Rescue Party ran the CPP extremely close in national general elections. Sustained protests and demonstrations followed, in which the opposition claimed that the CPP had rigged the election and called for Hun Sen to resign. Worryingly for the ruling party, it appeared particularly unpopular amongst young people—an increasingly large and influential section of the electorate—many of whom had graduated through the education system, but had been unable to find the kinds of jobs to which they aspired (*Cambodia Daily* 2013).

Impending ASEAN economic integration has amplified educational concerns. As of the end of 2015, ASEAN nationals were theoretically able to take jobs in Cambodia, with Cambodians able to take jobs elsewhere. Given Cambodia's lagging educational status, the former appears much more likely than the latter, especially when it comes to well-paid, professional jobs. Further tightening of an already straitened labour market for Cambodian graduates is

[8] Un (2012) argues that, although educational attainment in Cambodia remains poor, it has nevertheless marginally improved, despite massively expanded access. This distinguishes it from some other expanded access countries, for example Uganda. Un explains this by reference to Cambodia's greater centralization and more effective control of rent-seeking. Our take on this would be that although Cambodia and Uganda are both weakly dominant settlements, Uganda's is weaker.

[9] As of February 2017, 3,932 schools had been supported by the Prime Minister and his wife (MoEYS 2013, 16).

bound to have negative consequences for the ruling party. Concerns about educational quality have also been voiced by employers and business associations (Kotoski 2015; *Global Times* 2013). The response has been an increased interest in adopting ASEAN educational norms, for instance a 12 + 4 teacher-training system, as we will see (FG1, NM1, NM5, EA10).

In September 2013, the Prime Minister announced a cabinet reshuffle, prominent in which was the appointment of Dr Hang Chuon Naron to the education portfolio. Naron is a well-respected scholar, economist, technocrat, and trusted advisor to Hun Sen. Previously he had worked at the Ministry of Economy and Finance, and at the Supreme National Economic Council, the government's economic thinktank. His appointment to the education portfolio was interpreted as a sign that the Prime Minister recognized that a new approach to the sector was needed (FG1, NGO3, NM1). It can also be seen as part of a wider attempt to shift the political settlement away from its patronage roots and towards more programmatic, higher-quality, public goods provision (a move that is apparent in the domain of health as well as education, see Kelsall and Heng 2016), which at least some high-ranking CPP stalwarts now consider necessary.

The Politics of Cambodia's Education Domain, 1998–2013

A more granular understanding of the political economy of educational outcomes in the period 1998–2013 can be gained by examining the policy domain of education itself, as illustrated in Figure 7.2.[10] The main 'policymaking actors' are coloured in white, with the main 'implementing actors' in grey.

In the inner circle of power are the Minister (a post held during this period by Tol Lah, Kol Pheng, and Im Sethy), and the most powerful Secretary of State (whom we will call SOS A). SOS A began his professional life in the teacher-training department, where he still retains his strongest power base, working his way up the hierarchy over time. Observers attributed his rise to being in the right place at the right time when the Education for All and Child Friendly Schools policies were introduced, demonstrating his competence to development partners, and subsequently being chosen by the Minister to handle donor relations. He has since amassed an enormous portfolio of responsibilities and undoubtedly has the largest patronage base in the Ministry (EA6, EA7). Also

[10] The diagram is the result of a 'political settlements mapping' exercise, carried out amongst education NGOs, development partners, and CDRI (Cambodia Development Research Institute) researchers, held at the CDRI in January 2015. The mapping exercise used a tool adapted by Effective States and Inclusive Development Research Centre (ESID) from Parks and Cole (2010).

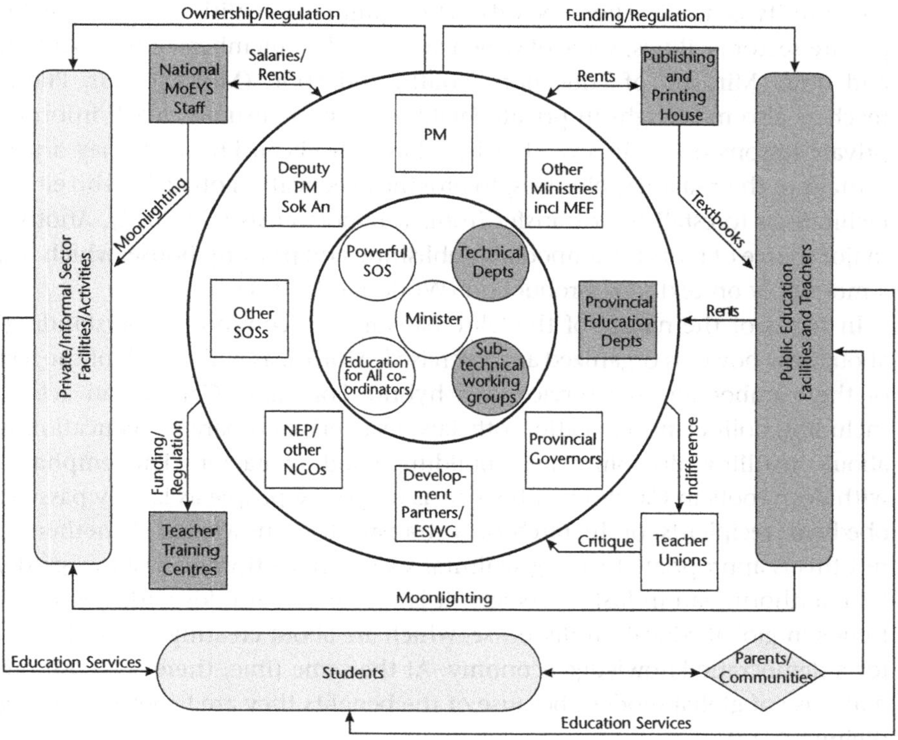

Figure 7.2 Politics of Cambodia's education domain, as of 2013

present are the Education for All coordinators (who worked closely with SOS A), the technical departments (with primary implementing responsibility), and the sub-technical working groups.

In the outer circle of power are the Prime Minister the late Deputy Prime Minister other ministries for whom education policies have implications, in particular the Ministry of Economy and Finance (MEF), more junior secretaries of state, provincial governors, and provincial departments of education, development partners—the most important of whom, such as UNICEF, UNESCO, JICA, Sida, and the World Bank, sit on the Education Sector Working Group—and NGOs, the most influential being, perhaps, the umbrella group, NGO Education Partnership. Teacher associations, both pro- and anti-CPP, exist, but they are forbidden to strike and are not particularly influential (CITA 2012; see also CITA 2013; Pereira 2014).

Between them, members of the dominant coalition fund, regulate, and try to improve the public education facilities that supply education services to teacher trainees and students, and are monitored, to some extent, by community-centred school boards. The dominant coalition also regulates private-sector facilities, some of which are owned by members of the coalition and other Ministry of Education, Youth, and Sport (MoEYS) staff. Public teachers also moonlight in private facilities or, more usually, teach informal private lessons on their own. Teachers have also been known to pay a percentage of their salaries, plus fees, to provincial education officials, who either facilitate or forestall their transfer from/to remote areas (Un 2012). Another major source of rents is Cambodia's publishing and printing house, which has a monopoly on textbook production (World Bank 2011).

In terms of the nature of the 'elite bargain', or 'common understanding' about how power is organized and exercised, MoEYS, as with much of the rest of the Cambodian civil service, is a hybrid. For many Cambodian actors, including politicians, education officials, teachers, and parents, education is about instilling discipline and building good character. The emphasis, with deep roots in Cambodian history, is on young people as largely passive, obedient recipients of hierarchically transmitted knowledge. Whether or not this is appropriate to an agricultural society transitioning to a low-grade, semi-authoritarian industrial society, it is very much at odds with dominant trends in global education discourse, which are about creating active citizens for a democratic knowledge economy. At the same time, there is a desire to make use of global models, because of the benefits they are believed to bring (Reimer 2012).

Administration is also of a mixed type. Although efforts have been made over the past twenty years to increase professionalism, some of which have undoubtedly borne fruit (McNamara 2013), much of the Ministry still runs on personalized, clientelistic, rather than legal-rational lines. At the local level, meanwhile, many senior officials are said to have paid hefty bribes to obtain their positions, and are thus dependent on illicit revenue streams from practices such as exam cheating and re-stationing teachers from remote areas, to recoup their investments (Un 2012, 110–47) (EA1, NE6, NGO3).

Development partners do try to make a difference to this scenario, with various projects to build capacity around either general or specific programmatic goals. However, the typical capacity-building intervention involves a set of lofty ambitions operationalized through a series of workshops or trainings, often held at attractive venues outside the capital. MoEYS officials often welcome these initiatives with open arms, since they bring resources into the ministry, fuel patronage networks, and can, to some extent, be skimmed. And while it would be unfair to say such trainings are useless, they usually fall well short of their aims, since most trainees fail to apply what they have been taught to their daily duties (EA2, EA4, NGO7). A 2002 study, for example, could find no relation between in-service training and classroom outcomes, describing most programmes as, 'short, irrelevant, irregular and conducted in a cascade system' (Chhinh and Tabata 2002).[11] Neither donors nor the government have shown much commitment to ensuring more effective forms of knowledge transfer.

Put differently, the ethos of the ministry, to quote one informant, 'is activities rather than outcomes based' (EA2). Many development partners recognize this but have, by and large, failed to find more successful ways of working.[12] Matters are not helped by donor fragmentation (only partially alleviated by coordinating bodies such as the Education Sector Working Group), and the tendency of most development agency staff to work on programmes and contracts that are only two to three years long (EA1, EA2, EA4). A report from the turn of the millennium commented that lack of coordination between donors created confusion in schools (Care International 1999).

Child Friendly Schools

Many of these trends are exemplified by the Child Friendly Schools (CFS) approach, which is an international initiative, promoted primarily by UNICEF, as a 'pathway to educational quality'. In Cambodia, CFS was piloted by UNICEF, Sida, SC-Norway and local partners in several provinces in the early 2000s. Based on these pilots' apparent success, it became national policy in 2007, with enthusiastic support from MoEYS and the World Bank. Amongst its objectives, CFS promotes child-friendly schools, effective learning, and the participation of children, families, and communities (Reimer 2012).

Evidence suggests, however, that inculcating a genuinely child-friendly approach has been challenging. For example, teachers have sometimes been found to have child-friendly lesson plans, which they can teach in the presence of inspectors, but which they rarely use for normal classes. Group work is used frequently, but mainly as a means of giving the teacher a rest. Teachers realize that corporal punishment is banned, though they still sometimes use it, while others resort to shaming practices instead. Gender equality is acknowledged as an ideal, but there is little attempt to challenge traditional gender roles, or to ensure that girls stay in school (Reimer 2012). While it has been adopted at a policy level, its key tenets—alien to dominant currents in Cambodian culture and education—have not been internalized at a practiec level, despite the expenditure of significant resources and technical support.

[11] Cited in McNamara (2013).

[12] An apparently successful capacity-building initiative around the Education for All initiative is detailed in Benveniste et al. (2008).

Its reasons for adoption, then, bear many of the hallmarks of what has elsewhere been called, 'isomorphic mimicry' (Andrews 2013):

> First, there is widespread recognition that the Cambodian public education system is of low quality and something must be done—no local options have presented themselves, so an international model is adopted. Second, CFS comes with significant funding resources and technical advice. Third, Cambodians are very conscious of wanting to appear competent on the regional and global stage and do not want to be regarded as 'backward' and 'not modern'. (Reimer 2012, 422)

A high-ranking Cambodian official admitted to us that the policy has been most successful in improving school environments ('Easy to do; easy to see'), less so in promoting effective learning ('Easy to say; very hard to do!') (NM5). In 2008, a statistical study found that the effects of CFS were inconclusive, with the overall 'flavour' suggesting that CFS 'has not had an impact on student learning' (Reimer 2012, 311).

Teacher Quality in Cambodia

At the root of many of Cambodia's educational problems is the poor quality of teaching, which has long been a subject of concern. As we saw earlier, teacher salaries have increased throughout the 1990s and 2000s. Nevertheless, in 2008 a major report from the World Bank found that teachers were still underpaid (Benveniste et al. 2008, 40). Although the quality of teaching had improved over the years, thanks to increases in the entry requirements for teachers, the length of time spent in teacher training, and programmes to encourage 'life skills' and 'Child Friendly' pedagogy, classroom observations suggested that most teaching remained 'frontal' and focused on 'rote learning': 'overall, the picture that emerges is a teacher-centred classroom where students basically receive information and prompting but are not themselves active partners in the learning' (Benveniste et al. 2008, 72, 75). Further, many teachers, especially older ones, lacked 'pedagogical content knowledge', with the result that they were unable correctly to diagnose and respond to student errors (Benveniste et al. 2008, 77). These findings suggested that, whatever improvements recent decades had seen, problems with pre-service and in-service training remained. Monitoring of teacher performance also left much to be desired, being organized around, 'a bureaucratic (external), low stakes accountability mechanism' (Benveniste et al. 2008, 82). Further, few incentives were offered for teachers to improve the quality of their teaching, since they faced a highly compressed salary structure, and the bonuses and performance-related incentives that did exist seemed not to be linked in any systematic way to performance in the classroom (Benveniste et al. 2008, 98). In response, the authors of the report urged the adoption of a 'Teacher Standards Framework', incorporating a range of teacher competencies tied to behaviours linked to student learning, which could be observed and evaluated (Benveniste et al. 2008, 100).

Since the 2008 report was written, base salaries continued to rise at the rate of 15–20 per cent a year (Pereira 2014), and the teaching workforce continued to expand. However, many of the problems identified in 2008 proved persistent. A 2015 World Bank study found that, on average, teachers earned only 60 per cent of what other professionals earned, and that a typical teacher, married, with a two-person family, found themself below the poverty line. The profession continued to fail to attract the most talented students, with the majority of teacher trainees having scored C, D, or E on their grade 12 exams, and private tutoring was still rampant (Tandon and Fukao 2015). Other research found teachers were unable or unwilling to teach the full curriculum during normal school hours, thereby driving students to take extra lessons (Un 2012). Typically, poorer students cannot afford these, and do less well in exams as a result (Brehm and Silova 2014).

Teacher training continued to require a significant overhaul (Tandon and Fukao 2015). Monitoring also remained an issue. Schools were supposed to be monitored by officials at district and provincial level, but evidence suggested that such officials, although they sometimes visited schools, rarely observed what was going on in the classroom. Teachers were also eligible for a number of performance-related bonuses, but respondents felt that these were small, and unrelated to good teaching practice (Tandon and Fukao 2015).

Interestingly, the Teacher Standards that were recommended by the 2008 report, piloted, and adopted as national policy in 2010, were in many cases ignored. Many teacher trainers, teachers, and principals had not heard of them, and many of those that had did not use them. Consequently, they were rarely incorporated into lesson plans, or used as a basis for monitoring and evaluation (Tandon and Fukao 2015). Although at one stage they had the enthusiastic backing of both donors and SOS A, it seems that ultimately they were not given sufficient political backing or resources to prioritize their introduction in TTCs and schools.

As we have seen, the quality agenda within the education policy domain received new impetus with the appointment of a new Minister in 2013. On coming to office, Dr Naron made a number of changes signifying the seriousness of the reform effort. Into the inner circle of power he brought a new actor, the newly created Education Research Council (ERC). The ERC comprises, on one side, educational specialists from the university and civil society, and on the other, ministerial staff, especially secretaries of state. The aim, apparently, is to inject fresh ideas into the Ministry, create a capacity for evidence-based research, and to provide a national counterbalance to the influence of development partners (NE1, NE2, EA3, NGO4). The Minister also brought into the Ministry a number of trusted aides with whom he had previously worked in finance, who immediately began to introduce reforms such as results-based budgeting (NE2, EA3, NM1).[13] He also made school visits, in which he listened to teachers' ideas and complaints, as well as establishing a Facebook page on which the public could air their views (FG1). Informants stressed that, unlike the previous minister, the new minister was genuinely curious about the state of affairs in education (FG1). By September of 2014 he had produced an eight-point reform agenda, prioritizing:

> 1. The reform of personnel, meaning the qualifications of teachers and their salaries; 2. Public financial reform at the ministry; 3. The issue of education quality; 4. A think tank to assist the ministry in policy recommendation and feedback; 5. Higher education reform; 6. Examination reform;[14] 7. Giving young people skills; and 8. Reform of physical education and sport. (Barron 2014b)

The Teacher Policy Action Plan

The new minister's main response to the problem of teaching quality is the Teacher Policy Action Plan (TPAP). Cambodia has had an official Teacher Policy since 2013 (MoEYS 2013), but shortly after taking office, Dr Naron decided that the Ministry needed a 'Plan'. After intense discussions, consultations with donors, revisions, and a national workshop chaired by the Minister, the TPAP (2015–20) was approved and published in January 2015 (Teacher Training Department 2015).

The Plan is based on the understanding that teacher quality is the most crucial ingredient in educational outcomes, and the most pressing problem facing the education sector is attracting high quality candidates to the teaching profession: 'Success in recruitment and training of teachers is the key to fundamentally reforming the teacher-training system and ensuring that the status and roles of the teaching profession rise significantly' (Teacher Training Department 2015, 3). It aims to establish a new vision for the teaching profession, improve educational quality at all school levels, reform teaching education institutions, raise the status of teachers, change teaching and learning practices, and lay the foundation for even deeper reforms post-2020. To this end, it outlines nine strategies, thirty-four sub-strategies, and over 100 tasks or activities. They include: strengthening teacher education and

[13] Apparently MoEYS was previously notoriously bad at constructing budgets, and partly for this reason MEF had reduced its share of spending over the years (EA3).

[14] The Minister has spoken of the exam reforms as a diagnostic tool for the education sector, from which the main takeaways were the need to focus on maths and science, retraining teachers, and strengthening the inspection system (Barron 2014b).

recruitment by improving the financial and social benefits of teaching, automatically admitting top-grade students into teacher-training colleges, and implementing a new set of Teacher Education Provider Standards; strengthening professional development by upgrading teacher qualifications via a Bachelor of Arts fast-track into the profession, while institutionalizing a system of in-school training; updating teacher-training systems by creating a Bachelor of Education 12+4 curriculum; and improving the school environment by revising textbooks, strengthening the accountability of teaching staff, and, once again, properly implementing the Teacher Professional Standards (Teacher Training Department 2015).

Yet in mid-2015, when most research for this chapter was conducted, progress on TPAP implementation was uneven. Dr Naron was widely acknowledged to have injected a new sense of dynamism and urgency into the ministry, and initiatives such as exam reform, for which the Anti-Corruption Unit was brought into the inner circle, had created a stir (FG1, NE1, EA2, NM1). It was not clear, however, that he had the critical mass of support to achieve his more ambitious aims. Upon taking office, there was said to be a tussle between the Minister and SOS A, although signs were that the former had subsequently gained the unswerving support of the latter. Most informants, meanwhile, felt that the Minister did not really have the support of the technical departments, though he was trying to change this by seeding them with his own supporters (FG1, NE1, NE2, NM2, EA3). And while some informants opined that the new ERC was working well, others claimed that the privileged financial position of the academics on the Council was creating resentment amongst MoEYS staff (NM2). Dr Naron was also said to be under criticism from the Cabinet for paying too much attention to foreigners (EA10). Certain national- and provincial-level officials, meanwhile, had their interests undermined by the exam and pay reforms, and it was unclear how supportive they would be of more far-reaching measures. To give one example, the ex-Minister, who allegedly had substantial vested interests in, amongst other things, textbook procurement, was said to be trying to poison staff against the reforms (EA7). Consequently, more than one informant said that Dr Naron may either become an icon of reform in Cambodia, or 'fall flat on his face' (EA1, EA2).

As of the end of 2016, there were signs that the Minister had consolidated his political position. A myriad of activities was being undertaken with the learning agenda in mind, including strengthening a Quality Assurance Department, creating a National Assessment Framework, providing additional training for monitoring and inspection, and beginning to administer standardized tests. Nevertheless, most of these initiatives were taking place on a small scale and were not yet translating into improved learning in the classroom (MoEYS 2016, 2017). A mid-term review of the Education Strategic Plan expected that rigorous implementation of the TPAP would strongly improve this situation (MoEYS 2016, 5). In 2017, the Ministry secured a large increase in its budget (Sokhean 2017), and teacher salaries were again raised—necessary but not sufficient conditions for improving the quality of learning. At the time of completing this chapter (March 2018), however, we were unable to access hard evidence on either the extent of TPAP implementation or classroom performance, although at least some education specialists had a positive impression of progress.

Be that as it may, it remains the case that the TPAP is an extremely ambitious undertaking that would be challenging to implement, even with a highly capable, coordinated bureaucracy. As we have seen, MoEYS, for historical reasons, falls some way short of this ideal. In light of this, perhaps the main thing the Cambodian leadership has on its side is time. Weathering the political storm of 2013, the CPP has, more recently, aggressively repressed and disorganized the political opposition, cementing its dominance as it heads into the 2018 election. Although some of its tactics in this respect have been unsavoury, they do reduce the electoral incentives to concentrate on visible infrastructure over learning reforms. Indeed, during the course of research, one of Dr Naron's close aides opined, in an aside, that reforming education in Cambodia would take at least twenty years.

Conclusion

The power domains framework predicts that in dominant, personalized political settlements, leadership coalitions sometimes emerge with an interest in promoting developmental outcomes, and—providing the policy domain is suitably aligned—their strong hierarchical institutions allow them to make rapid progress in this regard. Since independence, Cambodia has experienced a succession of political settlements of varying degrees of dominance, with leaders able to make a big difference to the education sector, though not in the interests of educational quality. Until recently, the constituencies concerned about quality—international donors, and a small number of ministry technocrats in the education policy domain—have been neither strong nor single-minded enough to make the agenda count. Instead, other educational ideas and interests, around national greatness, socialist refashioning, post-conflict state-making, and popular legitimacy, usually flowing down from the top leadership or up from a predominantly rural population, have driven widening access. In the early years of the millennium, the access agenda was also at the forefront of donor concerns, creating an alignment of political interest and donor funding that drove a particularly rapid expansion in schooling, with learning a secondary, if not irrelevant, consideration.

That is now beginning to change. The CPP political settlement has always been premised in part on earning legitimacy through ongoing economic growth, and there is a realization amongst elements in the leadership that better quality education is necessary to this. In addition, a community of interest that includes employers' associations, underemployed youth, international donors, and education NGOs are directly or indirectly applying pressure on the government, contributing to the appointment of a new Education Minister and a sweeping programme of reform, with quality at the centre. Here, the CPP's renewed dominance of a hugely uneven electoral playing field may prove to be an asset, since reformers are freed from the need to respond to short-term electoral pressures. At the same time, it needs to be remembered that the Cambodian political settlement is essentially a stitching together of a group of disparate elements under the CPP umbrella, united by little more than a shared interest in physical survival and rent-seeking. Power within the state itself, including the education bureaucracy, is somewhat dispersed. To succeed, Dr Naron needs not just to change the culture of the Cambodian classroom, but to win a political struggle against vested interests which prioritize personal ties, patronage, and rent capture over competence and performance. In this respect, the continued support of the Prime Minister and the Finance Ministry will be essential. Given MoEYS' internal weaknesses, Dr Naron's hand could also be strengthened by donors and civil society, providing horizontal support and bottom-up pressure for his reforms. That said, care must also be taken to provide solutions that are adapted to local circumstances and realistic in the context, as opposed to best-practice approaches appropriate to a very different type of state.

References

Andrews, M. 2013. *The Limits of Institutional Reform in Development: Changing Rules for Realistic Solutions*. Cambridge: Cambridge University Press.

Ayres, D. M. 2000. *Anatomy of a Crisis: Education, Development, and the State in Cambodia, 1953–1998*. Honolulu: University of Hawai'i Press.

Barron, L. 2014a. 'Woeful Failure Round Two'. *The Phnom Penh Post*, 31 October 2014.

Barron, L. 2014b. 'Meet the Man Behind the Exams'. *The Phnom Penh Post*, 8 September 2014.

Benveniste, L., J. Marshall, and C. M. Araujo. 2008. 'Teaching in Cambodia'. Report. Phnom Penh: World Bank and Ministry of Education, Youth, and Sport.

Brehm, W. C. 2014. 'Cambodia Grade 12 Examination: Lessons Learned?' Blog, http://willbrehm.com/cambodia-grade-12-examination-lessons-learned/, accessed 10 May 2018.

Brehm, W. C., and I. Silova. 2014. 'Hidden Privatization of Public Education in Cambodia: Equity Implications of Private Tutoring'. *Journal for Educational Research Online*, 6(1): 94–116.

Cambodia Daily. 2013. 'Protestors Unite Around Demand for Hun Sen's Resignation'. 30 December 2013.

Care International. 1999. 'Study on Effective Teaching Hours in Cambodian Primary Schools. Findings and Recommendations'. Phnom Penh: Ministry of Education, Youth, and Sport. Department of Planning.

Chhinh, S., and Y. Tabata. 2002. 'Teacher Factors and Mathematics Achievement of Cambodian Urban Primary School Students'. *Journal of International Development and Cooperation*, 9(1): 69–71.

CITA (Cambodian Independent Teachers' Association). 2012. 'Submission by the Cambodian Independent Teachers' Association (CITA) to the Committee of Experts on the Application of the Recommendations of Teachers (CEART)'. Phnom Penh: CITA.

CITA. 2013. 'Teachers' Salary and Terms and Conditions. Position Paper'. Phnom Penh: CITA.

Craig, D., and K. Pak. 2011. 'Party Financing and Local Investment Projects: Elite and Mass Patronage'. In *Cambodia's Economic Transformation*. Edited by Hughes, C., and K. Un, 199–218. Uppsala: Nordic Institute of Asian Studies Press.

Global Times. 2013. 'Lacks of Skilled Labor, Quality Human Capital Major Concerns for Cambodia: Survey'. 12 March 2013.

Gottesman, E. 2004. *Cambodia After the Khmer Rouge: Inside the Politics of Nation Building*. Chiang-Mai: Silkworm Books.

Hughes, C., and T. Conway. 2003. 'Understanding Pro-Poor Political Change: The Policy Process—Cambodia. Second draft, August 2003'. London: Overseas Development Institute.

Hughes, C., and Un, K. 2011. 'Cambodia's Economic Transformation: Historical and Theoretical Frameworks'. In *Cambodia's Economic Transformation*. Edited by Hughes, C., and K. Un, 1–26. Uppsala: Nordic Institute of Asian Studies Press.

Kelsall, T., and S. Heng. 2014. 'The Political Settlement and Economic Growth in Cambodia'. ESID Working Paper 37. Manchester: Effective States and Inclusive Development Research Centre, The University of Manchester.

Kelsall, T., and S. Heng. 2016. 'Inclusive Healthcare and the Political Settlement in Cambodia'. *New Political Economy*, 21(2): 238–55.

Kotoski, K. 2015. 'CAMFEBA on Industrial Relations and the Cambodian Economy'. *The Phnom Penh Post*, 8 April 2015.

Madhur, S. 2014. 'Cambodia's Skills Gap: An Anatomy of Issues and Policy Options'. CDRI Working Paper 98. Phnom Penh: Cambodia Development Resource Institute.

McNamara, V. 1999. 'The Education System of Cambodia: National Context and Development Issues'. In *Higher Education in Cambodia: The Social and Educational Context for Reconstruction*. Edited by Sloper, D., 99–122. Bangkok: UNESCO Principal Regional Office for Asia and the Pacific.

McNamara, V. 2013. 'Cambodia: From Dependency to Sovereignty: Emerging National Leadership'. In *Education in South-East Asia*. Edited by Pe Symaco, L., 23–45. New York: Bloomsbury.

MoEYS (Ministry of Education, Youth, and Sport). 2013. 'Teacher Policy'. Phnom Penh: Ministry of Education, Youth, and Sport.

MoEYS. 2014. 'Education Statistics and Indicators 2013–2014'. Phnom Penh: EMIS Office, Department of Planning.

MoEYS. 2016. 'Mid-Term Review Report in 2016 of the Education Strategic Plan 2014–2018 and Projection to 2020'. Phnom Penh: Ministry of Education, Youth, and Sport.

MoEYS. 2017. 'Education Congress—The Education, Youth and Sport Performance in the Academic Year 2015–2016 and Goals for the Academic Year 2016–2017'. Phnom Penh: Ministry of Education, Youth, and Sport.

Pak, K. 2011. 'A Dominant Party in a Weak State: How the Ruling Party in Cambodia has Managed to Stay Dominant'. PhD thesis. Canberra: The Australian National University.

Parks, T., and W. Cole. 2010. 'Political Settlements: Implications for International Development Policy and Practice'. Occasional Paper No. 2. The Asia Foundation.

Pereira, J.-F. 2014. 'The ILO-UNESCO Recommendations on Status of Teachers 50 Years On'. 17th UNESCO-APEID International Conference—The Powerhouses of Education: Teachers for the Future We Want. Bangkok, 29–31 October 2014.

Ponniah, K., and C. Heng. 2014. 'Three Quarters of Students Receive a Failing Mark'. *The Phnom Penh Post*, 30 August 2014.

Reimer, J. K. 2012. 'Local Negotiation of Globalised Educational Discourses: The Case of Child Friendly Schools in Rural Cambodia'. D.Phil thesis. Vancouver: University of British Columbia.

Roberts, D. W. 2001. *Political Transition in Cambodia 1991–99: Power, Elitism and Democracy*. Richmond: Curzon Press.

Sloper, D. 1999. 'Higher Education in Cambodia: An Overview and Key Issues'. In *Higher Education in Cambodia: The Social and Educational Context for Reconstruction*. Edited by Sloper, D., 1–24. Bangkok: UNESCO Principal Regional Office for Asia and the Pacific.

Sokhean, B. 2017. 'Government Proposes $6B Budget for 2018'. *The Phnom Penh Post*, 30 October 2017.

Tandon, P., and T. Fukao. 2015. *Educating the Next Generation: Improving Teacher Quality in Cambodia*. Washington, DC: World Bank.

Teacher Training Department. 2015. 'Teacher Policy Action Plan'. Phnom Penh: Ministry of Education, Youth, and Sport.

Un, K. 2005. 'Patronage Politics and Hybrid Democracy: Political Change in Cambodia, 1993–2003'. *Asian Perspective*, 29(2): 203–30.

Un, L. 2012. 'A Comparative Study of Education and Development in Cambodia and Uganda from the End of their Civil Wars to the Present'. PhD thesis. Amsterdam: University of Amsterdam Faculty of Social and Behavioural Sciences.

UNESCO. 2010. *UNESCO National Education Support Strategy, Cambodia 2010–2013*. Report. Phnom Penh: UNESCO.

World Bank. 2011. 'Cambodia: More Efficient Government Spending for Strong and Inclusive Growth. Integrated Fiduciary Assessment and Public Expenditure Review'. Public Expenditure Review (PER). Washington, DC: World Bank.

8

The Political Economy of Education Quality Initiatives in Uganda

Anne Mette Kjær and Nansozi K. Muwanga

Introduction

Uganda's success in broadening access to education is well documented (Ssewamalaa et al. 2011; UNESCO 2015). The introduction of universal primary education (UPE) in 1997 was widely welcomed by parents, especially the poor in rural areas, where the majority could not afford private schools or the charges levied in public schools by parent–teacher associations (PTAs) that had become the de facto school managers. The sharp rise in primary school enrolment, from an estimated 3.1 million in 1996 to 8.4 million by 2013, put Uganda on track to meet the Millennium Development Goals (MDGs) targets. However, these widening access achievements under UPE have been undermined by low literacy and numeracy levels and high dropout rates. There has been growing frustration with the dismal quality indicators amongst a cross-section of education stakeholders, including politicians, education practitioners, researchers, and the public. This has, in recent times, been echoed by the President, who has expressed frustration with the high dropout rates.

Despite the consensus that the quality of primary education is poor, and despite several policy initiatives to try to address the issue, there has to date been little progress in raising education standards in Uganda. This chapter offers an analysis of why this may be the case. The analysis is rooted in an understanding of how Uganda's political settlement has interacted with the education policy domain to shape the adoption, and variable implementation, of initiatives to improve the quality of education in government primary schools.

We rely on a careful reading of existing data and information on the education sector in Uganda, as well as on fifty-one key informant interviews. At the national level, we interviewed members of Parliament, Ministry of

Education (MoE) officials, education NGO staff, education researchers, and teachers' union representatives. At the district level, we interviewed district officials, local councillors, headteachers, teachers, and NGO staff in the districts of Mayuge and Mukono—chosen because one scores poorly on quality learning, while the other performs comparatively well. In each district, we chose a comparatively high- and low-performing school, based on a mix of local actors' assessments and the combined objective scores on the primary leaving exams, in order to identify whether school-level governance made a difference in otherwise matching contexts. Although it may be that the factors shown to explain performance across such different districts and schools can also explain performance more widely across the system, proving this would of course require the application of our approach to a wider sample.

This chapter finds that Uganda's dominant political settlement has features of competitive clientelism, which means that there are only weak policy coalitions to push for quality reforms within the education sector. The policy of fee-free primary education in effect prevents schools from practising cost-sharing with local communities, not least as it is tied to a populist promise made by a President who has become increasingly vulnerable to competitive pressures. In practice, this means that schools that manage to perform well within this system tend to be those that successfully raise incomes due to their position within local patronage networks, including through strong headteacher relations with local elites and politicians. The weakly dominant nature of the ruling political coalition means that quality reforms remain off the agenda, while only schools with strong local relationships can overcome the financial constraints of fee-free UPE policies to raise learning outcomes.

The Problem of Education Quality in Uganda

The Ugandan government introduced UPE in 1997, resulting in a dramatic increase in enrolment rates, from about 65 per cent in the early 1990s to over 90 per cent a few years later. Literacy rates rose to 56 per cent and 73 per cent in 1991 and 2010, respectively, as more children were enrolled, but not as much as predicted by the rise in enrolment (World Bank 2015). The Uganda National Household Survey found that literacy rates actually *declined*, from 71 per cent in 2010 to 68 per cent in 2013 (UBOS 2014). A series of assessments revealed that improvements in access had not been accompanied by an improvement in the quality of education, despite increased budgetary allocations to the sector (Guloba, Magidu, and Wokadala 2010; Hubbard 2007; Makaaru et al. 2015; UWEZO 2012). The pupil–teacher ratio increased after the introduction of UPE, and has declined only slightly since.

Table 8.1 Uganda education performance compared with Tanzania and Kenya

	Uganda	Tanzania	Kenya
Gross enrolment rates, primary, male and female, 2009 (UNESCO)	130	90	105
Pass rates numeracy and English combined (ages 10–16), 2012 (UWEZO)	38	45	70
Primary completion rate, 2009 (UNESCO)	53	58	85
Percentage of grade 6 pupils reaching level 5 difficulty in reading, 2009 (UNESCO)	16	25	22
Percentage of grade 6 pupils reaching above level 4 (basic reading ability), 2007 (UNESCO)	55	90	80

Sources: UWEZO, East Africa and UNESCO data at: http://epdc.org/sites/default/files/documents/eastafrica.pdf (accessed 16 April 2018).

Furthermore, the proportion of children passing the primary leaving exams is low. The government's policy of automatic promotion, which allows children to go on to the next grade without passing tests, is partly responsible for the decline in standards. For example, UWEZO Uganda,[1] an East African Education NGO which carries out regular assessments on the status of primary education in the country, estimates that only three out of ten children in Primary 3 to Primary 7 were able to read and understand a Primary-2-level story (UWEZO 2012, 13). It is clear from Table 8.1 that while Uganda, Kenya, and Tanzania all struggle with quality education, learning outcomes are poorest in Uganda. For example, numeracy and English pass rates in Uganda are at 38 per cent for ten to sixteen year olds, compared with 45 and 70 per cent in Tanzania and Kenya, respectively.

The Political Settlement and the Education Policy Domain

In order to understand why the performance of the Uganda education sector has this striking gap between access and outcomes, even when compared with countries with similar budget constraint challenges and poverty levels, we adopt a political settlement approach. This analysis helps us to understand why the expansion of education is more politically attractive than policies to improve its quality, and the factors that impede the uptake and implementation of learning reforms.

[1] Uwezo means 'capability' in Kiswahili. UWEZO was originally a five-year initiative, which has been consolidated into an organization that aims to improve competencies in literacy and numeracy amongst children aged six to sixteen years old in Kenya, Tanzania, and Uganda. It does so by taking an innovative approach to using educational assessments for social change in ways that are citizen-driven and accountable to the public (www.uwezo.net, accessed 23 February 2018).

All Ugandan post-independent rulers have had to struggle with how to construct a stable ruling coalition, given the many ethno-regional, religious, and socio-economic cleavages in the country. The current National Resistance Movement (NRM) government of President Museveni has largely achieved and maintained this difficult balance since taking power in 1986, at least in terms of preserving stability and promoting poverty reduction. Uganda's political settlement under the NRM can be characterized as dominant, in the sense that President Museveni and his ruling party maintain a strong hold on political power, and dominate the policymaking process. In power since waging a bush war against the Obote regime in the aftermath of the 1980 elections, the NRM built on an alliance between south-western and central Buganda factions, primarily from the previous kingdoms of Ankole and Buganda (Goodfellow and Lindemann 2013).

President Museveni and the NRM won elections under a no-party system in 1996 and 2001. In 2006, constitutional presidential term limits were lifted, allowing the President to contest and win the elections under a multi-party system in 2006, but with opposition candidates winning a higher share of the vote than in the past. In the 2011 election, the NRM won again, this time with an increased electoral margin, explained in part by an increase of support in the North, where peace had been restored after 2006. In the 2016 elections, the President once again won, but with a lower margin (60 per cent for Museveni; 35 per cent for the main opposition candidate, Besigye) (Kjær and Therkildsen 2013; Golaz and Medard 2014; Kiggundu 2016). NRM support remains stronger amongst the rural and poorer majority population than amongst wealthier, educated, and urban voters (Kiiza 2014).

Winning elections by a big majority has been an important concern to the regime, because a narrow margin would make the opposition a credible threat, and could induce lower-level factions to leave the coalition to join the opposition. The 2011 and 2016 elections showed the opposition as weak and disorganized compared with the ruling party, which is both better-organized and better-resourced (Golaz and Medard 2014; Kiiza 2014). The ruling NRM elite has taken several measures to weaken the opposition, including the regular arrest and harassment of the main opposition candidate. Elections have also strengthened lower-level groups of the ruling coalition, such as local army units, local council chairpersons, and local NRM chairmen. The role of lower-level political units is important in the mobilization of votes at that level (Kjær and Therkildsen 2013), which, in the lead-up to the 2016 elections, could translate into the co-option of opposition supporters with financial and other incentives.

Therefore, although the settlement is 'dominant', local factions have some power, and the maintenance of the coalition means that policies that run against powerful lower-level factions are unlikely to be implemented (Kjær

2015). There is enough factional competition within and outside the coalition to raise the cost of staying in power, a phenomenon Joel Barkan (2011) has labelled 'inflationary patronage'. Patronage is used to hold the coalition together, and government programmes can be used to appease lower-level interest groups. For example, the agricultural extension reform programme was used not only to give advice to farmers, but also as a source of patronage (Kjær 2015). Another important way in which these lower-level factions are kept 'in the fold' is by being allowed to use their positions to derive advantages and resources, so-called 'decentralized rent-management' (Khan 2010; Booth 2012). Decentralized rent management often takes place in settlements with strong lower-level groups; these groups can then derive rents from their positions in lower-level governments, or in various line ministries, or the army. In all, the ruling elite has been able to remain in power through a combination of repression, co-optation strategies, including decentralized rent management, and a broad appeal to the rural poor (Golooba-Mutebi and Hickey 2013, 2016).

Prior to 1997, the school system in Uganda had not been reformed since the near collapse of government functions in the 1970s and 1980s. Schools were primarily run by parents through PTAs, and government had limited capacity to provide direction (Muwanga 1999; Hubbard 2007; Makaaru et al. 2015). Parental contributions went towards school maintenance, and included partial support to teachers' salaries. Although government tuition fees were low, PTA dues meant that many poor parents were unable to enrol their children in school. On taking power in 1986, the NRM promised to build a broad-based system, built on inclusion and equality. Central to the rapid reforms, which the NRM introduced in the public sector and the economy, was the need to rebuild the education sector, to make it more accessible and equitable. The Education Policy Review Commission, 'Education for National Integration and Development' (Senteza-Kajubi 1989), and the government white paper on education (Government of Uganda 1992) provided the basis for the introduction of UPE in 1996. UPE fitted in well with the government's egalitarian and inclusive agenda. More importantly, however, it was a way of gaining control over an important social service that people identified with progress and social mobility. Providing free education meant reasserting centralized control over education and thus curbing the perceived influence of PTAs, largely controlled by more well-to-do parents, which had effectively appropriated the delivery of education services.

In 1996, the NRM government pledged to provide UPE, abolishing school fees and promising free education for four children in each family in 1997. After 1997, there were significant increases in funding for implementing the UPE programme, including with the support of new and important players in the education system, such as aid donors, particularly the World Bank. The number of schools and primary school teachers increased (Hubbard 2007;

Kjær and Therkildsen 2013; Stasavage 2004), but budgetary allocations for education expenditure have stagnated since 2002 (Hedger et al. 2010). The implementation of UPE from 1997 onwards fitted into the NRM's political agenda, and with the poverty reduction strategies emphasized by development partners and the MDGs in the making. This 'fit' between the ruling NRM elite, donors, and the rural poor formed a formidable policy coalition for universal access to primary education—a coalition which has not to date been evident in the support for quality improvement.

The political dividends of the UPE initiative were clear: any service improvement, such as expanding access to education to those previously disadvantaged, would be credited to the NRM government, thus increasing its popularity. The introduction of UPE and the abolition of school fees also coincided with the country's first elections under the new constitution, and UPE became an important government campaign pledge (Stasavage 2004; Kjær and Therkildsen 2013). Thus, the public funding that was pumped into the primary education sector after 1996 was basically to improve access (such as payment of capitation grants, building schools, or recruiting teachers), with little attention paid to the quality of education (such as improving inspection and monitoring, curricular activities, provision of materials, or training teachers). Although the country was still operating under a no-party system, the President used UPE as part of his election pledge in the 1996 elections, making it part of his political agenda (Muwanga 1999; Stasavage 2004). Implementing the UPE programme was about making good on that election pledge that had struck a chord with voters. The abolition of PTAs' financial contributions in schools effectively signalled a fundamental change in the power relations between the government, school management, and parents; the NRM and President Museveni specifically could take credit for broadening access and the inclusive delivery of education services (Muwanga 1999). The focus on numbers, rather than quality, in education continues to have political dividends, as we show in the next section, which focuses on why reforms targeting education quality and learning have only been implemented to a limited degree.

Education Policy Reforms Aimed at Improving Learning: Implementation at National and Local Levels

The government has acknowledged that the quality of education is poor in UPE schools. As early as 2003, an evaluation of the Teacher Development and Management System (TDMS), set up in the mid-1990s to provide pre-service and in-service training, revealed that the system and the 23 primary teacher colleges were inadequately staffed and funded, which undermined their overall contribution to improving the quality of education (USAID 2003, 6).

As the government's financial allocations remained low, the education sector largely relied on the support of development partners. The United States Agency for International Development (USAID)-supported UNITY programme, launched in 2006, focused on quality, with a large teacher-training component that also sought to strengthen the TDMS (USAID 2008). Similarly, the 2010 Quality Improvement in Primary Schools through Basic Requirements and Minimum Standards Implementation programme, supported by UNICEF, sought to support the TDMS and the school inspectorate function. Another initiative, supported by Oxfam and the teachers' union, is the Quality Educators for All Programme, which focused on developing competence profiles for teachers in northern Uganda. These initiatives, however, have so far not resulted in any significant improvements in the quality of primary education or learning outcomes. Arguably since 2006, the political emphasis has been on expanding the UPE programme into secondary education by universalizing secondary education to absorb the large UPE intake, rather than on improving the quality of primary education.

During the 2006 elections campaigns, the first multi-party elections under the NRM government, Universal Secondary Education featured strongly in President Museveni's campaign (Werner 2011; Hedger et al. 2010.) However, according to the teachers' union, this has resulted in automatic class promotion, which is largely responsible for students completing the seven-year cycle without attaining the required literacy and numeracy competency levels (UNATU 2013). In addition, since 2003, a larger proportion of donor funding has gone to the Uganda Post Primary Education and Training Program, a programme that also focused on secondary education and vocational training (Hedger et al. 2010).

The political settlement framework draws attention to three features of the policy domain that help explain why elite commitment to implementing initiatives to enhance quality has been weak in Uganda. First, both formal and informal governance arrangements allow for a system of decentralized rent management that serves to appease lower-level factions. Second, the policy legacy of UPE traps the NRM government in the rhetoric of free education, in an appeal to rural constituencies; this impedes local fund-raising and parental participation in school management, with adverse implications for local accountability and school governance. Third, weak policy coalitions in favour of learning at multiple levels translate into relatively weak pressure to push through quality-enhancing reforms.

Decentralized Rent Management

The management and provision of basic education in Uganda is largely in the hands of district administrations. At the district level, the chief administrative officer (CAO) is responsible for monitoring and ensuring full implementation of all government programmes. The CAO is expected to contribute to the development of education policies, setting up and supervising performance of education departments, supervising the construction of schools, and mobilizing communities to send children to school. At the school level, the headteacher and the school management committee (SMC) are supposed to support the UPE programme by mobilizing communities to send and keep children in schools, and to monitor the work of teachers.

While the formal arrangements seem adequate, in reality, the monitoring systems are weak, with several points of leakage. The public expenditure study by Reinikka and Svensson (2004) showed that the publication of releases of capitation grants for schools greatly decreased leakages, as did the transfer of capitation grants into designated district accounts, although some of these gains have been eroded over time (Hubbard 2007). In addition, the multiplication of districts, itself a manifestation of efforts to decentralize rent management, has served to undermine districts' financial, monitoring, and inspection capacities, opening up possibilities for abuses of the system (Green 2010).

Funds are allocated directly to schools from central government, and salaries paid directly to teachers. However, it is estimated that there is considerable leakage of resources at several levels. The leakage that occurs between central government and schools is principally through the payment of 'ghost teachers' and the misuse of UPE grants at the district level. Interviews with headteachers' association leaders indicated that local councillors and district officials may, for instance, use their discretion to allocate teachers or grant licences to set up private schools. Within schools, public spending on education is 'leaked' or wasted through high rates of absenteeism by pupils, teachers, and headteachers. Leakages and inefficiencies of this kind are predictable in a political settlement characterized by decentralized rent management.

In addition to central transfers, a school facilitation grant at the district level may be allocated if the district government has its own revenue sources. According to the regulations, the district is responsible for allocating school facilities grants. The technical team led by the CAO and the district planner agrees on priority sites following analysis of school workplans and reports from monitoring and inspection visits (Makaaru et al. 2015). But in practical terms, the capacity of local governments to carry out such functions has been weakened by the multiplication of districts that are generally underfunded, and lack the human resources to undertake the needed analyses for prioritization.

The increase in the number of districts[2] has increased public administration expenditures and presented a particular challenge for new local governments,

[2] This trend is widely perceived to be driven by the need to gain and consolidate the NRM's electoral support (Green 2010).

which typically lack staff, offices, and equipment to carry out basic functions (Kjær and Katusiimeh 2012). As a result, the districts often lack the capacity to carry out the required inspection and monitoring of schools. The district councils' technical planning committees and education sector committees provide citizens and civil society organisations (CSOs) with an opportunity to participate in education planning and budgeting at the local level. The district education office appoints SMCs, which are also supposed to be representative of different education stakeholders. The two local governments researched for this study displayed a general lack of capacity, with school monitoring and inspection functions particularly under-prioritized. In both Mukono (the high-performing district) and Mayuge (a low-performing district), the inspectorate was evidently underfunded, with insufficient staff, and no means of transport to inspect the large number of schools under their control.

One obstacle to stronger governance arrangements in this decentralized rent management system is that the political centre has to date failed to prioritize or mandate specific departments for quality reforms within the MoE. While the Education Sector Investment Plan emphasizes the need to improve the quality of education, it does not clearly spell out the aspects of quality to be addressed, nor does it detail the measures needed, nor the source of the funding to implement quality improvement programmes. According to one Ministry official, 'What happens in terms of initiatives in quality is largely accidental, and depends on whether there is a donor project'.[3] The lack of a clear and strong political priority around quality was highlighted by several interviewees, who noted that the former Minister of education had been an army officer and an NRM party loyalist, but nevertheless lacked the clout to instigate and implement quality reforms, and was widely viewed as having been uncooperative with key Ministry staff.[4]

Sector budget support has assisted the MoE to build its implementation capacity. However, evaluation reports and interviews indicate that the ministry lacks a strong implementation agency capable of pushing through quality reforms. Initiatives to improve monitoring and evaluation systems have the potential to highlight the leakages and inefficiencies of decentralized rent management, and thus to undermine the material basis for regime support amongst political actors at lower levels of the system. In an evaluation of sector support, Hedger et al. (2010, xi) observed that, although sectoral budget support had succeeded in supporting the achievement of UPE targets, it had

[3] Interview, MoE, January 2015.

[4] Following the February 2016 elections, Rtd Col Jessica Alupo was replaced by Mrs Janet Museveni as Minister of Education and Sports.

been less successful in strengthening accountability for financial management and service delivery at the district and local levels.

In sum, the political settlement has interacted with the policy domain to ensure weak elite commitment to building capacity and authorizing quality reforms in the MoE, in particular in the departments and functions associated with improving learning outcomes.

The Policy Legacy of Fee-free Education

Substantial investments are required to improve the quality of education through recruitment, training, monitoring, and assessing teaching and learning. One avenue for increased school funding—that of user fees and/or parental contributions—is blocked, however, by the strong policy legacy of the UPE drive, with its emphasis on fee-free education, which has been an important part of the government's base political support and electoral advantage.

However, the lack of initiatives to address quality by central government has meant that solutions have largely been left to the innovation of districts and school administrators. In practice, many schools elicit contributions from parents in order to attract teachers or provide other school services, such as meals for students. District and school responses to the decline in quality of education present an interesting departure from the UPE policy as it was introduced and has been implemented for more than two decades. One common view is that parents misunderstood their role under UPE, giving rise to creative reinterpretation at the level of implementation. For example, although government made it clear from the outset that SMCs were to assume all functions previously carried out by parents in schools, many local school administrators are reported to rely increasingly on parents to make financial contributions to ensure that schools have sufficient resources to provide an adequate education.

For the most part, the directive that parents should not be required to make financial contributions in school is ignored, and local leaders actively mobilize parents to contribute to supporting their local school. Furthermore, parents' financial contributions can facilitate linkages with the local political leadership to drive through the sorts of changes parents want in their schools. The result is an unofficial cost-sharing policy that is not officially condoned, but allowed to continue in practice. As one local political leader commented, 'We're encouraging the lower councils to come up with very good by-laws and they're coming up with them. But at the same time, the [national] laws are not looking into that.'[5] These by-laws permit parents to contribute through

[5] Interview, political leaders, Mayuge, May 2015.

the provision of food, paying for teacher accommodation, the costs of extra tutorials, or to supply boarding facilities.

While the NRM government tacitly condones such practices, during the last elections it confirmed that it had no intention of reopening the issue of cost-sharing. One education official reported that the MoE, together with the Ministry of Finance, Planning and Economic Development, had prepared a white paper on quality education that included discussion of user fees, but this never made it to cabinet out of fear that it would not have presidential support. It is understood that the President has no intention of going back on his pledge of fee-free education, which is seen as particularly important for poorer parents, as that would signal the government's inability to uphold its promises. Support for the policy remains widespread, particularly in rural areas. While it has become increasingly clear that UPE is not in practice free, local leaders, such as party chairmen, who dominate the lower-level factions of the ruling coalition, continue to promote public education as a free service. This reflects the nature of a dominant ruling coalition that depends on numerous local factions who are powerful because they can mobilize votes.

Weak Policy Coalitions to Push through Quality-focused Reforms

When the civil society group, Citizens' Action on Quality Public Education, took to the streets in 2012 to highlight the learning crisis in Ugandan schools, it was out of a sense of frustration about the lack of effort to address the quality of primary education. Its aim was to push MPs into taking a more active interest in education quality. However, the Parliament's education committee has remained passive, apparently more interested in trips abroad to examine schooling in other countries. An interviewee from the Parliament Watch civil society group stated that 'education has not preoccupied MPs a lot these past few years'.[6]

The teachers' union in Uganda, the Uganda National Teachers' Union (UNATU) has similarly tried to lead the push for quality education, but has largely failed to push through any significant initiatives. According to interviewees within the union and in school bodies, the union's struggle for salary increases was manipulated by the NRM government. On 10 July 2013, the MoE issued a press statement threatening to sack teachers involved in the quality education campaign and scheduled activities, and called upon the security agencies to investigate the NGOs behind the campaign. UNATU issued a counter press statement that the union was not part of the campaign, and presented a petition to the deputy speaker of parliament that was tabled

[6] Interview, NGO official, January 2015.

in parliament with wide media coverage.[7] The government responded with intimidation, as well as promises to pay lump-sum salary increases into UNATU's savings and credit organization, rather than committing to general salary increases. Some union members were alleged to have been co-opted by the government, disrupting the union's agenda and undermining its unity of purpose.[8] Overall, the lack of initiatives to raise the quality of primary education reflects the weakness of the policy coalition to push for learning reforms.

Variation in School Performance

The generally poor performance of UPE schools masks interesting and significant variations. The consensus amongst different district actors interviewed as part of this research was that better learning outcomes required parents to contribute to, and participate in, their children's schooling, the introduction of refresher courses for teachers, and strengthening of school inspectorates, in addition to the introduction of patriotism training for teachers.[9] In both the districts studied, the local councils (LCs) were passing by-laws (or ordinances) to allow schools to compel parents to contribute to schooling in different ways. For example, in Mayuge, parents contributed substantial quantities of maize, in addition to a financial contribution for processing it, a move endorsed by the resident district commissioner (RDC), whose role is to oversee the implementation of government policy.[10] This suggests that the NRM government silently supports these local policies to introduce an element of cost-sharing, even if this is against official government policy.

An elected local council V (LCV)[11] chairman explained how the council campaigned and explained to parents why they should contribute: 'Some of us have interacted with the President informally, talking about this and raising these issues, but you know, sometimes for better or for worse, politics comes on board.'[12] The LCV chairman's comments suggest that the President is aware of the problem and the fact that these local policies are not publicly renounced indicates that they are indirectly endorsed at the national level. 'Politics' here refers to electoral politics specifically, and to the President's concern to preserve the rural support base. Interviewees noted that the Ugandan government has described primary education as 'free' since the 1996 elections,

[7] Forum for Education NGOs in Uganda News, 4 February 2013. https://fenuexample.wordpress.com/2013/02/04/action-for-quality-public-education/ (accessed 16 April 2018).

[8] Interviews, teachers and union members, January 2015.

[9] Interviews conducted in January and May 2015 and June 2016.

[10] Interview with RDC Mayuge, May 2015.

[11] The local council V is the district level. Below, there are counties (LC4), sub-counties (LC3), parishes (LC2) and villages (LV1).

[12] Councillor, interviewed May 2015.

and that this has been interpreted to mean that all aspects of schooling should be free. All those interviewed were of the view that the government cannot correct this view, for fear of losing popularity. The message that education is free is then interpreted by local politicians, particularly at the LCIII (sub-county) level, who are important political mobilizers during elections, to mean 'everything is free'—a message that is then conveyed to parents.

Parents in a focus group discussion (FGD) at a well-performing school openly supported cost-sharing practices that were against official NRM government policy. According to a disgruntled but highly engaged parent:

> ...we [parents/teachers] agree on something in the meeting, but because politicians need the votes, they go to the parents and tell them the contrary to what we agreed upon. They confuse the parents because they need votes in the next election....parents need to be helped to appreciate that children are not Museveni's—the children will fail, but Museveni will remain the President of Uganda.[13]

The tacit condoning of parents' contribution in practice created significant variations in the performance of UPE schools, variations that reflect local contextual factors.

In Mayuge district, we visited two government (UPE) schools, one well-performing (School A) and one less well-performing (School B). In School A, 33 pupils had passed in the best category, Division 1, and none failed in 2014, whereas School B had no pupils in Division 1, and 18 out of the 64 pupils failed the primary leaving examination in 2014. Other visible differences between the two schools included infrastructure development and innovations: School A had many buildings, a *matooke*[14] plantation, and a chicken project, whereas School B had half-built buildings, and very few students.[15]

School A appeared well organized and managed. At the time of our visit, UNATU had just announced a general strike over an unfulfilled government promise to increase teachers' salaries. The strike was not fully endorsed by all teachers, as we found out during our visit to School A, where teaching was going on. At the time of our visit, a couple of new parents had left a private school to register their children in School A because they had heard about its good performance. The school boasted several teachers' houses, in addition to large dry storage rooms where maize, beans, and other dry foods were kept.

[13] FGD with parents in Mukono in 2015.

[14] *Matooke* is the staple food and having a plantation makes the school self-sufficient.

[15] Mayuge has a 50 per cent primary school dropout rate. In School B, however, the problem relates to the mismatch between the interests of parents and the headteacher. As a result, many parents who regard the school as academically inferior prefer to take their children elsewhere, irrespective of the distance (interviews, district education official and district politician, June 2016).

It was clear that School A had managed to 'get the parents on board'. Contrary to official government policy, they were taking a number of initiatives to raise parental contributions. Teachers at School A seemed engaged and motivated, because their conditions were relatively good, due to parents' contributions. Of course, contributions alone do not automatically convert into improved quality in education, and there is a risk of corruption and leakage of funds. However, at School A, there was transparency in the way parents' contributions were used. For example, the headteacher, the SMC, and the teachers had together worked out a system whereby the collected payments for extra tutoring were allocated on a weekly basis to an appointed teacher, who was responsible for administering the funds. This form of accountability, we were told, ensures that funds are spent according to a set plan agreed upon by the headteacher, teachers, SMC, and parents.

The teachers were also motivated by the fact that the school provided them with breakfast and lunch, in addition to accommodation. There were weekly checks to see if the teachers had carried out the necessary tests. But teachers were adamant that their performance had nothing to do with regular control by the director of studies or the headteacher. In response to our question of whether there were penalties for teachers' non-performance, one teacher answered: 'Teachers here know what to do. It's just in our blood; we're self-driven.'[16]

At School A, the fact that the headmaster was answerable to the PTA and SMC for school performance had, according to teachers, been amongst the factors that made a significant difference to the quality of teaching and learning in their school. Teachers were also held accountable for their performance, including for being present in class with lesson plans that were jointly prepared with the headteacher and some of the school directors. Appraisal forms were used to give teachers feedback on their lesson plans and performance. Teachers noted that the cooperation of both parents and teachers in contributing to the purchase of books and paying towards teacher allowances of between UGX 30,000 and UGX 60,000 to reward good teaching had helped motivate teachers, leaving no room for indiscipline. The school's good performance had also created a good relationship between teachers and parents.

The interview with the chairman of the SMC revealed what he saw as the key to the school's success, including their ability to mobilize parents to contribute to the school. He noted that the interpretation of the UPE policy as free education was the problem, because it implied that parents should abdicate their responsibility for their children, including expecting the

[16] FGD with teachers, May 2015.

government to feed them. In his view, the government needed to acknowledge that the policy was problematic and to reverse it, including by telling parents that 'they [parents] should feed them [their children in schools]'.

By contrast, in School B, there were no teachers present at the time of our visit and it was our impression that their absence was not solely due to the teachers' strike. Only the headteacher was present, but we suspected she only came because she had an appointment with us. Another teacher arrived an hour later and did not seem clear on what she was supposed to do. The school inspector's report noted that the school was well-known for teacher absenteeism. School infrastructure was poor, with only one school building that was divided into three large classrooms, which were poorly maintained and disorganized. The storage room used to store, amongst other things, maize for pupils, was in the headteacher's office; it smelt of mould and was infested with rats. Parents had contributed bricks, with which the headteacher had tried to build teachers' houses, but the construction had not progressed beyond the external walls. Parts of the foundation seemed to have been eroded by rain, and grass was growing in the centre. Interviews with the headteacher indicated that there was no clear or regular system for collecting parents' contributions and allocating these resources to various school needs.

One conclusion is that the difference between the schools reflects differences in the headteachers' ability to mobilize local communities. However, the better-performing school was also better situated in terms of links to the local council and the DEO than the poorly performing school, which arguably enables them to attract a better headteacher in the first place. The headteacher of School A had been able to influence the DEO to post good teachers, for instance. He had also used connections to make the council contribute to constructing teachers' quarters and boarding facilities. By contrast, in School B, the headteacher had been trying to gain access to the local council through letters about school needs, but these had gone unanswered.

The political connections of School A were not just limited to the headteacher. The treasurer at the school was a member of the SMC and the foundation body, and was also a member of other local committees.[17] Local government officials confirmed that the school had managed to establish close ties with the district, which had ensured that the headteacher was not transferred, inspection was regular, and support for different initiatives was forthcoming.[18]

The findings on cost-sharing and school management in Mayuge were similar to those in the better-performing school in Mukono district, School C. School C is a Church of Uganda-founded mixed boarding school, enrolling

[17] Interviews, headteacher and the school treasurer, May 2015.

[18] Interview, June 2016.

860 pupils at the time of our visit. According to teachers, students were learning well; the school was regularly inspected, and the headteacher actively and closely monitored their performance, including through assessments three times a term and through weekly meetings. The teachers were happy with the school's progress and overall performance compared with other schools, both public and private.

During the FGDs with teachers in School C in Mukono, all the teachers attributed their performance to a combined effort by parents, teachers, the district, and the community. According to one teacher, 'you find that when you do something good, different people come in to assist. So by our children performing very well, it [the school] has attracted the parents.'[19]

The importance of political connections was also evident in Mukono, where the well-performing school was considerably better connected politically than the low-performing School D. School C had several members of Mukono local council on its SMC.[20] As the chair of the SMC in the well-performing school in Mukono noted:

> We have got some politicians on board, we brought them also on this committee of ours. We have Mrs Ssozi, the LCV women district councillor, we also have the LCIII, he's also on board with us.
>
> Q: You mean on the SMC?
>
> A: Yes. Then the chairman of this area is also with us. So when we talk, it is a combined voice.[21]

As in Mayuge, the better-performing School C also appeared to have good relations with the foundation body, that is, the Church. Hence a group of closely connected persons, such as the LCV, LC III, the Church members, the headteacher, and SMC members made sure that the school's efforts were supported by the local government; the school also housed the local Catholic diocese.

Mirroring the experience with the poorly performing School B in Mayuge, Mukono's School D was poor in terms of its primary leaving examination results, teachers' own assessments, and in relation to basic infrastructure, and teaching and learning materials. Teachers lacked basic teaching materials, and had inadequate accommodation; notably the headteacher of School D did not use the house provided for him, preferring to commute daily from his home 15 kilometres away. Teachers lacked the necessary qualifications and motivation. The previous headteacher (the incumbent had only been in post a year or two) had frequently been absent and had made no effort to engage with teachers and parents. While the new headteacher had some personal contacts in the DEO, she used these contacts to help cover up her absenteeism, rather than to

[19] FGD Mukono, May 2015. [20] Interviews, Mukono, 2015. [21] Interview, June 2015.

pressurize the local council for resources or to enlist their help in mobilizing parents and resources for the school.[22] Interaction with parents was limited and of poor quality. The overall poor performance of School D was attributed by many interview respondents to the headteacher's inability to garner the support of different stakeholders. Her regular absence had alienated parents and district officials, who had decided to engage a dynamic deputy to sensitize parents to—and build consensus around—school and community roles and responsibilities. So, while headteacher leadership qualities matter for school quality, recruitment to the better-performing schools was also linked to the SMC's connections with the local council and the foundation body.

In both districts, the weaker schools were not well positioned in the local elite networks and had little success in improving their schools. This suggests that, in the absence of strong learning reform initiatives from the centre, a strong SMC and a strong foundation body with close connections to the local council is instrumental in recruiting a competent and visionary headteacher capable of mobilizing parents to contribute and support school governance. The emergence of such a local coalition around the school appeared not only to be the result of the personal characteristics of the headteacher, but also an outcome of a combination of factors, amongst which the place in the local political economy networks was important. Interviews and consultations at the national and district levels, and within schools, revealed the importance of political consensus around education and cost-sharing. In the instances where this political consensus was arrived at and worked to improve the quality of education—through ordinances, the mobilization of parents, and local leaders (religious and community)—there is evidence that performance in schools can improve to an extent, even without strong political or policy support for learning reforms from within Uganda's weakly dominant political settlement.

Conclusion

We have shown that in Uganda's political settlement, which is dominant but with many features of competitive clientelism, there are weak political incentives to undertake reforms to enhance quality learning. A system of decentralized rent management renders quality improvements arbitrary; the success of such initiatives depends on the presence of aid donor-driven projects or, at the local level, on the presence of resourceful and politically well-connected schools and individuals. At the local level, the school administrations in the high-performing schools were able to draw upon resourceful networks in

[22] Interviews, June 2015, June 2016.

order to mobilize local council funds, as well as funds raised from parents' contributions, in order to improve on different aspects of schools that together extended to improved school performance as a measure of quality.

The political leadership continues to believe that UPE, and specifically the idea of 'free' education, is an important part of the electoral appeal of the NRM for rural voters. While it has become increasingly clear that UPE is not in practice fully free, local leaders—including sub-county chairmen, who are predominantly NRM members and are important in terms of political mobilization—continue to frame it as such. The government is aware that cost-sharing by parents in schools is already practised, and that schools that perform well rely on the support and input of parents, as well as their political connections with local council governments. However, these facts are not publicly acknowledged; as the lead-up to the February 2016 elections demonstrated, the NRM continues to campaign on access to 'free' education under UPE. Finally, the pressure to push through education quality-enhancing reforms, whether from civil society, powerful interest groups, or parliament, is too weak to overpower the incentives within Uganda's political settlement that currently distract ruling elites from addressing the learning crisis head-on.

References

Barkan, J. D. 2011. 'Uganda: Assessing Risks to Stability'. CSIS Report. Washington, DC: Center for International and Strategic Studies.

Booth, D. 2012. 'Development as Collective Action Problem. Addressing the Real Challenges of African Governance'. *Synthesis Report for the Africa Power and Politics Programme*. London: Overseas Development Institute.

Golaz, V., and C. Medard. 2014. 'Election Results and Public Contestation of the Vote: An Overview of the Uganda 2011 General Elections'. In *Elections in a Hybrid Regime: Revisiting the 2011 Ugandan Polls*. Edited by Perrot, S., S. Makara, J. Lafargue, and M.-A. Fouéré, 54–109. Kampala: Fountain Publishers.

Golooba-Mutebi, F., and S. Hickey. 2013. 'Investigating the Links between Political Settlements and Inclusive Development in Uganda: Towards a Research Agenda'. ESID Working Paper 20. Manchester: Effective States and Inclusive Development Research Centre, The University of Manchester.

Golooba-Mutebi, F., and S. Hickey. 2016. 'The Master of Institutional Multiplicity? The Shifting Politics of Regime Survival, State-building and Democratisation in Museveni's Uganda'. *Journal of Eastern African Studies*, 10(4): 601–18.

Goodfellow, T., and S. Lindemann. 2013. 'The Clash of Institutions: Traditional Authority, Conflict, and the Failure of "Hybridity" in Buganda'. *Commonwealth and Comparative Politics*, 51(1): 3–26.

Government of Uganda. 1992. 'Education for National Integration and Development'. Government White Paper on the Education Policy Review Commission Report. Kampala: Government Printer.

Green, E. D. 2010. 'Patronage, District Creation and Reform in Uganda'. *Studies in Comparative International Development*, 45: 83–103.

Guloba, M., N. Magidu, and J. Wokadala. 2010. 'Public Spending in the Education Sector in Uganda: Evidence from Program Budgeting Analysis'. Global Development Network Working Paper.

Hedger, E., T. Williamson, T. Muzoora, and J. Stroh. 2010. *Sector Budget Support in Practice: Case Study, Education Sector in Uganda*. London: ODI and Mokoro.

Hubbard, P. 2007. 'Putting the Power of Transparency in Context: Information's Role in Reducing Corruption in Uganda's Education Sector'. Working Paper 136. Center for Global Development.

Khan, M. H. 2010. 'Political Settlements and the Governance of Growth-Enhancing Institutions'. SOAS Working Paper.

Kiggundu, E. 2016. 'How Uganda Voted in 2016'. *The Observer*. 22 February 2016.

Kiiza, J. 2014. 'Opinion Polls in the Spotlight: An Exercise in Deception? Opinion Polling in a Semi-Authoritarian African Polity'. In *Elections in a Hybrid Regime. Revisiting the 2011 Ugandan Polls*. Edited by Perrot, S., S. Makara, J. Lafargue, and M.-A. Fouéré. Kampala: Fountain Publishers.

Kjær, A. M. 2015. 'Political Settlements and Productive Sector Policies: Understanding Sector Differences in Uganda'. *World Development*, 68: 230–41.

Kjær, A. M., and M. Katusiimeh. 2012. 'Sustaining Fiscal Decentralisation in a Neo-Patrimonial and Aid Dependent State: The Case of Uganda'. In *Public Administration in Uganda: Theory and Practice*. Edited by Karyeia G. K. Kampala: Makerere University Press.

Kjær, A. M., and O. Therkildsen. 2013. 'Elections and Landmark Policies in Uganda and Tanzania'. *Democratization*, 40(4): 592–614.

Makaaru, J., K. Cunningham, K. Kisaame, S. Nansozi, and G. Bogere. 2015. 'Public Expenditure Governance in Uganda's Education Sector: Application of an Innovative Assessment Framework'. ACODE Policy Research Series 67. Kampala: Advocates Coalition for Development and Environment.

Muwanga, N. 1999. 'The Politics of Primary Education in Uganda: Parent Participation and National Reform'. PhD thesis. Toronto: University of Toronto.

Reinikka, R., and J. Svensson. 2004. 'Local Capture: Evidence from a Government Central Transfer Programme in Uganda'. *The Quarterly Journal of Economics*, 119(2): 679–705.

Senteza-Kajubi, W. 1989. 'Education for National Integration and Development'. Report of Education Policy Review Commission. Kampala: Ministry of Education.

Ssewamalaa, F. M., J. Shu-Huah Wangb, L. Karimlib, and P. Nabunyac. 2011. 'Strengthening Universal Primary Education in Uganda: The Potential Role of an Asset-Based Development Policy'. *International Journal of Educational Development*, 31(5): 472–7.

Stasavage, D. (2004). 'The Role of Democracy in Uganda's Move to Universal Primary Education'. *Journal of Modern African Studies*, 43(1): 53–73.

Uganda Bureau of Statistics. 2014. 'Uganda National Household Survey 2012/13'. Kampala: Government Printer.

UNATU (Uganda National Teachers' Union). 2013. 'Mobilising for Quality Education for a Better Uganda'. Uganda National Teachers' Union.

UNESCO. 2015. 'Education for All 2015. National Review Report Uganda', http://unesdoc.unesco.org/images/0023/002317/231727e.pdf, accessed 10 May 2018.

USAID (United States Agency for International Development). 2003. 'Strategies for Enhancing Basic Education System Performance. The Role, Performance, and Contribution of Coordinating Centre Tutors to Education Quality'. EQUIP2.

USAID. 2008. 'The Mid-Term Evaluation of USAID/Uganda's UNITY Program Report'. Uganda Monitoring and Evaluation Management Services (UMEMS).

UWEZO. 2012. 'Are Our Children Learning? Annual Learning Assessment Report'. Kampala: UWEZO Uganda.

Werner, J. 2011. 'Teacher Support for Universal Secondary Education in Uganda'. PhD thesis. Minneapolis MN: University of Minnesota.

World Bank. 2015. World Development Indicators online databank.

9

Identifying the Political Drivers of Quality Education

A Comparative Analysis

Sam Hickey, Naomi Hossain, and David Jackman

Introduction

This volume provides yet more evidence of the serious nature of the learning crisis in developing countries. The country case studies presented here offer accounts of systems that are failing at scale, where teachers lack the training to teach, let alone the motivation to show up; students spend demoralizing years in poorly equipped and overcrowded classrooms with little learning to show for it; and where parents' faith in the promise of education is shattered by the poor quality of the services on offer. Behind this crisis on the frontline of education service delivery, each country chapter documents a crisis of policy-making and implementation. Few country governments are taking on the challenge of even trying to raise educational standards with any conviction; and education bureaucracies are ill-equipped or weakly incentivized to deliver even those learning reforms that get through the policy process.

Yet the analysis here also shows that this crisis is neither inevitable nor permanent, even in countries where universal primary education (UPE) is a comparative novelty. Much more is now known about how learning outcomes can be improved in developing countries, going beyond the necessary investments in classrooms, textbooks, and teachers. Examined closely, it is clear that a 'misalignment' between learning goals, policies, and practices feature across education systems that are failing to enable children to learn, even by their own standards (World Bank 2017). The amount of time that well-trained teachers spend on task, the quality of school leadership, and the strength and legitimacy of accountability mechanisms in ensuring higher levels of performance at multiple levels of the education domain have emerged as particularly critical (UNESCO 2014; Bruns, Filmer, and Patrinos 2011).

There is also a growing consensus that politics largely determines whether or not reforms aimed at improving learning outcomes are adopted and implemented (Kingdon et al. 2014; Bruns and Schneider 2016). Yet there has to date been little knowledge of the political conditions under which ruling elites become committed to, and capable of delivering on, such reforms, and none of the analytical tools that would help us understand this. Assumptions that a mixture of electoral competition, decentralization, and stronger downward accountability would do the trick, in part by countering the oft-cited malign influence of teacher unions in blocking reforms that might damage their interests, have rarely been grounded in comparative evidence of how the politics of education reforms has played out in practice.

This book set out to examine the politics of the learning crisis within the global South, in societies where learning outcomes have stagnated or worsened, despite remarkable achievements in widening access since the 1990s. The introductory and theoretical chapters at the start of this volume argued that, although politics is increasingly recognized as an important explanation of how education systems perform, there has to date been no robust framework within which to examine the critical features of the politics of education. Inspired by the small number of comparative political analyses of education in developing countries (in particular, Grindle 2004; Kosack 2012), we became convinced that any such framework would need to capture the multiple incentives and ideas that shape elite behaviour. Crucially, this was a task that entailed moving beyond a focus on formal institutions, to capture the significance of informal power relations and practices; the ways in which material aspects of a country's political economy shape the capacity of different groups to make demands; the particular forms of political agency (e.g. leadership, coalitions) required to navigate these structural conditions at multiple levels; and the role of governance arrangements and relationships within the state, as well as between the state and citizens.

We responded to this need for an analytical framework through which to investigate the politics of education, by developing what we term a 'domains of power approach'. This was then applied to understanding the conditions under which elites commit to education reforms, and how these reforms unfold in practice (see Chapter 2). This approach posits that elite commitment to education is influenced by the interaction of two domains of power. The first is the political settlement, which we conceptualize in terms of the balance of power between contending social groups and how this interacts with institutions. The second is the dynamics of the education policy domain, which is partly embedded within and defined by the political settlement, but which also has distinctive sectoral characteristics, such as the specific governance arrangements associated with education service delivery, and the legacies of past policies, in particular those from earlier periods of rapid expansion of schooling provision. We deployed this 'domains of power' approach through a comparative case study analysis of elite commitment to promoting improved learning outcomes in six countries, each of which was chosen to represent particular types of political settlement. Our country research teams carefully traced the interaction between these two domains of power from top to bottom, examining elite commitment to enacting and implementing reforms through multiple levels of governance, from the national level down to comparisons of high- and low-performing districts and schools. The insights generated by this approach have, we believe, helped to deepen our collective understanding of how politics shapes the learning crisis in developing countries. In particular, our case study chapters have demonstrated the following.

Elite Commitment to Education Reform is Shaped by the Political Settlement

Political settlements have a direct bearing on education policy and practice, shaping the extent to which elites commit to adopting and implementing reforms aimed at improving learning outcomes, and the nature that this influence takes. This analysis has helped to problematize a current tendency to assume that getting the formal political processes (electoral competition, decentralization, 'bottom-up' mechanisms of accountability) right will be enough to improve the quality of education in developing countries. We accept that there are strong arguments for such institutional reforms. However, our analysis suggests that deeper forms of politics and power relations tend to (mis)shape these institutional forms and undermine their potential gains for social service delivery in general, and education in particular.

Informal Power and Politics are Critical

There are two reasons why less visible and formal forms of power and politics are so important in explaining the persistence of the learning crisis. First, the interaction between formal institutions of political competition and pre-existing informal and often clientelistic forms of politics can—and frequently does—generate incentives that undermine, rather than support, elite commitment to development. Such tendencies are particularly apparent in the domain of education, which offers the rents and legitimacy required to help keep ruling coalitions in power, and which makes the domain of education particularly prone to being politicized. Second, this interaction between politics and institutions is closely shaped by the balance of power between contending social groups (di John and Putzel 2009).

Diverse Actors Play Important Roles

For the most part, the coalitions of actors in favour of improved learning outcomes (including business and middle-class parents) are less powerful than those in favour of maintaining a focus on reforms that widen access, but do little to address quality (including populist leaders and teachers' unions). Our analysis also questions the extent to which teacher unions should be the central focus of the political economy analysis of education in developing countries (cf. Moe and Wiborg 2017), in part because the evidence that unions are a powerful obstacle to promoting learning seems to rest on a specific handful of country cases. Instead, we find in our country cases that teacher unions play positive as well as negative roles in advancing learning reforms, and that focusing exclusively on unions risks overlooking the highly significant roles played by other key players, particularly politicians, bureaucrats, and other politically salient stakeholders, such as aid donors and teachers associations, in shaping education reforms.

Levels of Political Competition Influence the Incentives and Constraints to Reform

While political settlements play a significant role in shaping the level of elite commitment to delivering higher-quality education, our aims have also been to explore how different types of political settlement influence this in specific ways. How power is distributed and maintained creates varying elite incentives, opportunities, and constraints to reform, depending on whether and how the education domain helps maintain political order and secure the survival and legitimacy of ruling elites. We distinguished here between political settlements characterized by more or less political dominance or intra-elite competition in terms of political power, and between those with institutions organized along more or less personal or impersonal logics. Comparative analysis of our cases, each of which represented different types of political settlement, suggests that consistent dynamics can be discerned which indicate that settlement types relate systematically to the capacity and commitment of elites to improve educational outcomes.[1]

[1] Note that we did not set out to explain different levels of learning outcome in our cases, but rather to understand the extent of elite commitment to adopting reforms focused on raising learning outcomes. Any generalizations we make from our comparative analysis here are to the heuristic types of political settlement that our cases represent, rather than to developing countries as a whole. Even here we acknowledge that any such generalizations are necessarily tentative, given the relatively small number of cases we have looked at here, and the likelihood that there will be variation within each political settlement type.

Political Competition and Dominance Influence Reforms in Complex Ways

These dynamics are multiple and complex: while political dominance is associated with the effective delivery of educational access, and may enable ruling elites to overcome resistance from powerful interest groups to drive through reforms aimed at improved outcomes, the top-down accountability mechanisms associated with dominant settlements struggle with more 'transactional' tasks of improving frontline educational quality (Pritchett 2013). Meanwhile, higher levels of competition can lead to short-termism and a tendency to appease vested interests. Only where high levels of bureaucratic capacity already existed did we find that high levels of political competition helped to also motivate quality reforms (i.e. in South Africa's Western Cape), and even here the hierarchical governance structure limited the advances made in delivering on this transactional policy agenda. Further down the delivery chain, the absence of national-level dominance can, when combined with decentralized governance arrangements, enable more space for problem-solving innovations at lower levels. However, the emergence of developmental coalitions capable of devising such institutional fixes can be more difficult in local contexts, where intense levels of competition amongst political elites lead them to politicize local governance arrangements. This further underlines the importance of undertaking a close analysis of the interactions between overlapping domains of power and formal governance arrangements in the education sector at multiple levels.

We Need to Acknowledge Idiosyncratic Factors

While settlement types thus tend towards particular dynamics in the education domain, education quality reform and educational provision are also an outcome of highly contextual and idiosyncratic factors that shape the domain of education in different countries. These include policy legacies, the local political economy, and the sociology of citizen–state relations. The main drivers of education reform thus derive from a combination of variables and actors from both the political settlement and the policy domain of education.

The following sections in this chapter integrate analysis across these two domains to synthesize and further develop the key findings emerging from the empirical country cases. The next section examines the significance of political competition or dominance in enabling reform. This is followed by an exploration of how micro and sub-national variations influence education performance. The chapter concludes with an outline of the intellectual and strategic agenda emerging from our analysis.

Elite Cohesion, Drivers and Limits to Education Reform

Weak Coalitions for Quality Reform

Political elites across settlement types exhibit a high level of commitment to mass basic education, which they appear to see as vital to the achievement of a modern, productive, and governable population. The fact that there are high levels of investment in education, and an accompanying tendency to reform initiatives, suggests that across political settlement types a commitment to mass education is important to the legitimacy of successive ruling coalitions. Following Schmidt (2008), we would characterize this commitment as a 'paradigmatic' idea: it is not just a general norm, but an organizing principle that has been binding across political (and other) elites in these countries since before independence.[2] In key respects, elite ideas about education in these case studies are consistent with Corrales' (2006, 244) view that the 'idea that education is a public good, in the national interest of every state, is one of the most significant paradigmatic shifts of the twentieth century'.

However, across all of our cases, the strength of the political and social coalitions in support of expanding schooling provision is more powerful than that of the coalitions in support of reforms to improve learning outcomes. Coalitions for educational access involve powerful alliances between populist leaders and their rural constituencies, teachers' unions, and (historically, at least) international development agencies, whereas the actors that could potentially form coalitions for learning—including business groups (to the extent that business depends on a steady supply of labour with at least basic educational attainments), teachers associations and middle-class parents, have so far failed to coalesce. Donors have relatively recently turned their attention to the quality agenda, but have so far failed to identify and form alliances with influential domestic actors.

In these contexts, political entrepreneurs have yet to offset the collective action problems faced by groups with an interest in raising the standards of public education, in contrast to the coalitions that emerged in favour of increased access in many developing countries during the 1980s and 1990s (cf. Kosack 2012). The civil society-led groups that have tried to do so have

[2] Literature on the post-colonial politics of education in developing countries highlights the significance of the experience of colonial and Western education for nationalist political elites and ideas about education reform as part of the nationalist development project; see in particular comparative analyses of Kenya's *Harambee* education movement and Tanzania's Education for Self-reliance initiative (see, for instance, Cooksey et al. 1994; Buchmann 1999; Court 1976; Buchert 1994). See also Fuller and Rubinson (1992) on the motives and roles of political elites in expanding mass basic education; Hossain and Moore (2002) on why contemporary developing country elites favour mass education over public health; Tikly (2001) on education and post-colonial state-building; and Benavot and Resnik (2006) on how international organizations such as UNESCO established ideas about the education-economic 'black box' amongst post-colonial leaderships.

largely failed to push issues of quality onto the political agenda, in part through being either too co-opted (Uganda) or too excluded (Bangladesh) from the ruling coalition. Business plays a critical role in each of our ruling coalitions, but none of our countries seem to have reached a stage where capitalists actively demand more skilled labour (as white capital eventually did in South Africa), although there are early signs that this may be emerging in Cambodia and Bangladesh, and some vocational agendas are emerging in Rwanda which respond directly to the demands of the economy. As a result, the policy coalitions that Grindle (2004) describes as central to driving through reforms against similar obstacles in Latin America are not present in our parts of Africa and South Asia.[3] This suggests that new class configurations may be a necessary precursor to demands for higher-quality governance in the sector to emerge. Aside from the absence of structural transformation,[4] a significant obstacle here is that the educated middle-class groups most likely to press for higher-quality provision and help ensure this (via school management committees [SMCs], parent–teacher associations [PTAs]) are exiting the public sector for private schools.

Reforms addressing the quality of education provision are thus difficult to get on the agenda, and are often fragmented and poorly implemented, failing to confront the entrenched interests and constituencies empowered by previous reforms aimed at widening access. While elite commitment to improving education access is therefore strong, commitment to educational quality is weak, and this can be at least partly explained by the opportunities and constraints that different political settlement types bring to bear on political elites and the education domain.

Rents and Competitive Pressures

A critical factor determining the relationship between the political settlement and the education domain is the degree of elite cohesion, or the degree of political dominance or competition within the political settlement. The

[3] Of our six cases, Cambodia, Ghana, and South Africa depend substantially on exports, while Bangladesh depends substantially on labour-intensive exports for its foreign currency earnings. In the two Asian countries, in particular, there are objective reasons for educational quality investments to matter, even if those are not as yet manifest in education policy debates. Actual demand for skilled labour may help to explain why quality has at least gained a position on the education policy debates in these countries, even if this has yet to be articulated as a political 'demand'.

[4] Structural transformation tends to lead not only to new class configurations and different demands from capital, but also to the increased levels of domestic revenue required to invest in education from tax receipts. For example, it may be that Kenya is doing better than Uganda and Tanzania on literacy/completion rates, in part because it has a larger 'middle-class' and also more domestic revenue to invest.

education domain is likely to be an important source of rents, votes, and legitimacy for any ruling coalition in a developing country. Exerting control over it can be a means by which ruling coalitions seek to exercise or consolidate power. As a result, the dynamics seen in the domain, including its organization, modes of delivery, and the potential for collaboration and coalitions, can all be closely linked to how a particular political settlement is maintained. The extent and way in which any given policy domain has this political salience relates to the structure and nature of the ruling coalition, as well as the ideological commitment of ruling elites to education. Our cases indicate that the education domain is particularly prone to being politicized in competitive clientelist settlements, and in those where ruling elites are only weakly dominant, and which have a greater need to appease lower-level factions or maintain a popular support base. This aligns with Levy's (2014) argument that competitive clientelist political settlements display a stronger tendency for the public bureaucracy to be subjugated to the imperatives of ruling coalitions, which may use key policy sectors to distribute rents, often in partisan ways, and to maintain popular legitimacy.

This dynamic can be seen in diverse ways across our cases. In more competitive political settlements, such as Ghana and Bangladesh, there was evidence of the partisan allocation of jobs and other rents at different levels of the education system. Access to free education was seen as important to maintaining the rural electoral base, and to some extent the bloc support of teachers' unions. But even dominant settlements with elements of competition featured politicized and clientelistic practices, such as the appointment of education sector personnel in Cambodia on the basis of personal connections rather than professional competence, and of official positions being used as a springboard for income-generating projects in the private sector. In Uganda, the persistence of an officially 'fee-free' policy reflected ruling party fears that the introduction of cost-sharing would undermine rural political support, even though cost-sharing is believed to be necessary to raise the very low educational standards there. A system of decentralized rent management was also implicated in failures to install stronger accountability mechanisms within the system: lower-level political factions tend to benefit from weak governance on the education frontline, giving the national leadership little incentive to change matters.

Competitive clientelism tends to incentivize reforms that offer tangible benefits, while undermining efforts to implement the politically difficult reforms associated with improved learning outcomes. Unlike the expansion of school systems, efforts to raise quality are difficult to 'see' politically. In more competitive political contexts, improving quality lacks the political salience of the tangible goods of widening access or building schools. The universalistic nature of the education sector also appears to lend itself to a particular form of populist policymaking in clientelistic political settlements, where executive fiat overrides or ignores bureaucratic policy processes, leading to short-termism and policy incoherence. As a result, high levels of political pressure and influence over bureaucracies mean that administrative authority is weak: attempts to impose top-down reforms within such settlements can face opposition throughout the educational hierarchy, perhaps most critically amongst the political elite. This dynamic can be reproduced at the local level (as seen in the case of the poorer performing district within our Ghana study) in ways that can fracture local-level interests and prevent collaborative partnerships from emerging.

At the national level, however, we also find some evidence that under certain circumstances increased competitive pressures can persuade ruling elites to adopt reforms aimed at improving quality. In Cambodia, the close-run 2013 election and the strength of the opposition party, the Cambodian National Rescue Party, indicated weak electoral support amongst the youth, which seems to have bolstered the commitment of the government to education reforms. This was reflected in the appointment of a Technocratic Minister to drive quality reforms through. Electoral concerns can thus result in higher or lower levels of commitment to learning reforms, depending on the political salience of relevant constituencies. While in Cambodia, political competition appears to have spurred some commitment to improving education quality in part because of the political salience of urban youth, in Uganda, one of the least urbanized countries in Africa, the President relies heavily on support from the rural majority. There the political calculus has been that more citizens are interested in a free school place than in the quality of learning. Rather than appoint a Technocratic Minister to the post of Education Minister after the last election in 2016, the President deepened his personalized approach to both the education domain and state institutions more generally by appointing his wife as Minister, an experienced political campaigner but with no sectoral experience or track record of delivery.

Political Dominance: Constraints and Opportunities

Our analyses of more dominant party political settlements reveal a complex relationship between political dominance and a commitment to education reform. Elite-level political dominance, as seen most clearly in Rwanda, can reduce the tendency for systems of decentralized rent management to impinge on the functioning of the bureaucracy, and enable effective and efficient implementation of certain policies, notably those around improving access. However, there are also signs that the top-down hierarchical system of accountability that political dominance enables is a blunt tool with which to undertake the more transactional task of securing accountability and performance on the frontline of education.[5] In Rwanda, this reflects how the education sector has come to form a key part of the government's performance legitimacy, relying on measurable indicators that do little to raise the quality of services, and may in practice drain the capacity of education sector actors. This suggests that a functioning hierarchical, impersonal bureaucracy may work very well in terms of establishing rational, technocratically sound, and even politically viable policy, as well as in implementing that on the ground. But, when it comes to quality, 'education may be the kind of craft-based activity for which hierarchy is not the appropriate response' (Levy and Kelsall 2016, 12; also Pritchett 2013), and which relies on 'horizontal' governance, and localized mechanisms of accountability and authority to deliver high quality outcomes (Levy and Kelsall 2016, 12; also Pritchett 2013).

Political dominance can have a questionable impact on education systems and delivery if the policies imposed are themselves misaligned with the changing needs of the society in relation to the domain of education. The sudden decision to switch the language of instruction from French to English in Rwanda, for example, has resulted in incoherent forms of educational delivery, as the decision behind the switch was disconnected from the abilities of frontline staff. These challenges can become exacerbated when education has an ideological significance, as it clearly does in President Kagame's vision of 'high modernism'. As with competitive clientelist settings, education policymaking can therefore be subject to short-term political pressures, such as when President Kagame scheduled policy reforms expanding access to education in line with the electoral calendar, overriding bureaucratic policymaking processes in much the same way as in Ghana. Moreover, it is harder to challenge bad policies in dominant political settlements, where political space is limited, and where critique of the leadership can be risky. The same is arguably true of President Museveni's commitment to offering 'free' UPE in Uganda, at a time when the National Resistance Movement (NRM) had a dominant hold on political power. This policy brought significant benefits in terms of wider access. However, the policy was introduced in a highly personalized way (as a gift from the President, rather than as a right) and was designed to displace local accountability structures, which had been based in part on co-financing arrangements with local communities, with a more direct line of control from the headteacher through to the ruling party.[6] The political logic of

[5] A similar problem is apparent in South Africa, where the strong belief in hierarchical modes of governance is undermining efforts to promote learning, even in relatively high-capacity and well-governed regions such as the Western Cape (see Levy, Hirsch, and Woolard 2015; Levy et al. 2018).

[6] The fact that Universal Primary Education in Uganda (as elsewhere) was funded by external sources rather than through a tax bargain with citizens, has likely further undermined the potential for virtuous circles to be established between the politics of education and democratization in contexts such as Uganda.

these reforms, as tied directly to the personal promise of a particular leader and premised on the return of political loyalty, undermined active local involvement in school governance, and has made it politically difficult to discuss alternative financing arrangements that might improve school performance at both national and local levels.

It remains feasible that, once a dominant leader turns their attention to the question of learning and quality, as now appears to be occurring in Rwanda and Cambodia, this level of coherence and capacity to exert top-down forms of discipline will enable swifter progress than in more competitive clientelistic countries. This contention is buttressed by the evidence that the statistical outperformers in education league tables have tended to be led by countries (including Japan, South Korea, Singapore, and Vietnam) which would all have been described as 'dominant' during the period of their most significant advances on this front (see Chapter 10).

Furthermore, our cases also indicate that political dominance, rather than competition, can better enable productive coalitions to emerge at the school and sub-district level. In the Ghana case, intense political competition undermined relationships between politicians and key members of the bureaucracy and resulted in an incoherent and fragmented response to the problem of teacher absenteeism. By contrast, in the district characterized by political dominance and low levels of inter and intra-party competition, 'development coalitions' emerged. These incorporated actors at different levels of the bureaucracy and ruling party, enabling creative and consistent responses to the problem of teacher absenteeism, and thereby ensuring appropriate levels of teaching. The only direct example we found of intense electoral competition playing a positive role was within certain parts of South Africa, a finding best understood in relation to historical legacies of state building. This is in line with the wider finding that electoral competition can tend to exacerbate the politics of patronage, unless a longer-term process of state building has already taken place (Fukuyama 2016; Grindle 2012).

Institutional and Policy Legacies

The influence of political settlements on the education domain is also mediated by the institutional and ideational legacies within society. The significance of political competition or political dominance for elite commitment to education reform, and how these reforms unfold in practice, is partly influenced by institutional arrangements such as bureaucratic capacity, pre-existing in any given context at both the national and sub-national levels. Similarly, policy legacies stemming from previous iterations of the political settlement also influence the nature of pressures for reform that develop, and how reforms are implemented.

Comparative analysis of the performance of school systems in the Western and Eastern Cape provinces of South Africa underscores the significance of sectoral or domain governance in explaining learning outcomes (Chapter 6, also Levy et al. 2018). Both provincial school systems are regulated by the same national policy framework and receive the same per capita resourcing, but differ widely in learning outcomes: the Western Cape performs at the top and the Eastern Cape near the bottom of the country's educational assessments. The difference can be substantially explained by the better performance of the relatively impersonal education bureaucracy in the West, buttressed by a competitive multiparty system. This is in contrast to the more personalized and politicized bureaucracy in the East, where an apparently dominant party system has in practice been subject to fragmentation and intra-elite competition (Levy et al. 2018). Notwithstanding the argument that less hierarchical and more locally oriented forms of governance arrangements may be required for the Western Cape to generate even higher levels of learning, this suggests that performance in the domain of education is closely shaped by the dynamic interactions between institutional arrangements and the political settlement to shape performance.

Policy legacies also shape the room for manoeuvre for alternative policy reforms and agendas, and are themselves outcomes of earlier political settlement dynamics that have now become entwined in contemporary iterations. The major reforms undertaken to promote increased access to primary education were often directly linked to critical junctures within the political settlements explored here, from the establishment of post-independence governments through the resolution of conflicts to the deepening of competitive pressures in the 1990s. One outcome of this is that these reforms also frequently strengthened the position of stakeholders, whose interests may be inimical to aspects of quality reforms. For example, the expansion of education has meant more teaching jobs and school building, helping to grow teacher unions, and creating interest around procurement contracts that have enabled rent-seeking behaviour within school management processes.

The means of financing the costs of schooling and the implications this has for performance in the education domain has been politicized in different ways in the case countries: in Uganda, debate continues about user fees as a means of raising quality by re-engaging parents in school performance, in a context in which UPE also abolished PTAs. In Bangladesh, financing has been politicized to ensure that poorer children get stipends to offset direct costs, and constitutes a major part of public spending on education. While the state officially pays for schooling in all these countries, parental involvement is expected, informally or not; additional fees may be charged for extra tuition at the school level to raise examination performance. Those willing and able to pay for a better service may pay for additional private tuition or exit to the private sector. However, some private schools perform on average worse than public schools, including secondary schools in Rwanda and Bangladesh.

The strong emphasis placed on abolishing user fees to achieve the important goal of enabling poorer families to send their children to school may also have undermined the mechanisms that historically played a role in local oversight, for example, through cost-sharing with local communities and their representatives in school management processes (e.g. PTAs). Poor, uneducated people struggle to hold educators and officials to account (Kingdon et al. 2014; Dunne et al. 2007), not helped by the fact that most developing country education systems are highly but ineffectually centralized (Pritchett 2013). We find some evidence that improved levels of performance are correlated with schools forming co-productive arrangements with parents around cost-sharing, in ways that run counter to the dominant narrative of education being 'free'. The abolition of fees is the easy way for governments to signal commitment to UPE, but out-of-pocket spending tends to be significant, even without official school charges.

Policy legacies thus influence the terrain on which reform agendas emerge and are implemented. Yet political settlements themselves also differ in the political space they enable for alternative policy agendas and ideas to develop within the education domain. Weak dominant Uganda and the competitive clientelist cases seem to display similar levels of policy (in)coherence and short-termism, but the dominance of a single political principal in Uganda makes it even harder to challenge certain policies which are holding back improvements in quality. The continued presence in power of the party that brought in 'free' UPE, and the growing power of lower-level factions who frequently exploit the popularity of 'free UPE' for their political gain, makes it difficult for school-level actors to resolve resource-based constraints (e.g. through co-financing agreements with parents). Local political entrepreneurs, keen to make political capital from (false) promises of 'free education' and to align themselves with the dominant leader, often prevent other stakeholders from exploring creative solutions to pressing problems of school financing. Better-performing schools have tended to ignore the presidential commitment to 'free' education and have entered deals with parents whereby they share costs in return for greater oversight by parents, in so doing, behaving more like schools in the more competitive and de facto decentralized systems of Bangladesh and Ghana. In key respects, this marks a reversion to how the education domain functioned prior to Museveni's populist move to install 'free' UPE (Dauda 2004). Political settlements thus shape the room for manoeuvre in terms of alternative agendas and approaches. Our cases of dominant or weak dominant settlements demonstrate how such settlements can inhibit alternative voices, and opportunities for reform. Alternative policy coalitions are unlikely to emerge in dominant Rwanda in ways that could significantly alter the course of educational policy. The political space to discuss alternative policy agendas is more open in our competitive settings.

Understanding Micro Variations in Education

Across many of our cases, there is significant variation in school performance between and within districts, demonstrating that the local context is critical to educational outcomes. As explored above, these differences stem in part from variations within societies between district- or regional-level political settlements, indicating the need to give analytical and empirical attention to how settlements differ regionally. These local political settlement domains can closely shape how formal institutions of governance actually function, and influence whether or not developmental coalitions are likely to emerge. The final domain of power to which our research drew attention concerned the micro-sociology of schools themselves.

Accountability and Local-level Partnerships

With respect to the functioning of accountability mechanisms at the frontline, school-level analysis indicates that school governance matters, perhaps even more than sub-national governance. The characteristics of the sector mean that headteachers are better equipped to monitor teaching and learning on a day-to-day basis than are district administrators. However, where schools were effectively supervised, the critical actors were often those operating at the interface of local government and school-level management structures, as with circuit supervisors in Ghana. Monitoring and supervision activities are always under-resourced, and their costing is notional, so that budgets are easily cut or re-purposed. Although we found little evidence of synergies between the long and short routes to accountability identified in earlier work (World Bank 2003), informal downward accountability mechanisms appear to work better under the competitive clientelism of Ghana and Bangladesh, where better-performing schools tend to be those where communities take control in decentralized or weakly centralized settings. In Bangladesh, the focus has been on 'carrots not sticks' for teachers, and policy reforms to increase bottom-up accountability through school-based management have been implemented in a weakened form. Ghana and Rwanda also illustrate the problems that arise where lines of oversight, accountability, and incentives are misaligned on the central/local axis. For instance, teacher training and advancement are controlled centrally, while other aspects of oversight are nominally 'decentralized'. Yet while decentralization and accountability reforms have been stymied from the centre in Ghana, they have created space for local-level reform at school level, involving SMCs and PTAs. There is some evidence to suggest that top-down pressure combined well with bottom-up accountability measures in Uganda (Hubbard 2007), but as the focus of the executive is on quantity rather than quality, efforts to promote higher quality remain off the agenda.

The detailed Western and Eastern Cape comparative analysis again offers confirmation of the significance of school-level governance in learning outcomes. Although the Western Cape outperforms the Eastern Cape by some distance, when socio-economic status is taken into account, it is no longer clear that the 'good enough Weberianism' of the education bureaucracy adds much value. When compared with the performance of far poorer Kenyan children in far less well-resourced Kenyan schools, the notion that education in the Western Cape is delivering comparatively high quality becomes questionable. It is also clear that parental involvement, in terms of contributing to school building and maintenance, is more important in the Eastern Cape, suggesting a far higher degree of local participation. Tracing these processes down to paired school-level comparisons, the analysis indicates that:

> a well-functioning bureaucracy can support success; but that there are limits to the ability even of well-functioning bureaucracies to shape what happens at the school level... [and] even where bureaucracies work relatively well, the presence or absence of engaged parents and communities can be key to sustained strong performance. (Levy et al. 2018, 29)

In Chapter 6 of this volume, Levy et al. argue that horizontal governance mechanisms at the level of schools can play different roles within different sub-national political settlements, offering complementarity within contexts of higher bureaucratic functioning, and playing a replacement role in more dysfunctional contexts. In line with these reflections on the more sociological dimensions of the challenge and prospects of improving school quality, our analysis draws attention to aspects of the educational domain that shape learning, but which are more clearly shaped by factors that are not directly linked to the political settlement per se, particularly in terms of how social relations and basic issues of capacity affect quality outcomes.

Citizen–State Relations: The Sociology of Schools

The status and social relations of teachers play a role in accountability and motivation, and therefore performance, at the local level. Where teachers are accorded a high social status within the communities they serve, poorer and, in particular, less educated parents may struggle to hold them to account for their performance (Westhorp et al. 2014). But relative declines in teacher status may be demoralizing and also have adverse effects (Barrett 2005;

Avalos and Assael 2006). One example to emerge from our cases is the expansion and feminization of the teaching workforce in Bangladesh, promoted as a means of improving girls' access to education, but implemented chiefly through lowering teacher qualifications. This has contributed to a notable decline in the authority and position of teachers in the social system, but also (therefore) to an equalization of (poor, rural) communities, vis-à-vis school authorities. It also appears, however, to have changed official perceptions of accountability for performance within the teaching profession, in that perceptions of women teachers' social reproductive roles contribute to effective lenience with respect to teachers' attendance and classroom performance.

The pull exerted by the private sector on parents and teachers alike has a powerful and probably negative effect on public sector performance, largely through the exit of educated parents able to hold schools to account for their performance. Although this to some extent reflects the nature of the political settlement (in terms of the absence of capitalists pressing for higher skilled workers, the relative holding power of 'middle-class' parents, as against the rural majority within our ruling coalitions, and the neoliberal ideas of political elites), there are wider factors at play here, including the logics of class reproduction and status, which create incentives for middle-class parents to remove their children from public schools that educate poor children.

The sociology of education matters also in helping to explain the interplay between demand and supply, in determining the conditions under which parents can in practice exert accountability pressures on schools. Under the tightly controlled conditions of education provision in the dominant party settlements (notably Rwanda), there is considerably less room for local manoeuvre, so that poorer parents systematically lack power at the local level, despite policies intended to promote their participation in school-level governance. In the effectively deconcentrated settings of the two competitive clientelistic settlements (Ghana and Bangladesh), there is more scope for local collective action, where the governance of teachers and other school resources can be coordinated and co-produced.

Human Resource Capacity

The problem of quality in education is cyclical and self-reinforcing, because the graduates of poor schools go on to become the teachers in poor schools. This is why teacher training has been a priority in most of these countries. But teacher-training facilities are typically also sites of capture, as in Ghana, where training has become a perk because of the allowances it involves. In all of the better-performing schools in each of the countries studied here, it emerged that good teachers can emerge out of, and teach well, even within poorly governed systems with weak policies on teaching and learning quality.

The analysis here supports education sector research that finds that innate and professional motivations are vital incentives in all contexts (Bruns and Luque 2014). Headteacher leadership is critical. In the weakly dominant and competitive clientelist cases, strong headteacher leadership emerged in situations where they were sufficiently embedded to be responsive to local community needs, but not so embedded that they lacked autonomy to discipline teachers and enforce rules. The significance of such local relationships and personalities to school performance indicates the importance of creative and local responses to the challenges of improving learning outcomes (Pritchett 2013). Economic stability through small businesses (agriculture and livestock) can enable improved school conditions, and the discretionary power of headteachers (including informal pressures, such as shaming), are often contextually important ways in which staff are motivated and discipline ensured.

Strategic and Analytical Implications

This volume reinforces the growing recognition that political economy factors critically shape the adoption and implementation of reforms aimed at improving learning outcomes. The domains of power framework employed here, with the emphasis on the links between the political settlement and domain of education, can be deployed in other studies, in part to explore how far these results are representative of the politics of education within other similar types of political settlement. We reflect on how our approach and empirical cases can inform the education reform agenda.

Realigning the Reform Agenda within Political Settlements

The fact that it is difficult to identify elements of the education sector that are somehow free from the tendencies generated by the political settlement takes on particular significance regarding the next steps that policy actors may seek to take to promote higher levels of learning in developing countries. This lack of relative autonomy is a considerable constraint to achieving significant reforms in the sector, and suggests that responses will need to be closely attuned to what is politically feasible, rather than to what might be seen as technically optimal. In particular, and in the absence of system-wide pressures to institutionalize the quality agenda in developing countries, we are wary of advocating system-wide reforms as the solution in contexts where the configuration of power that shapes the incentives of the system is not changing in progressive directions. The dynamics of political settlements mean that the broad and ambitious scope of educational reforms, which are sometimes facilitated and encouraged by international donors and development agencies, can lead to policy incoherence, delivery failures and despondency. Such reforms are often insufficiently considerate of how politics influence the education domain, and can thus be distant from, and misaligned with, the operational contexts for which they are intended.

Where the quality agenda is under-emphasized (e.g. in Rwanda and Uganda) policy changes may be required, although even here the first step may not be to promote off-the-shelf policies associated with improved learning outcomes, but to identify the actors and ideas around which coalitions in support of higher-quality education might emerge. But in most cases the problem is not policy per se, but implementation. There is also a case for governance reforms in cases where the current configuration of decentralization creates a great deal of incoherence at regional, district, and school levels (such as in Ghana). The need to redress the balance between centralized and decentralized mechanisms for oversight and accountability generally accords with Pritchett's (2013) warning that:

> School systems in many countries are centrally controlled by large, top-down national or state/provincial bureaucracies that hand down decisions about which schools get built, where teachers get assigned, and what subjects are taught. Well-functioning centralized systems can efficiently carry out logistical tasks and scale up quickly and inexpensively, as the success in expanding the number of school buildings shows. But a centralized system cut off from the judgment and concern of local parents and teachers is doomed to succeed at schooling but fail at education. [The lesson is]: don't force centralized systems.

This would involve moving towards combining 'thin' forms of centralized accountability (performance pressures) with 'thick' forms of localized accountability (involving politically salient stakeholders), alongside measures to reduce the tensions between such top-down and bottom-up mechanisms. However, such ambitious reforms are unlikely to be successful in the short to medium term, given the nature of political pressures within each system and the absence of coherent, high-capacity policy coalitions pushing for higher-quality education. This echoes the sense that

> ...for certain development problems the quest for the solution is itself the problem, and this is especially so in matters pertaining to political, legal and organisational reform, where combinations of high discretionary decision-making and numerous face-to-face transactions are required to craft supportable solutions (plural). (Pritchett, Sen, and Werker 2013, 11)

As we go on to argue, the capacity to craft supportable solutions to contextualized problems has often been best achieved by coalitions of politically salient stakeholders within localised contexts.

Attempts to impose system-wide reforms within competitive and weak dominant settlements are therefore highly unlikely to succeed, given (a) the incentives for politicians to use the sector for political purposes, and (b) the wide range of veto players. System-wide reforms may in theory be more feasible in dominant settings, to the extent that political principals turn their attention to this policy goal, but they need to be geared towards matching strong top-down forms of accountability with stronger bottom-up forms that empower decentralized systems and actors at both local government and school level.

Building Coalitions

Our findings and analysis underscore the significance of focusing on the role that coalitions play in shaping the extent to which reforms aimed at improving learning outcomes are adopted and delivered. We deepen and extend existing work on coalitions in relation to the politics of education (Grindle 2012) and development (Leftwich 2010), by (a) showing that their roles differ according to different types of political settlement, and (b) highlighting the critical role of local-level coalitions in driving up performance at district and school levels.

Coalitions play a critical role at multiple levels of governance in ensuring the adoption and implementation of reforms aimed at improving learning outcomes. This suggests that support for such coalitions might be the best first step for those seeking to promote institutional reforms. An important constituency here would be business actors, particularly those with requirements for a more highly skilled labour force and which have sufficient autonomy from ruling coalitions to be able to make demands for reforms around educational upgrading (Doner and Schneider 2016). Donors were critical actors within the earlier policy coalitions that helped establish the access agenda, and there is evidence that their focus has, belatedly but increasingly, turned to issues of quality. Their difficulties in promoting the quality agenda may reflect a lack of clear focus on this issue, as well as their generally declining influence over developing country governments. Although their continued high level of involvement in funding social sectors holds open the possibility of greater influence in this domain than in some others, it suggests a need for more creative (and arm's-length) approaches to building alliances and coalitions, with political as well as technical actors. Donors can play particularly important roles here as knowledge brokers, helping to create and promote a credible evidence base around learning outcomes, and actionable means of improving them. Civil society, particularly in the form of teachers' associations, which are mandated to work towards producing a higher-quality workforce, could constitute a further ally within such coalitions. Shifting political settlement dynamics may provide windows of opportunity (e.g. elections or other periods of vulnerability) for reformers to promote reforms aimed at improving learning outcomes. A further implication of our analysis is that future studies should build in a strong focus on the potential role of business and middle-class parents to form coalitions in support of higher-quality education, within the context of a given country's political economy profile and integration within the global economy.

Decentralization and Accountability

The gap between policy formulation and implementation needs to be narrowed in terms of the range of actors involved in each process. Greater coherence is required between centralized and decentralized arrangements for (a) teacher training and career advancement, and (b) monitoring performance and accountability. Top-down forms of performance management and accountability are insufficiently embedded in local contexts and poorly attuned to the specific challenges therein. These need to be joined by (and joined up with) bottom-up and horizontal forms of accountability that empower those working within both local government (e.g. circuit supervisors) and civil society to hold frontline service providers to account. This focus on decentralized forms of performance management and oversight, from local government down to the school level, largely accords with the most recent work on the links between governance and educational quality (e.g. Pritchett 2013).

We would add, however, that there needs to be a stronger emphasis on ensuring that accountability reforms fit with particular contexts. While we know a lot more now about how accountability reforms operate—including reforms to improve school-based management and to hold teachers to account for performance (Bruns et al. 2011)—we also know that the success of such reforms depends a great deal on the local political context into which they are introduced (Gaventa and McGee 2013; Hickey and King 2016). Our chapters on Ghana and South Africa suggest that different particular settlements at sub-national levels can offer very different incentives and opportunities for elites to adopt particular accountability mechanisms; this implies that reform-minded implementers need to have a solid grasp of political economy dynamics before promoting particular approaches. Capacity building is also essential here: a government has to be capable of doing something before it can be meaningfully held to account for performing a given task. Local government bureaucrats are a key constituency to be engaged here.

Connected to this, accountability and performance mechanisms need to be as much about carrots as sticks, primarily in the form of non-financial awards for performance, and the building of professional norms and cultures of performance at multiple levels. As noted earlier, teaching associations can play important roles in generating and reproducing professional norms, and could benefit from external support. The critical attention paid to teacher unions in the literature may have inadvertently drawn attention away from the strong potential for a progressive role to be played by teacher associations in making the case for, and helping to deliver on, higher-quality education.

Local-level Initiatives

In line with the arguments that reforms need to be more cognisant of how local-level coalitions and accountability systems emerge and function to improve educational systems, our cases also suggest that other local-level initiatives to improve commitment to educational outcomes are important. This may involve practices and coalitions that do not adhere to 'best-practice' models. Coalitions exist at district as well as school level, and help reveal the extent to which informal fixes represent the kinds of 'best-fit' solutions increasingly advocated within the new governance agenda (e.g. various funding mechanisms in Uganda or the employment of party loyalists as an auxiliary teaching force in Ghana). These appear to be most common in contexts where formal arrangements are regularly undermined by the informal power relations that underpin political settlements. While acknowledging the limitations to such arrangements, particularly in terms of the degree to which they can be institutionalized and remain stable, our analysis suggests the need for openness to working with these.

Finally, our cases also suggest that political settlements contain varying political dynamics at the regional or district level, pointing to the analytical and empirical need for moving beyond national-level settlement analysis. This indicates that national-level reforms will not only differ between settlement types, but also lead to different outcomes across regions, interacting with the dynamics of political competition or cooperation present there, as well as the institutional and even policy legacy particular to specific regions. Future studies should thus be attentive to differences in the political settlement across regions, as well as to how these localized settlements interact with that at the level of society as a whole.

Conclusion

Rapid expansion alongside poor quality are characteristics of most mass education systems in most developing countries (World Bank 2017). Our focus here has been on the extent to which governments acknowledge and address the issue of learning, and whether, and how, this is shaped by the nature of the political settlement. The general failure to promote higher-quality education that we identify in our country cases directly reflects the dominant incentives and ideas generated by the political settlement, both of which emphasize the quantity of provision in terms of access, rather than the quality of provision via improved performance in the educational sector. The political logics (popular legitimacy, votes), coalitions (populist leaders, rural poor, teachers' unions, global actors and agendas), and governance arrangements (centralized) that underpin the strong focus on access are more powerful, and are also more or less opposed to the drivers of a stronger focus on quality. A drive for quality education would likely require long-term investments beyond a given electoral cycle, a coalition that includes non-poor parents and capitalists that need skilled workers, and decentralized mechanisms that help ensure localised oversight of performance.

Many aspects of the politics of education seem to play out in the same way across all of our different types of political settlement, although the room for manoeuvre in terms of future reforms is more constrained in dominant than in competitive settings. At the same time, the ways in which competitive forms of electoral politics can exacerbate clientelistic tendencies underline the need not to assume that democratization alone will eventually solve the learning crisis in the global South. Arguably, the most powerful drivers of educational quality in our countries come from the ways in which elements of the two domains on which our framework centres—namely, the political settlement, and the policy domain of education—combine with each other over time. This in turn closely circumscribes what is possible in terms of undertaking reforms aimed at improving learning outcomes in developing countries. It also suggests the need for more politically attuned approaches that focus on building coalitions for change and supporting 'best-fit' types of problem-solving fixes, rather than systemic change. Higher levels of performance at the frontline seemed to emerge as localized solutions to specific problems, often against the grain of dysfunctional sectoral arrangements and the national-level political settlement, but in line with the contextualized fixes devised by progressive local coalitions of politically salient stakeholders.

Our approach and findings converge strongly with the few comparative studies of the politics of education in developing countries that exist, and which also go beyond formal institutional analysis to include a focus on underlying forms of power (Kosack 2012; Grindle 2004). We have attempted to go further here by bringing together an analysis of national-level and domain-level politics. We have also engaged with the governance arrangements that operate at multiple levels of the education sector; on this our conclusions largely support Pritchett's (2013) suggestion that decentralized systems are better suited to the transactional governance task of improving levels of learning, rather than schooling. We would, however, add that supporting developmental coalitions may be a more realistic first step than undertaking systemic change within contexts where the configuration of power runs counter to formal institutional arrangements being allowed to function effectively. By bringing these disparate strands of the literature together, we have tried to offer a more holistic and multi-levelled account of the politics of promoting higher-quality education in developing countries and (in so doing) establishing a more realistic basis for policy interventions to tackle the learning crisis in the global South.

References

Avalos, B., and J. Assael. 2006. 'Moving from Resistance to Agreement: The Case of the Chilean Teacher Performance Evaluation'. *International Journal of Educational Research*, 45(4–5): 254–66.

Barrett, A. M. 2005. 'Teacher Accountability in Context: Tanzanian Primary School Teachers' Perceptions of Local Community and Education Administration'. *Compare: A Journal of Comparative and International Education*, 35(1): 43–61.

Benavot, A., and J. Resnik. 2006. 'Lessons from the Past: A Comparative Socio-Historical Analysis of Primary and Secondary Education'. In *Educating All Children: A Global Agenda*. Edited by Cohen, J. E., D. E. Bloom, and M. B. Malin, 123–229. Cambridge, MA: MIT Press.

Bruns, B., and J. Luque. 2014. *Great Teachers: How to Raise Student Learning in Latin America and the Caribbean*. Washington, DC: World Bank.

Bruns, B. and B. R. Schneider. 2016. 'Managing the Politics of Quality Reforms in Education Policy: Lessons from Global Experience'. *The Learning Generation Background Paper*. New York: The Education Commission.

Bruns, B., D. Filmer, and H. A. Patrinos. 2011. *Making Schools Work: New Evidence on Accountability Reforms*. Washington, DC: World Bank.

Buchert, L. 1994. *Education in the Development of Tanzania, 1919–90*. Melton: James Currey Publishers.

Buchmann, C. 1999. 'The State and Schooling in Kenya: Historical Developments and Current Challenges'. *Africa Today*, 46(1): 95–117.

Cooksey, B., D. Court, B. Makau, and J. Barkan. 1994. 'Education for Self-reliance and Harambee'. In *Beyond Capitalism versus Socialism in Kenya and Tanzania.* Edited by Barkan J. D., 201–33. Boulder, CO: Lynne Rienner.

Corrales, J. 2006. 'Political Obstacles to Expanding and Improving Schooling in Developing Countries'. In *Educating All Children: A Global Agenda.* Edited by Cohen, J. E., D. E. Bloom, and M. B. Malin, 231–99. Cambridge, MA: MIT Press.

Court, D. 1976. 'The Education System as a Response to Inequality in Tanzania and Kenya'. *The Journal of Modern African Studies*, 14(4): 661–90.

Dauda, C. L. 2004. 'The Importance of De Facto Decentralization in Primary Education in Sub-Saharan Africa PTAs and Local Accountability in Uganda'. *Journal of Planning Education and Research*, 24: 28–40.

Di John, J., and J. Putzel. 2009. 'Political Settlements: Issues Paper'. Birmingham: Governance and Social Development Resource Centre (GSDRC), University of Birmingham.

Doner, R. F., and B. Ross Schneider. 2016. 'The Middle-Income Trap: More Politics than Economics'. *World Politics*, 68(4): 608–44.

Dunne, M., K. Akyeampong, S. Humphreys, and Transitions and Equity Consortium for Research on Educational Access. 2007. *School Processes, Local Governance and Community Participation: Understanding Access.* Brighton: Consortium for Research on Educational Access, Transitions and Equity.

Fukuyama, F. 2016. *The Origins of Political Order.* London: Profile Books.

Fuller, B., and R. Rubinson. 1992. *The Political Construction of Education: The State, School Expansion, and Economic Change.* New York: Praeger.

Gaventa, J., and R. McGee. 2013. 'The Impact of Transparency and Accountability Initiatives'. *Development Policy Review*, 31(S1): S3–S28.

Grindle, M. S. 2004. *Despite the Odds: The Contentious Politics of Education Reform.* Princeton, NJ: Princeton University Press.

Grindle, M. S. 2012. *Jobs for the Boys: Patronage and the Politics of Public Sector Reform.* Cambridge, MA: Harvard University Press.

Hickey, S., and S. King. 2016. 'Understanding Social Accountability: Politics, Power and Building New Social Contracts'. *The Journal of Development Studies*, 52(8): 1225–40.

Hossain, N., and M. Moore. 2002. 'Arguing for the Poor: Elites and Poverty in Developing Countries'. IDS Working Paper 148. Brighton: Institute of Development Studies, University of Sussex.

Hubbard, P. 2007. 'Putting the Power of Transparency in Context: Information's Role in Reducing Corruption in Uganda's Education Sector'. Working Paper 136. Center for Global Development.

Kingdon, G. G., A. Little, M. Aslam, S. Rawal, T. Moe, H. Patrinos, T. Beteille, R. Banerji, B. Parton, and S. K. Sharma. 2014. 'A Rigorous Review of the Political Economy of Education Systems in Developing Countries. Final Report'. *Education Rigorous Literature Review.* London: Department for International Development.

Kosack, S. 2012. *The Education of Nations: How the Political Organization of the Poor, Not Democracy, Led Governments to Invest in Mass Education.* Oxford: Oxford University Press.

Leftwich, A. 2010. 'Beyond Institutions: Rethinking the Role of Leaders, Elites and Coalitions in the Institutional Formation of Developmental States and Strategies'. *Forum for Development Studies*, 37(1): 93–111.

Levy, B. 2014. *Working with the Grain: Integrating Governance and Growth in Development Strategies.* Oxford: Oxford University Press.

Levy, B., and T. Kelsall. 2016. 'Working Contextually: What Works in Different Types of Political Settlements'. Effective States and Inclusive Development Research Centre, The University of Manchester. (Mimeo).

Levy, B., R. Cameron, U. Hoadley, and V. Naidoo. 2018. *The Politics and Governance of Basic Education: A Tale of Two South African Provinces.* Oxford: Oxford University Press.

Levy, B., A. Hirsch, and I. Woolard. 2015. 'Governance and Inequality: Benchmarking and Interpreting South Africa's Evolving Political Settlement'. ESID Working Paper 51. Manchester: Effective States and Inclusive Development Research Centre, The University of Manchester.

Moe, T. M., and S. Wiborg. 2017. 'Introduction'. In *The Comparative Politics of Education.* Edited by Moe, T. M., and S. Wiborg, 1–23. Cambridge: Cambridge University Press.

Pritchett, L. 2013. *The Rebirth of Education: Schooling Ain't Learning*. Washington, DC: Center for Global Development Books.

Pritchett, L., K. Sen, and E. Werker. 2013. *Deals and Development: The Political Dynamics of Growth Episodes*. Oxford: Oxford University Press.

Schmidt, V. A. 2008. 'Discursive Institutionalism: The Explanatory Power of Ideas and Discourse'. *Annual Review of Political Science*, 11(1): 303–26.

Tikly, L. 2001. 'Globalisation and Education in the Postcolonial World: Towards a Conceptual Framework'. *Comparative Education*, 37(2): 151–71.

UNESCO. 2014. *Teaching and Learning: Achieving Quality for All. Education for All 2013/14 Global Monitoring Report*. Paris: UNESCO.

Westhorp, G., B. Walker, P. Rogers, N. Overbeeke, D. Ball, and G. Brice. 2014. *Enhancing Community Accountability, Empowerment and Education Outcomes in Low and Middle-Income Countries: A Realist Review*. London: Department for International Development.

World Bank. 2003. 'Making Services Work for Poor People: World Development Report 2004'. Washington, DC: World Bank.

World Bank. 2017. 'World Development Report 2018: Learning to Realize Education's Promise'. Washington, DC: World Bank.

10

Understanding the Politics of the Learning Crisis

Steps Ahead on a Long Road

Lant Pritchett

Education has been a core component of the development agenda since before there was a development agenda. In 1948, the UN Declaration of Human Rights declared: 'Everyone has the right to education'. In the seventy years since there has been both massive action to expand education systems and a massive academic literature from a variety of disciplines devoted to education. What could a new drop add to this ocean of ink? This new volume of case studies introduced and edited by Hickey and Hossain makes three distinct and valuable contributions.

First, they orient the key question from the politics of 'schooling'—explaining why governments choose to expand children's 'time served' in a building called a school—to the politics of learning—why is it children learn so much more in some countries' schools than others? They address the question with six country case studies: four African (Ghana, Uganda, South Africa, and Rwanda) and two Asian (Bangladesh and Cambodia) using a common analytical framework.

Second, their framework allows for a 'policy domain' approach that acknowledges that 'just because the tyre is flat doesn't mean the hole is on the bottom'. That is, many approaches to the politics of education assume that if the education sector is dysfunctional in producing learning the fault must lie in the education sector as a policy domain itself—some deficiency in the operation of the sector explained by characteristics or ideas or capabilities in the sector. But the 'domains' approach suggests that perhaps the fault may really lie in the stars—that the failures to promote universal learning are the result of structures in the larger domain of national politics that lead politicians to have other goals and purposes for schooling (Panglayan 2017).

Third, the six country case studies assess how a particular approach to 'political settlements' helps explain successes and failures in orienting the education sector around not expanding schooling but actually promoting learning. The lessons are salutary, but bracing, as none of the 'types' of political settlement reliably lead to an effective politics of learning. Some political settlements that involve electoral democracy produce 'competitive clientelism' that makes it difficult to operate on the long-view of learning performance and hence formulate and implement effective programmes versus the use schools for short-term political advantage. While 'dominant' settlements have potential advantages in this regard over 'competitive clientelism' in being able to enact longer-term reform agendas, this may or may not lead to effective, learning-enhancing reforms as opposed to engaging in other political agendas via schools, like Rwanda's abrupt adoption of English as medium of instruction.

From Schooling to Learning

In 1960, the typical adult (over age 15) in the developing world had only 2.1 years of schooling and 87 per cent of the population had not completed primary schooling. But, by 2010, the typical adult in the developing world had 7.5 years of schooling and only 40 per cent had not completed primary. There was more expansion in schooling in these countries in the last fifty years than the previous 5,000. Today nearly every child will, at some stage, enrol in a school. This expansion in formal schooling is a revolution and will be a milestone in human history.

While there are many studies about the politics of why governments have expanded schooling, a truly astounding feature of this expansion is how uniform it has been across countries. While everyone knows that the high-performing East Asian countries expanded schooling rapidly—Indonesia by 4.5 years, Vietnam by 3.4 years, Thailand by 3.3 years—it might surprise some to know that countries not widely known for stellar development performance such as Haiti expanded years of schooling by just as much as any of those stars: 4.4 years. Malawi expanded years of schooling completed by *more* than either Vietnam or Thailand.

So while a number of forays into the 'politics of schooling' want to explain why some countries did more and others less, in my view, the key puzzle for theories of *schooling* is why so many governments around the world—including countries with corrupt, non-democratic, human rights-abusing and otherwise pretty dismal and dysfunctional governments—chose to do so very much of it.

But the development goal was never 'schooling' for its own sake, the goal was education. The declared purpose of schooling was that children learn and acquire the skills, competencies, knowledge, and dispositions to be successful adults. On this front, tragically, there has been enormously less progress and the progress has been hugely more variable across countries. A couple of examples, which add to those in Chapter 1 of this book, motivate the very rapid recent shift in attention from 'schooling to learning'.

Recently the Indian NGO Annual Status of Education Report (ASER) carried out an assessment of Indian youth aged 14 to 18 to assess their skills (ASER 2018). While these youth were schooled—86 per cent had either completed grade 8 or were still enrolled in school—a shocking number lacked even rudimentary skills. Shown a picture of a girl going to sleep at 10:30 p.m. and then waking up at 5:30 a.m. less than 40 per cent of them could say how long she slept. Less than 40 per cent could calculate the price of a 300 Rupee shirt after a 10 per cent discount. And 27 per cent of those with grade 8 or higher schooling completed could not read a simple paragraph. A question arises: 'how can schooling be so awful that eight years of attendance produces so little in the way of conceptual mastery and competencies?'

The Demographic and Health Surveys (DHS) interview a national sample of women aged 15 to 45 and in the newer modules they assess whether women can read a simple declarative sentence such as 'Farming is hard work' in a language of their choosing. In Ghana only 7.6 per cent and in Egypt only 18.2 per cent of women who had completed grade 6 (but no higher) could read a single sentence versus 75.1 per cent Indonesia and 86.1 per cent in Tanzania (Kaffenberger, Pritchett, and Sandefur 2018). So while Ghana's completed years of schooling is 7.7 and is more than Indonesia (6.1) or Tanzania (5.5), a pressing question has to be why primary schooling's ability to convey retained literacy amongst women varies so widely across countries.

As a final illustration of the puzzle to be explained, a recent (and still preliminary) data set has attempted the Herculean task of piecing together all of the existing results from international assessments into a single comparable indicator of the 'average' learning in each country on a scale in which the average OECD country is 500.[1] Figure 10.1 shows the scatter plot of that learning indicator against gross domestic product per capita (GDPPC), just for those countries with (purchasing power adjusted) GDP per capita less than US$10,000. While there is a tendency for richer countries to have higher performance on learning, the differences across countries of similar GDP are striking. Vietnam, for instance, is estimated to have learning of 524

[1] This is the Altinok, Angrist, and Patrinos (2018) data in its May 2017 version. As this data is not yet finalized nor widely available the specific scores for specific countries may change but the rough points I make here are robust in the October 2018 version of the data.

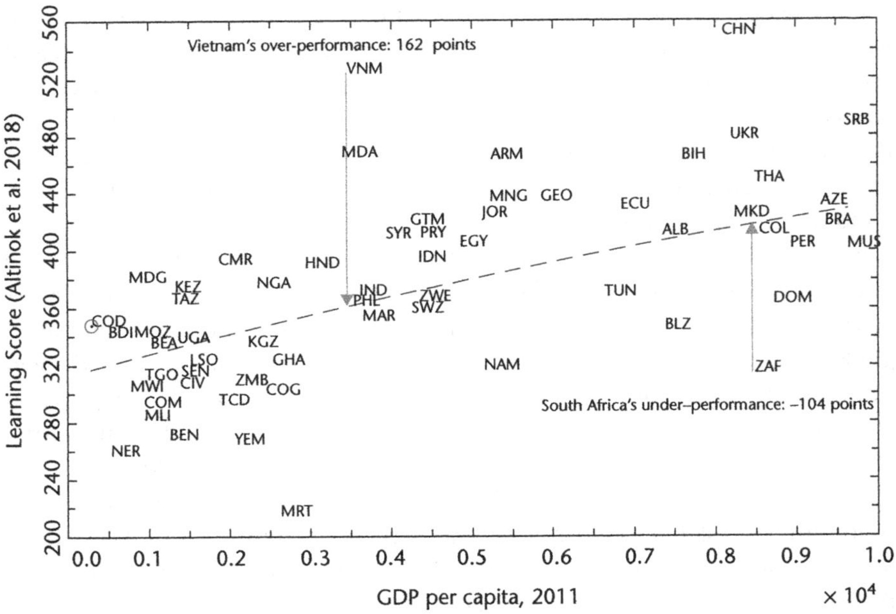

Figure 10.1 Learning score and GDP per capita (countries with GDPPC <US$10,000)

(equivalent or better than many rich countries) whereas based on its income alone we would have predicted 362, so it over-performs its income level by 162 points. In contrast, South Africa, with a GDP per capita more than twice that of Vietnam, scores only 314, whereas its income would predict 418 and hence under-performs its income level by 104 points. The Dominican Republic has a GDP per capita of $8,700 but a learning score of only 363, placing it below much, much poorer countries such as Kenya and Tanzania. Given the scale of this measure of learning and its typical distribution across students, a rough and ready calculation suggests that the average gap between Vietnam and South Africa of 210 points means that the distributions of student performance essentially do not overlap—that is, nearly every 9th grader in Vietnam has higher learning achievement than nearly every South African 9th grader.

The question this new book brings to the fore is: 'Why have the politics been such that (a) nearly all countries expanded schooling but that (b) some did so with very low learning achievement and some did so with high learning achievement (even at similar levels of national resources)?' There are many narratives about why expansion of basic schooling has become so widespread (and of the timing of that expansion)—and many simple 'response to citizens' or 'political pressure from citizens' models seem to explain that (although these cannot explain the timing or universality of these expansions as many, many, governments that were demonstrably not 'responsive to citizens' nevertheless expanded schooling (e.g. Pritchett 2004; Paglayan 2017)). But it is not at all clear why 'pressure from citizens' would lead to a rapid expansion of schooling but with schooling of persistently low learning quality. And, as the authors point out, it is pretty obvious that the 'high learning performance conditional on income' countries as shown in Figure 10.1 (where the top eight learning over-performers (largest regression residual) are: Vietnam, China, Moldova, Armenia, Singapore, Ukraine, Korea Republic, and Serbia) is not a list of 'well-functioning liberal democracies' or even stars in generic measures of 'good governance' (e.g. in the World Governance Indicators for 2011, Vietnam was in the bottom third on indicators for Voice and Accountability, Rule of Law, Control of Corruption, and Regulatory Quality).

This is very much the right question and, on the face of it a puzzling question as it means many countries expanded schooling but without accomplishing at least some of the priority education objectives that were touted as the purpose of expanding schooling—no country claimed they were trying to expand schooling but not learning. This is also very much the right question as one might hope it could lead to an answer of what might be done to accelerate progress in learning.

Policy Domains

A first component of this book's approach is to adopt a 'domain of powers' approach to explaining variation across countries in learning achievement. There is a domain of the general political settlement of a country and then the domain of education per se. This is important as it might seem natural to explain education failures (or successes) by education factors. Of course, on some proximate level in a causal chain that is near true by definition. That is, if we can specify what leads to learning (starting from proximate determinants as simple as 'time-on-task', and having teachers who know the material to be taught and students motivated to learn) then, on a proximate level we can 'account' for improved learning via these proximate pathways. It is a (near) truism that 'if education reform doesn't change what happens in the classroom it cannot change outcomes'. But to trace differences in the sufficient causes that explain persistent learning differences across countries one has to push to the proximate determinants of the proximate determinants and even to the proximate determinants of the proximate determinants of the proximate determinants.

Before you are convinced this is just excessive repetition of the word 'proximate', let me give a concrete example. The Service Delivery Indicator data have been collected on a nationally representative basis in seven African countries. Figure 10.2 and 10.3 show two proximate determinants of the

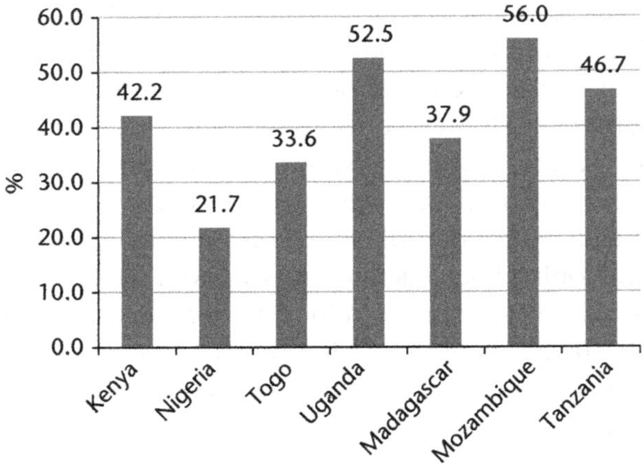

Figure 10.2 Per cent of teachers absent from the classroom during the scheduled period
Source: World Bank Databank, Service Delivery Indicators.

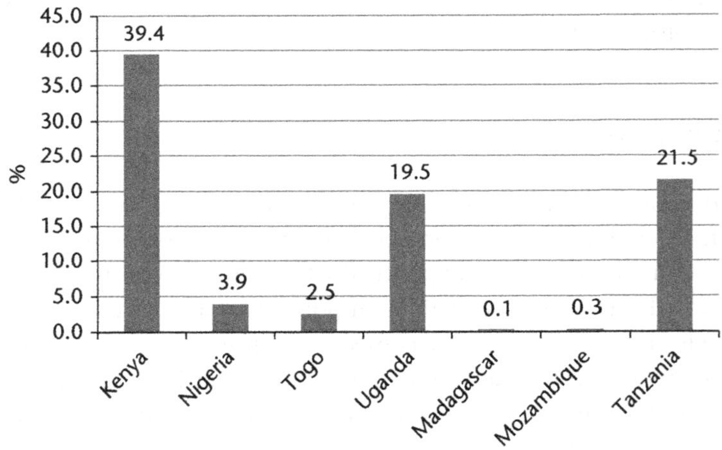

Figure 10.3 Per cent of teachers with minimum subject knowledge (as defined by SDI)
Source: World Bank Databank, Service Delivery Indicators.

classroom experience that are widely regarded to be relevant to student learning: whether a teacher is present (Figure 10.2) and whether the teacher has adequate subject matter knowledge (Figure 10.3).

As an explanation of why in the DHS data for Togo only 22.6 per cent of women who completed grade 6 could read a sentence it probably helps to know that at any given time there was a 1/3 chance the teacher was absent from the classroom, reducing time-on-task, and that there was only a 2.5 per cent chance the student was exposed to a teacher with minimally adequate content knowledge as those are *proximate* determinants of learning.

But this leads to the obvious question: why is it that Togo's education system is such that only 2.5 per cent of classroom teachers in Togo demonstrate minimum subject knowledge (versus, say, roughly 20 per cent in Uganda and Tanzania). Is this a feature of the education of the potential labour force—there simply are not adequate candidates? Is it a feature of something about the education sector and its policies that are the proximate determinant of the low level of this proximate determinant? Is teacher pay too low to attract good candidates to teaching? Are the methods of selection not present to screen out candidates with low subject knowledge?

But even if we could explain the low level of student performance in Togo as low subject content knowledge of teachers and even if that were explained as the result of identifiable policy stances in the education sector, one would still want to ask: What is it about Togo that leads it to have those education sector policy stances? Was it something specific to the configuration of ideas, interests and powers amongst the relevant actors within the education domain of Togo versus other places that explains the policy stance outcomes? Or what if those policy stances are not determined by features of the education domain unique to Togo but rather are determined by broader political factors outside the education domain? What therefore explains low student performance is both the low time-on-task and teacher subject knowledge (amongst other proximate factors), and that is itself explained by features of policy stances within the education domain that are themselves not exogenous or autonomous determinants, but are influenced by the general political context.

I think the 'policy domains' approach is a useful corrective. As one of the authors of the World Development Report 2004, which introduced an 'accountability' framework, we had in mind something very much like this. That is, in our framework outcomes of service delivery (and basic education was included as a paradigm case) were the result of four distinct relationships of accountability: *politics* (between citizens and the state), *compact* (between the executive actors of the state and organizational providers), *management* (between organizations and frontline providers) and *client power* (the direct relationship of service recipients and frontline providers and organizations). Our purpose in emphasizing an analytic approach with all four relationships was that, at the time (early 2000s), far and away the dominant discourse at the World Bank was to discuss only the 'management' relationship. That is, most deficits in service delivery were treated as technical problems in organizational design and implementation that were addressable by the leaders of the relevant provider organizations who, it was imagined, both had sufficient autonomy to act and could be induced to do so with sufficient evidence that specified action(s) of a policy, project or programmatic kind would lead to improved outcomes. This was a natural bias of the donor-driven discourse as the direct 'client/recipient' of donor loans and grants was the organization;

hence 'client-driven' behaviour was in 'partnership' with the provider organizations, and hence the natural focus was on what these organizations could do to improve the state of affairs, and the entirely natural (and not entirely undesirable) bias for optimism led to the idea that there was adequate space for action within the 'management' relationship.

The idea that the deep causal determinants of poor education performance is not in the 'policy domain' of education nor in the 'problem definitions' or 'policy ideas' within the education sector at all but is rather in deeper political determinants, such as the nature of the political settlement, is an important idea. This is a useful corrective to the (self-serving) bias of academics and researchers that 'rigorous evidence' about 'what works' is, in and of itself, an important causal binding constraint to improved performance.

Political Settlement

The main contribution of this volume is applying an instantiation of 'political settlement' to six country cases. As elaborated in Chapter 2 and drawing on work by Khan (2010) and Levy (2014) they stipulate that the political settlement is influenced by (1) power relations and orderings that structure the ruling coalition, (2) material incentives, and (3) paradigmatic ideas. They offer a two by two typology of political settlements with the dimensions of whether 'elite cohesion' is high or low and whether 'organizational and institutional complexity', by which they mean the extent to which administrative processes are personalized or determined largely by formal, impersonalized processes, is high or low. The result is a classification of the political settlement in a country at a point in time into a set of six categories (which I number by Roman numerals to indicate these are categories that are not ordered on any single metric or ordered on any expected sequence, for example, Type III is not 'better' nor necessarily comes after Type II).

This approach brings two important advances on what might be called the 'typical' approach of development experts. A description, perhaps a tad caricatured, of the 'typical' approach is to assume that problems can either (a) be solved 'technocratically' within a given 'policy domain' by sufficiently clever application of known sectoral approaches (something like 'best practice') or (b) that if the problem is 'politics' then well-functioning electoral democracy will, eventually, be sufficient to create the pressure for governments to adopt solutions (or authorize those in the policy domain to adopt solutions) for the quality of education.[2] Relative to that, this approach brings two advances.

[2] I owe this structuring of approaches into 'fix the sector technocratically' or 'fix the politics with democracy' to Agustina Paglayan.

Table 10.1 Typology of political orders

Closed-Access Orders (all except Type VI)				
Type I:	Stable Political Settlement (Types II-V)			Type VI:
No stable political settlement open conflict or instability (e.g. Yemen, Somalia, DRC, Syria)		Personalized (low organizational and institutional complexity)	Impersonal (high organizational and institutional complexity)	**Open access orders** ('Developed' polities, 'rules' systems with high state capability and stable democratic political processes (e.g. Denmark, Germany, Japan)
	High elite cohesion	Type II: **Dominant-personalized** (e.g. South Korea 1960s, Rwanda, Ethiopia)	Type IV **Dominant Rule-by-law** (e.g. South Korea 1980s–1990s, Singapore, South Africa post-apartheid)	
	Low elite cohesion	Type III: **Competitive clientelist** (e.g. Bangladesh 2000s, Malawi, Kenya, Ghana 1990s–2000s)	Type V **Competitive Rule-by-law** (e.g. India)	

Source: Adapted from Figure 10.2 and text, Chapter 2.

First, it essentially never uses the word 'democracy'. I think many have come to believe uses of the word are mostly hoary or hortatory and that, without predicates, the word 'democracy' conveys too little content to be of use. Note that it is possible that any of the six types in Table 10.1 could have held an election as a means of determining the current executive—but it is obvious that holding an election in the Democratic Republic of Congo (DRC) in 2006 did not, in and of itself, magically move DRC from Type I and create a stable country-wide political settlement. This book advances arguments, which have emerged in other policy domains, that elections in weakly institutionalized environments can produce 'competitive clientelist' conditions that are inimical to undertaking some type of reforms. The scatter plot in Figure 10.1 itself illustrates that 'democracy' is neither necessary (Vietnam counter-example) nor sufficient (South Africa counter-example) for high learning achievement in schools.

In contrast, 'dominant' settlements can create conditions in which major reforms can be undertaken and implemented. That said, it is not guaranteed that the reforms of dominant settlements will be conducive to improving learning. Their case study of the overnight move to English language as the medium of instruction in Rwanda is an example of the type of reform only possible in a dominant settlement but which is of at least dubious efficacy in improving learning in the short to medium run due to its disruptive effects.

Second, it is, in and of itself, a major advance to acknowledge that the very notion of 'the politics of X' (where, in this case, X is achieving high learning in basic schooling) needs to be made specific to the type of government. In particular, it is easy to assume that Type VI countries represent the 'normal' or 'paradigm' case and models and frames and tools developed for those cases can be transplanted, with perhaps only minor tweaks, to other cases (or, alternatively, that there is no useful 'politics of X' until a country reaches Type VI). I am stunned at the frequency with which, in academic seminars and the like, I hear the words 'median voter theorem' described as the 'standard' and expect the onus to be on the presenter as to why their predictions would differ from this 'standard'.

But to my view, the 'politics of X' are completely different in a 'deals' world (Types I to V) than in a 'rules' world (Type VI).[3] In a rules world politics is about rules which are expected to be neutrally and impersonally enforced by organizations that (roughly) enforce the rules—which is itself a mapping from facts to actions—with rough fidelity. Rules, by creating groups of people who are similarly affected, create 'interests' and 'interest groups' as people who have common costs and benefits from different rules. But this is precisely what 'low organizational and institutional complexity' or 'low state capability' undermine. Precisely what 'personalized' implies is that expected outcomes are indexed by *who* you are as a *person* not by *what* you do or by any determinant factual condition, like actually complying or not complying with a rule.

This means we need, and the book pursues the goal of, something like 'what are the politics of learning in Type III (competitive clientelist) countries' and 'what are the politics of learning in Type IV (dominant rule of law) countries' with no expectation that these are at all alike or that either is similar to the 'politics of learning in Type VI (open access order) countries'.

It is a truism that 'no battle plan survives contact with the enemy' or, as the sage Mike Tyson put it more recently, 'Everyone has a plan 'till they get punched in the mouth'. Having been involved in my academic career with a number of exercises that attempted to use a framework to structure case studies, my experience is that the raw phenomena of country/regional experiences in all their messy contextual complexity survive collision with analytical frameworks, but not always vice versa.

In this instance, I had three reservations.

The first concern, and one that the researchers cannot be held responsible for, is that there is just no data on learning performance that is comparable

[3] On 'deals', see Pritchett, Sen, and Werker (2018).

across countries or within countries over time. To do research on the question 'What are the conditions under which countries adopt reforms that are effective at promoting learning?' one would have to be able to have at least some rough ability to get at learning performance 'with' and 'without'. But precisely what the focus on schooling has done is create international and national systems in which data on schooling (e.g. enrolments, grade attainment) is widely available across countries and over time with at least modest reliability but data on learning is piecemeal, not widely comparable, and very, very few countries have comparable learning assessments spanning more than just a few years. This means all of the case studies can only really investigate 'what are the conditions in which countries adopt reforms which are claimed to be about learning (or which conventional wisdom or our beliefs think are likely to promote learning?)' which is perhaps an interesting question, but recent research encourages caution on that score. For instance, Indonesia recently doubled teacher wages on the not implausible premise that this would be 'quality improving' but so far the evidence is that this has been 'Double for Nothing' (de Ree et al. 2017). This is important because it is possible, if not plausible, that effective and ineffective reforms have different politics and it is possible, if not plausible, that effective reforms are more politically difficult than reforms that are putatively and rhetorically justified by learning but which are bound to be ineffective.

My second reservation is that one plausible conjecture from the distinction between 'dominant settlements—personalized' and 'Competitive clientelist' and the raw fact that many long-term authoritarian governments have better outcomes than 'democratic' governments (e.g. Indonesia versus India or Vietnam versus the Philippines) is that the longer-term horizon and more 'encompassing' interests of the 'dominant' settlements allow a greater latitude for creating and sustaining reform than do 'competitive clientelist' contexts. But this does not come through the case studies clearly at all—not a fault of method but of the sometimes very stubborn nature of the facts. So, for instance, while the South Africa case study contrasting Western Cape and Eastern Cape provinces is full of rich material (and draws on an additional volume just on South Africa (Levy et al. 2018)), in the end while the configuration of socio-economic, political settlement and inherited institutions between Western Cape and Eastern Cape (Table 6.4) may explain the superior learning performance of Western Cape, it is not clear why the Western Cape lags learning performance in say, Kenya (a much poorer place) nor why progress has proven so fitful, even in Western Cape. Similarly, the 'dominant settlements' of Rwanda and Cambodia had very different trajectories, but neither of them is a clear success nor do they reveal a particularly common 'dominant settlement' politics. I would rate the claim in the conclusion that 'Comparative analysis of our cases, each of which represented different types of political settlement, suggests consistent dynamics can be discerned...' as 'not yet proven'.

Third, the framework emerges as helpful, but not granular enough yet. I think the 'domains of power' and 'political settlement' approaches are an advance over the (implicit) idea that the 'politics of learning-oriented reforms' can be usefully approached without a political settlement (or 'nature of politics') typology and that the first 'lesson' in Chapter 9 that 'Elite commitment to education reform is shaped by the political settlement' is useful. However, other 'lessons' in Chapter 9 reveal the distance the research agenda has yet to go: 'Diverse actors play important roles', 'Political competition and dominance influence reforms in complex ways', 'Informal power and politics is critical', and 'We need to acknowledge idiosyncratic factors'. All of these statements are likely true (as their negation seems false) and perhaps useful correctives—perhaps previous approaches thought informal power was not critical or that only limited actors played important roles—but it is not clear how such statements can inform concrete action.

The book makes a creditable and credible start down the path to identifying the political drivers of the learning crisis. That it does not both start and arrive fully in the same journey is my judgement from the reading of the six cases, but cannot be taken as criticism, and I would encourage each reader to form their own judgement.

References

Altinok, N., N. Angrist and H. P. Patrinos. 2018. 'Global Data Set on Education Quality 1965–2015'. Policy Research Working Paper 8314. Washington, DC: World Bank.

ASER (Annual Status of Education Report). 2018. 'Beyond Basics: Annual Status of Education Report 2017 (Rural)'. New Delhi: ASER.

De Ree, J., K. Muralidharan, M. Pradhan, and F. H. Rogers. 2017. 'Double for Nothing? Experimental Evidence on the Impact of an Unconditional Teacher Salary Increase on Student Performance in Indonesia'. Policy Research Working Paper 8264. Washington, DC: World Bank.

Kaffenberger, M., L. Pritchett, and J. Sandefur. 2018. 'Estimating the Impact of Women's Education on Fertility, Child Mortality, and Empowerment When Schooling Ain't Learning', https://riseprogramme.org/sites/www.riseprogramme.org/files/publications/Kaffenberger.pdf, accessed 3 Oct. 2018.

Khan, M. 2010. 'Political Settlements and the Governance of Growth-Enhancing Institutions'. Monograph. London: SOAS, https://eprints.soas.ac.uk/9968/, accessed 3 Oct. 2018.

Levy, B. 2014. *Working with the Grain: Integrating Governance and Growth in Development Strategies*. Oxford: Oxford University Press.

Levy, B., R. Cameron, U. Hoadley, and V. Naidoo (eds.). 2018. *The Politics and Governance of Basic Education: A Tale of Two South African Provinces*. Oxford: Oxford University Press.

Paglayan, A. S. 2017. 'Political Origins of Public Education Systems'. PhD thesis. Stanford, CA: Stanford University.

Pritchett, L. 2004. Towards a New Consensus for Addressing the Global Challenge of the Lack of Education. Center for Global Development, Harvard University. Working Paper Number 43.

Pritchett, L. 2013. *The Rebirth of Education: Schooling Ain't Learning*. Washington, DC: Center for Global Development Books.

Pritchett, L., K. Sen, and E. Werker. 2018. *Deals and Development: The Political Dynamics of Growth Episodes*. Oxford: Oxford University Press.

11

Similarities and Differences in Policy Reform Destinies

What Do Political Settlements and Domain Politics Explain?

Merilee S. Grindle

In Chapter 9, Sam Hickey, Naomi Hossain, and David Jackman compare the six case studies of education reform brought together in this volume. They ask to what extent a political settlements approach can explain how quality-enhancing reforms played out in discrete contexts. They demonstrate important ways in which a focus on distinct elite coalitions can explain differences across countries at a macro level. They are clear, however, that in order to explain more fully why countries followed unique paths towards reform, it is essential to explore politics and governance contexts within the education sector and to understand the ways that these policy domain interactions are influenced by the broader political settlement. By combining macro and meso levels of analysis, their insightful assessment of the six cases indicates that a theory of elite bargains and domain politics provides a convincing and nuanced story of how education reform happens—or fails to happen—across a significant number of countries.[1]

[1] Drawing on the work of Khan (2010) and others (Acemoglu and Robinson 2012; Levy 2014) on the importance of political settlements for the development potential of countries, recent studies have addressed the links between such agreements and the specific politics at sectoral levels (see, for examples Abdulai 2017; Bebbington et al. 2018; Hickey and King 2016; Hickey and Lavers 2016; Hossain and Hassan 2017; Levy and Kelsall 2016; Pritchett 2013). This effort responds to the concern that many political economy discussions of why some development initiatives succeed while others fail focus on either broad historical trends (a macro approach) or on specific interventions to improve performance (a micro approach). This recent work is notable for attempting to bridge this gap, and particularly for efforts to link macro and sectoral levels of analysis (a domain approach; see Grindle 2017).

In a separate reading of the case studies, this chapter confirms the importance of macro settlements and domain-specific interactions in explaining why 'politics matters' in education policy and, importantly, in showing '*how* politics matters' in accounting for differences across countries in what can be accomplished through policy change. However, here there is added emphasis on the observation that differences across the case studies are most apparent when efforts are made to implement new approaches to problematic conditions in the education sector. That is, this chapter suggests that the destinies of education reform initiatives in Ghana, Bangladesh, Rwanda, South Africa, Cambodia, and Uganda began to be most clearly determined when efforts were made to put them into practice. While the intent of the new initiatives was nowhere perfectly reflected in the policies activated, some countries demonstrated greater commitment and capacity to implement reform initiatives, and to sustain them for some period of time. Others were less able to manage effective national implementation of new policies, and the fate of the reforms in these countries was to lie fallow, to be promoted in diverse ways at the sub-national level, to have resources devoted to other ends, or to be replaced by renewed emphasis on alternative policies.

There were, then, clear differences across countries in terms of how new education policies were implemented. With a series of earlier education reforms emphasizing access, however, and with the initial phases of problem definition, agenda setting, policy design, and official adoption of quality-enhancing reforms, important similarities characterized the politics of education reform. Thus, by drawing attention to the histories of successful 'easy' education reform—those that provided schooling to large numbers of children, and to the early phases of 'hard' education reform—those that focused attention on improvements in learning, this chapter suggests that a generalized political economy of education reform can be advanced to explain some types of education initiatives and some parts of the policy process. But a general explanation proves wanting when efforts are made to implement policies, as the case studies and comparative analysis make clear. Understanding the implementation story when difficult policies are at stake requires a more nuanced approach, one that can be found by exploring political settlements and domain politics. Thus, the destiny of education policies can be understood in part as a function of policy content and process, although it is ultimately determined by the important political dynamics emphasized in this volume.[2]

[2] The distinction between access and quality in education achievement has received increased attention in the 2000s. Earlier, a focus on 'education for all' encouraged a significant expansion of the number of children enrolled in primary schooling (UNESCO 1990), but more recent assessments have drawn attention to the problem that 'Schooling Ain't Learning' and that quality has lagged in educational achievement in large numbers of countries (Pritchett 2013;

A General Story of Similarities

A useful explanation for the similarities in the experiences across countries lies in the nature of the political benefits and costs of distinct policy regimes in education. Moreover, most countries demonstrate significant similarities in the ways in which national education problems become recognized as important policy issues, are reflected in policy designs, and are adopted formally by political elites. Thus, there is a good *general* explanation in political economy for the ways in which Ghana, Bangladesh, Rwanda, South Africa, Cambodia, and Uganda followed similar paths in increasing access to education, recognizing the limitations of this policy, and setting out a new agenda for enhancing the quality of schooling. Regardless of the political settlement characterizing the country, all moved along a similar path of first addressing 'easy' education reforms. Then as evidence and pressures mounted about the limitations of the emphasis on access, political elites reacted similarly by adopting new policy ideas and encouraging their elaboration into national policy plans for 'hard' reforms.[3]

Of course, to call some education reforms 'easy' should not diminish the effort involved—increasing access to schooling involved massive efforts by public organizations and officials, often at multiple levels of government. It required bigger budgets for Ministries of Education; introduced a significant management challenge of transmitting policy goals into specific measures to be taken by numerous actors; occupied a large number of administrators overseeing specific initiatives; implied a Herculean effort to train a corps of teachers; entailed building many new schools and classrooms as well as providing desks, textbooks, chalkboards, and pencils; and called for extensive public information campaigns. Long chains of decisions and action extended from central policymakers and administrators all the way to schools, classrooms, teachers, students, and parents and had to be coordinated. Moreover, the goalposts moved over time, increasingly emphasizing the need to incorporate rural children and then other groups often marginalized in their societies, such as girls and cultural minorities. Efforts to undertake these changes were significant, not least for the political and bureaucratic elites who promoted such changes in their societies, and the way was studded with planning and logistical obstacles, mistakes, corruption, waste, and delay.

UNESCO 2006; World Bank 2017). The increased awareness of the difficulty of improving quality has encouraged greater attention to the political economy of education reform (Bruns and Schneider 2016; Corrales 2006; Grindle 2004; Kingdon et. al 2014; Kosack 2009; Moe and Wiborg 2017; Wales, Magee, and Nicolai 2016).

[3] The political differences between 'easy' and 'hard' education reform are described in Grindle (2004); (see also Bruns and Schneider 2016).

Nevertheless, from a political point of view, education advances tied to increasing access to schooling were by and large 'easy' because of the nature of the policies themselves—they provided a range of benefits that could be distributed amongst important groups and broadly to communities that desired and appreciated them. Universal education initiatives provided budgets to ministries to employ more officials to undertake more programmes, and to hire and train extensive numbers of teachers and school administrators—this kind of job expansion was an important building block of a foundational middle class in many cases. The reforms paid for the construction of teacher-training institutes and schools and the production of teaching materials. Efforts to get more children into school were visible and popular, and politicians and parties were eager to claim credit at ribbon cuttings for new infrastructure and the celebration of education campaigns. A paradigmatic idea for national advancement and material incentives for multiple actors were aligned in these kinds of reforms, regardless of differences in how political systems functioned.

Thus, in Ghana, Bangladesh, Rwanda, South Africa, Cambodia, and Uganda political elites were often eloquent in advancing education as a universal public good—for them, education was a national project directly related to the ability to undertake and achieve economic and social development. In many cases, commitment to the idea of universal education was strong across several decades and distinct political arrangements. And in fact, each country made great strides towards providing this public good. Often encouraged by international campaigns such as 'Education for All' and the Millennium Development Goals, by the 2010s, each country had managed to get an impressive proportion of its children into primary school; and in many cases a significant number of students had advanced to secondary schooling. These cases were not unusual; by early in the twenty-first century, a large majority of poor countries achieved similarly significant results in providing universal access to education. Where education policy had emphasized quality as well as access, getting more children into school was invariably the primary accomplishment.

By the early 2000s, elites in each of the six countries began to encounter mounting evidence that getting children into school was only part of the challenge of education. In the face of international and domestic concern about human and economic development, data-based evidence of education shortfalls, and middle-class flight from public schools, elites in each of the countries began to acknowledge that something needed to be done about the gap between two different measures of educational output—access and quality. The case studies show that in Ghana, Bangladesh, Rwanda, South Africa, Cambodia, and Uganda, the definition of the education problem, and the policy ideas needed to respond to it, began to shift in similar ways. Although the timing was distinct, political elites, technocrats, education specialists, and donors set about reframing education policy to address the learning crisis. Specific policy measures differed, but most new plans involved efforts to decentralize the management of education systems and to improve teacher training and accountability.[4]

At this point in the policy process, elites were responding to drivers such as the direction of international discourses on education, increasingly available data about failures of prior policies, the ideas of domestic policy reformers, and pressures from groups favouring change. Across the six countries, there were few political constraints on pulling together reform-minded officials, academics, planners, not-for-profit organizations, and donors to develop new policy initiatives such as the NERP and the 2008 Education Act in Ghana, the PEDP3 in Bangladesh, the MINEDUC 2007 in Rwanda, the ELRC in South Africa, the CFS or the TPAP in Cambodia, and the BRMS in Uganda—to invoke a veritable alphabet soup of reforms. These changes amounted to a new policy agenda for education. Again, these were not isolated cases, as the learning crisis became increasingly evident in many countries around the world and as the paradigmatic idea of universal public education was met by criticism of what that national project had not been able to deliver.

A Particular Story of Differences

But implementing quality-enhancing reforms and sustaining them was a much bigger challenge than getting more children in school or designing new national policies because, from a political perspective, they were costly to important political and bureaucratic interests. Ministries were no longer as flush with resources as they had been in earlier decades and they resisted pressures to become more efficient and accountable. School expansion slowed, harming construction firms and workers; ribbon cutting became less frequent; and political parties were deprived of many tangible resources and jobs to distribute. Educators and administrators resented being tested, measured, and judged on their performance and looked to their associations and unions to protect them from new standards. Parents and voters were asked to trust that in a number of years, their children would be better prepared for the future; many were unconvinced that this would occur. Middle-class and

[4] For discussions of efforts to improve quality in education, see Bruns, Filmer, and Patrinos (2011), Evans and Popova (2016), and World Bank (2017).

business interests—important in the development of public education in many now-rich countries—were not major players in such reforms either because they had deserted to private-sector schooling or because they did not envision better public education as important to their economic future. From a political perspective, commitment to these kinds of education reforms was much more vulnerable to resistance, often from the same organized groups—parties, politicians, unions, bureaucrats, local officials—that had benefitted from access-enhancing reforms.

And, because the actors important to policymaking differed significantly from those important in policy implementation, once an initiative addressing the learning crisis was formulated and approved, its future became extremely vulnerable to the nature of the political settlement and domain-level political interactions and governance structures. Thus, when governments in the case study countries—at least rhetorically committed to new policy initiatives—reached the point of trying to put more difficult reforms into practice, characteristics of their underlying political agreements emerged as important explanations in how well they were able to promote change. Multiple patterns of capacity and commitment across countries, and within countries at the sub-national level, became much more apparent. Teachers' associations, bureaucrats, local and regional elites and, in some cases, local communities became much more important drivers of political interactions, and their intent was to resist change rather than to promote it. This is when the legacies of prior policies, the differential capacity of implementing organizations, the strength and weakness of interests harmed through reform, and the degree of competitiveness in elections became part of a more nuanced understanding of the politics of education reform. In such cases, paradigmatic and policy ideas about what to do to address a problem were no longer in alignment with the material incentives to adopt change.

Thus, we find that Rwanda, with a dominant and development-oriented political settlement spearheaded by a powerful central actor and a cohesive party, had considerable capacity to introduce an education reform that had high priority for this elite. The rapid switch to English as a medium of instruction—and its unfavourable impact on education quality—can be tied to core concerns of the political elite about domestic peace and international alliances. But, despite rhetorical commitment to improved schooling, this same elite did not use its considerable top-down discipline to pursue teacher-training reforms; this initiative was not a high priority for it. In Cambodia, a top-down approach to implementation within a dominant but more personalized political settlement suggests relatively efficient management of the introduction of reform, but one more sensitive to personalistic trade-offs within the sector and across different districts and localities. The likelihood of increased trade-offs and negotiations with elite factions and lower-level political actors during implementation increased in the case of Uganda, where the elite settlement was less firmly dominant and personalism was more prominent; decentralization as a feature of reform governance increased the potential for variation across districts and localities by opening up room for manoeuvre by lower-level political and bureaucratic elites who were differentially motivated to accept or resist reforms.

Elite settlements in Bangladesh and Ghana were looser, and more competitive and discordant than in Rwanda, Cambodia, and Uganda, supporting a less cohesive implementation process characterized by more negotiation and conflict around policy objectives and resources. Not surprisingly, especially with governance measures that introduced more decentralization, greater autonomy for district and local actors led to significant variations in implementation at the community and district level, with the effectiveness of implementation depending much more on local and regional actors' incentives to adopt or reject the changes mandated by national policy. This same tendency towards implementation variability at sub-national levels was evident in South Africa, where decentralization combined with distinct legacies of bureaucratic capacity to emphasize not only provincial political settlements, but also differences based on the institutions of governance.

The cases illuminate not only differences amongst settlements and domain-specific politics but also distinctions in the implementation fault lines related to distinct elite settlements. In Rwanda, for example, the top-down style of decision-making and control also facilitated a misreading and mismatch between the reforms introduced and the realities of conditions within the education sector; the coherence of the dominant coalition interfered with the capacity to appreciate and respond to issues that emerged within the sector during implementation. Even in this case of a dominant developmental settlement, the implementation phase of the policy process was vulnerable; political and governance conditions in such contexts may be opaque to central policy implementers, distinct from situations in which ongoing negotiation and clientelistic arrangements are the norm. Conversely, the most insistent challenge to policy implementation in looser and more conflictful political arrangements is greater diversity in the capacity to implement as well as the use of policy resources for default options where resistance to change is greater. The outcome of less coherent implementation in these conditions can take the form of some resources being newly committed to access-type reforms; benefits increased to resistant stakeholders such as teachers and administrators without emphasis on performance accountability; or misuse for personal or partisan gain. In all cases, then, implementation was the most fragile part of the policy process in education reform, but for distinct political reasons.

When Politics Defeats Policy, What Can Be Done?

Similarities and differences in the dynamics of the policy process suggest that, for education policy, the point at which differences amongst political settlements and domain politics is most evident is not at the point of rhetorical commitment to change, the process of policy design, or even formal mechanisms of political approval, but at the point of implementing and sustaining important changes. With the exception of South Africa, the case study countries, like most poor countries across the world, have relatively insulated policymaking processes, weak formal institutions of governance, and important deficiencies in the hierarchical administrative capacity to exert compliance from multiple officials and to hold a variety of other actors to legal or administrative standards; South Africa demonstrates this reality at sub-national levels. In some cases, strong coalitions of elites substitute for institutional incapacities, a condition that does not occur in other countries. Thus, differences amongst countries cannot be captured on a simple strong state/weak state continuum but must address the nature of the coalitions constructed by national political elites and parties and the complex political interactions and governance structures that characterize the education sector.

A focus on the political interactions of implementing difficult policies suggests that, where policy change has a high priority for elites in dominant/developmental settlements, the potential to impose policy costs on important interests may be considerable. Nevertheless, policy initiatives under these more authoritarian settlements depend significantly on the priorities of the elite coalition—expanding their capacity to introduce policies they are particularly concerned about, but hindering opportunities for change in non-priority areas. Centralized power, then, can be advantageous for introducing quality-enhancing education reforms, but only when the elite itself is committed to using its capacity to promote such change. Where such commitment exists, democratic processes may be ignored or undermined. Certainly it is possible that, over time, more authoritarian coalitions might become more open and democratic—the example of South Korea is emblematic in this regard. Similarly, the historical experience of some countries such as Chile, Colombia, Brazil, and possibly Ghana, suggest that clientelistic systems can evolve over time into more coherent and programmatic democracies that have greater capacity for implementing hard policy choices. Moreover, the case studies suggest that while more cohesive and dominant coalitions might be more efficient in setting out on policy implementation processes, they share a common flaw in being less sensitive to what is happening at sub-national levels. More fragmented and clientelistic systems may be 'smarter' in terms of the ability to adjust and negotiate some implementation efforts.

Are there political avenues to encourage the implementation of 'hard' reforms, even in countries in which elite settlements are weak, fragmented, and contested? As Hickey, Hossain, and Jackman confirm, the cases indicate that for some countries, differences in political and governance arrangements at sub-national levels offer opportunities for improvements in education in at least some regions, districts, or localities. They suggest that one path towards building effective change in countries that cannot count on a dominant coalition to lead and implement reform is through initiatives to capitalize on favourable sub-national political dynamics, or to encourage them to be more supportive of quality-enhancing change. Building reform initiatives beyond sympathetic sub-national contexts, however, would require major efforts to create and strengthen parental, school-based, associational, political, and bureaucratic leadership across sub-national units, linking them in networks with national and international supporters of reform. Thus, to scale-up sub-national achievements, policy reformers would need to reassess where to focus their efforts—fewer, perhaps, on policymaking and processes at national levels, and more on building and linking more localized capacities and leadership.

A complementary path towards reform in contexts of national political weakness is suggested by the histories of education reform that initially promoted education as a universal right as part of a national project or paradigmatic idea. Such national projects have been important in many countries in encouraging the development of national identity, industrialization, public health, and the removal of barriers of discrimination against women and minorities. As Hickey and Hossain indicate in Chapter 2, paradigmatic ideas can 'bind elites together, securing their commitment to upholding a certain set of institutions whilst also being deployed more instrumentally by elites to secure loyalty among followers'. National projects are not easily undertaken, of course, but much of what promotes them is talk—insistent emphasis on the universal benefits to be gained from broad initiatives; the use of ideas and data in ongoing political communications; and the development of a narrative to capture a national audience and filter into the rhetoric of political parties, interest groups, and everyday conversation. These resources are available to reform proponents in many countries, even those that lack significant implementation capacity. This strategy can be useful over the longer term in building broad-based support for reform where political coalitions register rhetorical commitment to it but lack commitment and capacity; strong public discourse about the importance and direction of change in education policy can be critical support for beleaguered reformists in countries around the world.

The political facts of hard-to-implement reforms are stark, and perhaps nowhere more apparent than in efforts to introduce and sustain quality-enhancing education policies. However much reformers wish to see schooling enhanced by learning, they face major challenges that become most apparent when they attempt to put plans into practice. The challenges are greater in some countries than in others because political and bureaucratic conditions exacerbate rather than counteract resistance and chip away at capacity and commitment. Where the difficulties are greatest, pursuing implementation of 'hard' policies may ultimately be a function of strategies that work at subnational and national levels to substitute for weaknesses inherent in broad political settlements and specific policy domains. Policymakers and analysts alike might therefore focus additional attention on ways to subvert political vulnerabilities that become most evident while implementing change initiatives.

References

Abdulai, A-G. 2017. 'Competitive Clientelism and the Political Economy of Mining in Ghana'. ESID Working Paper 78. Manchester: Effective States and Inclusive Development Research Centre, The University of Manchester.

Acemoglu, D., and J. A. Robinson. 2012. *Why Nations Fail: The Origins of Power, Prosperity and Poverty*. London: Profile Books.

Bebbington, A., A-G. Abdulai, D. Humphreys-Bebbington, M. Hinfelaar, and C. Sanborn. 2018. *Governing Extractive Industries: Politics, Histories, Ideas*. Oxford: Oxford University Press.

Bruns, B. and B. R. Schneider. 2016. 'Managing the Politics of Quality Reforms in Education Policy: Lessons from Global Experience'. *The Learning Generation Background Paper*. New York: The Education Commission.

Bruns, B., D. Filmer, and H. A. Patrinos. 2011. *Making Schools Work: New Evidence on Accountability Reforms*. Washington, DC: World Bank.

Corrales, J. 2006. 'Political Obstacles to Expanding and Improving Schooling in Developing Countries'. In *Educating All Children: A Global Agenda*. Edited by Cohen, J. E., D. E. Bloom, and M. B. Malin, 231–99. Cambridge, MA: MIT Press.

Evans, D. K., and A. Popova. 2016. 'What Really Works to Improve Learning in Developing Countries? An Analysis of Divergent Findings in Systematic Reviews'. *The World Bank Research Observer*, 31(2): 242–70.

Grindle, M. S. 2004. *Despite the Odds: The Contentious Politics of Education Reform*. Princeton, NJ: Princeton University Press.

Grindle, M. S. 2017. 'Good Governance, RIP: A Critique and an Alternative'. *Governance: An International Journal of Policy, Administration and Institutions*, 30(1): 17–22.

Hickey, S., and S. King. 2016. 'Understanding Social Accountability: Politics, Power and Building New Social Contracts'. *The Journal of Development Studies*, 52(8): 1225–40.

Hickey, S., and T. Lavers. 2016. 'Conceptualising the Politics of Social Protection Expansion in Low Income Countries: The Intersection of Transnational Ideas and Domestic Politics'. *International Journal of Social Welfare*, 25(4): 388–98.

Hossain, N, and M. Hassan. 2017. 'The Problem with Teachers: The Political Settlement and Education Quality Reforms in Bangladesh'. ESID Working Paper 86. Manchester: Effective States and Inclusive Development Research Centre, The University of Manchester.

Khan, M. 2010. 'Political Settlements and the Governance of Growth-Enhancing Institutions'. Monograph. London: SOAS.

Kingdon, G. G., A. Little, M. Aslam, S. Rawal, T. Moe, H. Patrinos, T. Béteille, R. Banerji, B. Parton, and S. K. Sharma. 2014. 'A Rigorous Review of the Political Economy of Education Systems in Developing Countries. Final Report'. *Education Rigorous Literature Review*. London: Department for International Development.

Kosack, S. 2009. 'Realising Education for All: Defining and Using the Political Will to Invest in Primary Education'. *Comparative Education*, 45(4): 495–523.

Levy, B. 2014. *Working with the Grain: Integrating Governance and Growth in Development Strategies*. Oxford: Oxford University Press.

Levy, B., and T. Kelsall. 2016. 'Working Contextually: What Works in Different Types of Political Settlements'. Effective States and Inclusive Development Research Centre, The University of Manchester. (Mimeo).

Moe, T. M., and S. Wiborg. (eds). 2017. *The Comparative Politics of Education: Teacher Unions and Education Systems Around the Globe*. Cambridge: Cambridge University Press.

Pritchett, L. 2013. *The Rebirth of Education: Schooling Ain't Learning*. Washington, DC: Center for Global Development Books.

UNESCO. 1990. *World Declaration on Education for All*. Paris: UNESCO.

UNESCO. 2006. *The Quality Imperative: Education for All 2005 Global Monitoring Report*. Paris: UNESCO.

Wales, J., A. Magee, and S. Nicolai. 2016. 'How Does Political Context Shape Education Reforms and Their Success?' ODI Dimension Paper 6. London: Overseas Development Institute.

World Bank. 2017. 'World Development Report 2018: Learning to Realize Education's Promise'. Washington, DC: World Bank.

Index

Index